D1538688

OPPORTUNITY ZONE MILLIONAIRE

OPPORTUNITY ZONE MILLIONAIRE

LEARN HOW TO ATTRACT INVESTORS, RAISE CAPITAL, BUILD WEALTH AND CREATE POSITIVE SOCIAL IMPACT IN YOUR COMMUNITY

ROCCO FORINO

The Author is not an attorney or an accountant and does not provide legal, tax, or accounting advice. The author recommends that each reader prior to making any investments, take time to research legal, tax and investment advisory firms, investment advisory representatives, and the services and products being offered prior to establishing an investment advisory relationship with any firm or advisor.

To All Entrepreneurs

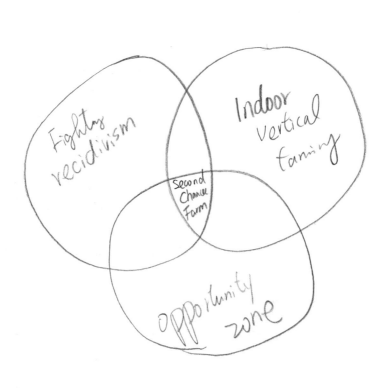

Fighting recidivism

Indoor vertical farming

Second Chance Farm

Opportunity zone

CONTENTS

INTRODUCTION

What do AT&T, Pfizer, Google, Kohl's, and Tesla share?[i] They were once start-up businesses founded by immigrant entrepreneurs. Founders of these—and thousands of other successful businesses across the country—put in incredibly long hours building products, testing prototypes, courting customers, and finding investors to reach the pinnacle of success.

Many experienced humiliating failures before hitting on the business idea that hit it big. As Thomas Edison put it: "I have not failed. I just found 10,000 ways that won't work."[ii]

Finally succeeding, after years of scraping by, juggling multiple jobs, and hustling for capital, most entrepreneurs believe the struggle was worth it. All the late nights, the take-out pizzas, the crummy apartments, and overdrawn bank accounts finally translate into the true meaning of freedom. When you own a successful business that has scaled, you've finally got the freedom to do what you want, whenever you want, without ever having to worry about money again.

Startup founders come from all walks of life. Many are fortunate to possess deeper safety nets than others. Maybe it's having not one but two educated parents. Or maybe it's learning a crucial skill at an early age. Maybe it's having immediate and easy access to investors. As for aspiring entrepreneurs from high-poverty communities, these safety nets are a luxury—even nonexistent. You must rely on a significant amount of hard work and hustle. Otherwise, failure could be a financial death sentence setting you even further back for years.

I know, because I've done it. My first start-up happened 20 years ago in a distressed city that is now a designated an opportunity zone (OZ), Waterbury, Connecticut.

Growing Up in an Opportunity Zone

I was born and raised in Waterbury, Connecticut, which is a blue-collar town surrounded by Connecticut's wealthier communities. I was raised by a single mother—a third generation Italian-American with a public high school education. Growing up, we lived with my grandparents. My grandfather—a second generation Italian-American who never finished high school—was a small business owner and owned his own a welding company called Nutmeg Welding. Beginning around the age of eight, I worked for my grandfather during summer breaks, snow days, and holidays. Rather than playing outside with friends like other children around my age, I was expected to provide for the family by doing everything from sweeping up metal shaving to cutting steel on a chop saw that would be welded together to form something unique.

What was great about working in this environment was that I can literally make anything I imagined... out of metal. In sixth grade, I made a Freddy Krueger Halloween costume from an old glove and some leftover flat-bent metal I glued onto a glove. It was identical to the actual Freddy Krueger glove and was cool because I made it. Every school project I made had some form of metal involved in it. Access to tools and raw material provided me with the ability to look at a problem and then envision and create a solution. When I wasn't at my grandfather's welding shop, I was usually dragged around from house to house by my mother who worked as a hairdresser cutting people's hair inside their homes and selling Avon—a few of her many jobs. While my friends in high school were busy getting taxied around by their parents from one sport event to the next in hopes of a college scholarship, I had to figure out how the world worked on my own.

Applying to college? As some kids were touring college campuses, I was reading college brochures, looking at photographs, and trying to narrow down colleges on paper. Neither my mother nor my grandparents had attended college, so they really didn't know the process. Throughout high school and school vacations, I worked from 8:00 a.m. to 4:30 p.m. for my grandfather. Then, I would head to work at a local Stop and Shop grocery store from 5:00 to 9:00 p.m. in the dairy department. In the summer, I would do this sometimes six days a week when overtime was allowed. When I got home from work, I smelled like a combination of cut steel and a slight tinge of milk sometimes when a gallon slipped out of my hand and exploded onto the floor and splashed up at me. While my other classmates were hanging out with friends and going to camps on their summer vacations, I was working two jobs—a sacrifice that still instilled a hard work ethic. I continued working two jobs even while attending Quinnipiac University until my junior year when I started several internships. One of these internships was at Oxygen Electronics—an electronic parts broker located near the green in New Haven, Connecticut.

Back then, electronic brokers would serve their clients the old-fashioned way—by phone. For example, if Apple needed a specific chip that was no longer being manufactured for their existing Macintosh line, they would call in and request for us to scan the globe of electronic suppliers that may have had extras in their inventory. Most companies would usually seek an older electronic component to keep prices low instead of finishing the product line with the newer, more expensive electronic component. However, in the case of older chips, which usually meant the chip was no longer currently being manufactured.

If we found an electronic supplier with the exact amount of parts, Oxygen Electronics would send someone on the next flight across the globe to retrieve the components, put it in a suitcase and hand-deliver these components to the customer in less than three days. Since the components were in-demand, the broker would charge an enormous amount of money, considering this was during the "dot-com era." Because of the recent technology boom, warehouses had a surplus of electronics and microelectronics components such as computer chips, capacitors, and transistors that were not easily searchable or in a digital database for public view. Websites were a new concept back then. The websites that did exist only possessed basic functionality.

E-Commerce Meets Entrepreneurship

While this method worked, it was slow and often inefficient, especially for the customer. But surely, there was a quicker, cheaper, and more effective way for customers to find and purchase obsolete electronic and microelectronic components. That's when I devised a plan for an e-commerce platform—echainOnline. echain stood for electronic supply chain. Unfortunately, the domain—echain.com—was already taken (yes, domain squatters started right from the get-go).

After graduating from Quinnipiac University in 1999, I started writing a business plan for how I envisioned the company would dominate the industry. On the echain platform, electronic suppliers would list their components while customers placed bids on these listings. This allowed suppliers to list their excess electronic inventory and allow customers to search and bid on obsolete components. Because these components were in high demand, a bidding platform was the best business model. echain would also expedite the whole process, unlike the old-fashioned way through telephone and long-distance flights.

However, building a bidding platform was complex. To start a business with complex software and database design, I needed to raise capital to get something tangible to show investors and customers. So, I raised under $20,000 from family and friends who could not afford to take the risk at the time, but did so anyway. Keep in mind that a decent Dell computer cost around $4,000 back then, so frugal use of cash was important. My initial plan was to build the most minimal viable product (MVP) and raise another round of capital after we had proven demand for the service.

Rather than head straight to the Bay Area like many other e-commerce ventures and like my partners suggested, eChain made its home at Waterbury's Bank Street.[iii] Waterbury was touting itself as a designated information technology zone (ITZ), promising to support technology ventures willing to make their HQ there. echain had promise and perhaps had the potential to become one of the first companies to contribute to Waterbury's potential tech economy. Development corporations such as Naugatuck Valley Development Corporation (NVDC) promised start-up ventures like us hundreds of thousands of dollars in grants if we located to their designated technology zone. Even the city's mayor promised to push for the development of Waterbury's economy as an ITZ.

However, things turned out differently than what we initially envisioned.

Waterbury Drops the ITZ Zone Ball

Soon after we located to an office space on 65 Bank Street in downtown Waterbury, things quickly became quiet. There was no more talk about the ITZ zone, these grants or how great the program would be for the future of the city's economy. When I initially met NVDC managers, they had a list of demands. First, they demanded that I assembled a team. I recruited the help of three partners—two recent Harvard graduates and a veteran computer programmer from India—to write software code. Then, they demanded financial statements from every individual on our team[iv] (we were all recent college graduates) and a thirty-page business plan that included a five-year plan prior to the product's release.[v] This was all for a grant of a measly $100,000. Meeting after unfruitful meeting followed. NVDC, despite advertising it would provide a $100,000 grant to help the development of new, local businesses, were ill-prepared. They promised to jumpstart their ITZ campaign and yet, kept pushing it back every month. It turned out it was bogus, the quasi-government agency comprising old guard, traditional bankers.

As the weeks turned into months, we realized the city, and its development agency, had no experience in venture investing. In fact, they didn't seem interested in investing at all. They would only allow 15-minute meetings before losing patience. The mayor at the time seemed just as clueless about the idea. No experienced local entrepreneurs or investors stepped up to provide guidance either.

Even though platforms such as Amazon and eBay were becoming more mainstream—e-commerce was still a new concept for most people in 1999. However, in 1996 Jeff Bezos was also experiencing difficulty raising capital for Amazon. "I had to take 60 meetings to raise $1 million, and I raised it from 22 people at approximately $50,000 a person," Bezos told CBS' 60 Minutes.[vi] "And it was nip and tuck whether I was going to be able to raise that money. So, the whole thing could have ended before the whole thing started."

Bezos took 60 meetings and was turned down by over 60 percent of the investors that he approached, showing how difficult capital raising was and still is. Of the 60 meetings he took he was able to convince 22 Seattle-based investors to invest $50,000 each in return for a little less than 1 percent equity in Amazon. Bezos' parents also invested a significant portion of their life savings.[vii] Amazon's one VC investment an $8 million Series A funding from Kleiner Perkins, was the only VC investment before it went public in May, 1997.[viii] It is estimated that the value of just one of the $50,000 investments, would have a value of more than $1.9 billion today.

Mark Benioff, who launched Salesforce in 1999, had no success raising capital from venture capitalists. Even in 1999, a year where technology start-ups were still benefitting from the tech-stock bubble, Benioff couldn't convince venture capitalists to invest in his vision for automating business development through cloud computing. [ix] "When we were raising money, no one would give us money," Benioff said in an interview with TechCrunch in October 2019.[x] Eventually, Benioff and his co-founders did raise money, but the entire $17 million came from private, individual investors, not venture capitalists.[xi]

Bezos' and Benioff's struggles to raise capital demonstrates that raising capital is a difficult endeavor, regardless of the economic and market environment. If you're a start-up founder, there may not be a professional investor community or venture capitalists in your city. However, there's a large potential market to tap in any community, which includes successful business executives, doctors and business founders that should make their investment interests known in their communities. Jeff Fagnan, founding partner of Accomplice, a seed stage venture capital firm points out that, "If you had success in your career you have a social responsibility to become an investor — whether you want to or not. We feel like if someone helped you, you need to pay it forward as well," he told Term Sheet.[xii]

Back in Waterbury, after several grueling and frustrating months, we withdrew our application for a grant. The officials we were working with did not take the idea of transforming Waterbury into an ITZ zone as seriously as we did.

In 1999, we were unaware of any venture capital (VC) or angel investors in Connecticut and there definitely were not any within the Waterbury area. One reason the ITZ plan failed was the lack of support for investment groups and accelerators, essential for facilitating start-ups.

Look at shows like *Shark Tank*. They have supported entrepreneurs by investing in their products and services and provided publicity that has helped entrepreneurs to gain needed exposure. While Ring Doorbell rejected an investment from a *Shark Tank* panelist, the exposure helped the company get other investors, including Richard Branson.[xiii] In 2018, Ring was acquired by Amazon for $1 billion.[xiv] Other successes include Scrub Daddy, a householder cleaner that has netted more than $100 million in sales, the Squatty Potty with more than $30 million in sales, and mobile app Groove Book that was acquired by Shutterfly for $14.5 million.[xv] As of October 2019 *Shark Tank* entrepreneurs have totaled a collective $6 billion in sales.

Not only have the hosts—known as sharks—facilitated the creation of successful businesses, they have also created jobs in countless communities across the United States. *Shark Tank* has also filled the investor void in the many communities across the United States that lack access to angel investors, investment clubs, and venture capitalists.

While we were trying to push for echain to become a successful venture, on the other side of the country, up and coming entrepreneurs in Silicon Valley were easily raising millions of dollars with decent business concepts, a couple of pitch deck slides, and a meeting or two. After our failed meetings in Waterbury, we also considered moving the company to the Bay Area to join these ventures. Since I barely raised enough capital to cover product development costs, there was not enough cash to cover the bills and the burn rate, let alone a move across the country. When the Dot-com bubble burst, it made what was already a virtually impossible venture even more difficult, considering that we were in a tertiary city and with little access to capital and experienced business mentors.

Since my college major was in international business and finance, my chances of landing a job locally or in Connecticut for that matter were slim. As a result, I took a full-time job in finance located in New York City's Rockefeller Plaza, commuting two-and-a-half hours each way to and from the city five days a week for two years. The commute wasn't all bad news—I discovered Brooks Brothers and Starbucks for the first time. Also, on my way to work, I walked by the *Today* Show, which was partly filmed outside and was an interesting distraction from the grueling commute every day.

Perhaps things would have fared better if we started off in the Bay Area. The tech bubble had already burst, which dried up most VC investments. A lack of VC funding led to a lot of spending cuts that affected tech companies who once were splurging on everything brand new were now forced to budget and purchase used obsolete electronic and microelectronic components that were cheaper than purchasing brand new ones. It would have been the perfect market for echain.

Despite the bursting of the Dot.com bubble, Silicon Valley has thrived due to an influx of massively successful technology companies. While there were busts, the many successful companies created an astounding boom. The median household income in Silicon Valley exploded since then with an estimated median income $118,314 in 2019.[xvi] And it's still growing every single year. Although this example demonstrates the openness and ease of investing in entrepreneurs in Silicon Valley, this area has morphed into an extreme concentration of wealth and gentrification that should not be the model for other start-up friendly cities to follow, but demonstrates the massive successes that investing in tomorrow's technologies can produce.

And what about Waterbury—my hometown? While Waterbury has certainly not prospered like Silicon Valley, there have been a few positive developments.[xvii] Between 2012 and 2019, 90 new businesses created 2,800 jobs, which represent only 2.5 percent of jobs created relative to the population of Waterbury. Of those 2,800 jobs it is unclear what percentage of those jobs pay their workers a living wage. Downtown Waterbury is in the process of a facelift after a renovation of the city green and the upcoming $8 million renovation and expansion of the Mattatuck Museum, an American art and history museum.[xviii] Post University, which enrolls approximately 7,800 students in on campus, online and hybrid bachelor's degree programs, moved their Information Technology Center to the newly renovated Howland Hughes Building in downtown Waterbury.[xix] The University of Connecticut UCONN which offers over 110 majors also has a Waterbury campus located in downtown Waterbury just a few blocks from the new Post University location.

Despite these developments the economic situation for many in Waterbury has not changed much with median income household declining to an average of $39,681.[xx] When I searched the list of opportunity zones (OZs) in Connecticut, I realized that the entire downtown area of Waterbury, including where my former office was located, was designated as an OZ. In the downtown Waterbury OZ, 59 percent of the households live in poverty with a median household income of $12,747.00, one of the lowest in the nation. In total, about 30 percent of Waterbury's land mass has been designated as an OZ. Unfortunately, after two years since President

Trump signed the TCJA into law that provides wealthy investors with significant tax incentives for investing in OZs nationwide, Waterbury has done nothing to promote its OZs. As of November 2019, there's no website, no outreach to qualified opportunity funds (QOFs) or investors and no mention, that I could find, of OZs in any city materials. What's worse is that one of the major tax incentives, the 15 percent tax exemption, is going to expire on December 31, 2019. All while investors who have made investment in tier one OZs have been attacked in the media for actually investing, many Tier-2 and Tier-3 cities are culpable for making little to no an effort to attract investors, QOFs, developers, and start-ups who can transform their cities. The few Tier-2 and Tier-3 cities that have built a marketing and investor outreach plan deserve credit for understanding the benefits this legislation can provide. The communities that have failed to capitalize on this legislation still have time to develop a plan to gain a competitive advantage, which, I will discuss later in this book.

There are thousands of entrepreneurs across the country that have stories similar to mine—where would-be entrepreneurs have no outlet or support for their innovative ideas. In most cases, these Americans go on to take jobs where they are underpaid and undervalued, giving up forever on the idea of running their own businesses and building wealth. Few have the ability to persevere and go onto succeed because the odds are so stacked against them. They've got to make a living, pay their bills, and support their families. It's not surprising that the cost of this bargain involves putting their entrepreneurial ideas on ice. While America will never know what inventions and advances were missed out on because of the start-ups that never got off the ground, I have no doubt that there has been a high cost attached to this failure. I'm not blaming those who have given up—what choice did they have? Without resources or support, they saw no way forward. The blame rests squarely on the communities, business leaders, and successful entrepreneurs who failed to provide the encouragement and assistance that these would-be start-up founders so desperately needed. Starting a business is an incredibly difficult endeavor and starting a business in a community that lacks investment infrastructure and ecosystems is virtually impossible. Without experience or support, start-up founders struggle to take crucial steps forward to grow their businesses. Even if they succeed in producing a MVP, scaling a business is very difficult without access to investors with capital and guidance. My experience in Waterbury wasn't unique—it's a national issue for the 8,762 OZs across the country that need to build the next generation of entrepreneurs. Successful businesses owe it to their communities to invest in the next generation of entrepreneurs by creating VC, private investment, or accelerator programs. Without this type of support, a huge void exists in a community, preventing the next generation from enjoying start-up success. Facilitating a start-up culture is critical because start-ups experience the fastest growth and wind up employing the most employees as they evolve through their growth stages. The start-up stage is where founders hire their core teams that receive decent salaries and equity stakes in the business that vest over time. This is how employees of start-ups build wealth. Companies in the later part of the business cycle typically fill mostly entry-level jobs with less upward mobility and no equity. Because so many existing businesses and successful entrepreneurs from OZ communities across the country failed to invest in the next generation of entrepreneurs, they have essentially isolated themselves in their own wealth and prevented others from succeeding and enjoying similar successes.

The fact that most of the United States is an entrepreneurial dead zone explains why *Shark Tank* is such a hit. Americans are enamored with the hosts—known as the Sharks—who offer entrepreneurs from all walks of life a chance at success. The lure of *Shark Tank* obscures the fact that the business leaders and successful community members who have already enjoyed great success have done little to build up the next generation of potential entrepreneurs; instead, they've only isolated and enriched themselves, ultimately creating one of the largest wealth gaps in American history. The time has come for businesses, business leaders, entrepreneurs, and community leaders within these distressed communities to seize this golden opportunity by marketing themselves to potential investors willing to invest in their community. Creating a supportive infrastructure for start-ups in OZs—including mentorship programs, accelerators, incubators and actual investment—are the building blocks to success for these communities. When investors take an active role in facilitating a start-up culture, they create opportunities to learn about the business ideas brewing in a community. They can then select the businesses that they believe are the best candidates for personal investment, in a similar way to what the Sharks do in *Shark Tank*. Just like the Sharks, these investors will take an equity stake in the businesses they invest in. Because their own capital is at stake, they take an active interest in the business, looking out for it and seeking to grow and protect for the future.

This type of investment ultimately benefits the surrounding community, enabling all to succeed and thrive. In order to attract businesses and investment, all OZ communities must discover their strengths by positioning, and marketing themselves appropriately to the investors, developers, and entrepreneurs they seek to attract. OZ investment incentives hold the potential to create significant economic impact by bringing countless jobs into high-poverty communities and bolstering America's entire economy in return. This is why the Tax Cut and Jobs Act, which President Trump signed into law on December 17, 2017, is so crucial to America's future.[xxi] OZs represent the chance for Waterbury and other high poverty communities to rebuild with the assistance of massive federal tax incentives, compensating for decades of neglect and under-investment.

Investing in entrepreneurs and their surrounding communities creates a force multiplier of social and economic impact. Consider the impact of current tech leaders Apple, Google, and Amazon. Starting in communities such as Silicon Valley and Seattle gave these companies the advantage of building a start-up in an economic hub that possessed an existing and supportive investment ecosystem. Their success was only possible due to investment from experienced investors and business leaders as well as the support of these communities in return. The creation of OZs offers a fair and potentially powerful solution to close the wealth gap that has divided this country for so long. If OZs succeed, they offer the potential to solve many of the problems of distressed communities through well-paying jobs, food security, and affordable housing to name just a few. In the coming chapters, I'll reveal the strategies and tactics that translate opportunity into success for OZs, QOFs, OZ investors, and OZ start-ups and entrepreneurs. But let's first identify all the moving parts and players to make sense of it all.

Chapter 1

BREAKING IT ALL DOWN

America's superrich have grown about $21 trillion richer, while those in the bottom 50 percent of the wealth distribution have grown $900 billion poorer.[xxii] During the same period since 1989—the poorest Americans slid into "negative wealth," a situation where their debts are larger than the value of their assets.[xxiii] These statistics vividly illustrate the widening income gap that has spread across America. While the net wealth and income of the richest Americans have grown to exceed those of the poorest Americans by a factor of 10, the net wealth and income of the poorest Americans have barely budged. Nowhere has this income inequality been felt more deeply than in America's most distressed communities.

In an effort to increase investment in inner cities and other poverty-stricken areas, the 2017 Tax Cuts and Jobs Act (2017 TCJA) included a provision to incentivize the investment of capital gains into America's poorest communities. Labeled as opportunity zones (OZs), 8,762 census tracts across the United States were designated by state governors and other officials as eligible for this type of investment. Many inner cities and other distressed communities are now designated OZs. Through OZ legislation, investors now possess the potential to create real transformative impact by investing an unprecedented amount of capital in communities and entrepreneurs. These investments are designed to generate well-paying jobs, build affordable housing, improve access to healthcare, and provide equitable education opportunities for all. In effect, this provision of the 2017 TCJA sought to leverage the U.S. tax code to bridge the gap between America's wealthiest investors and the entrepreneurs that desperately need investment capital to help transform their communities.

Investors—specifically family offices, ultra-high-net-worth individuals and wealth managers—can deploy their capital in one or multiple communities through specially designed qualified opportunity funds (QOFs). These types of professional investors are an ideal match for OZ investment deals because they are likely to possess sufficient investable capital in the form of capital gains to meet QOF minimum investment requirements. A family office is a private investment firm set up to serve ultra-high-net-worth individuals and their families. These firms offer a customized management solution that takes care of the entirety of these individual's financial and investment needs. Many founders of companies that have recently gone public or who have sold their businesses privately set up family offices to manage their new-found wealth. Minimum assets under management for a family office usually start at $100 million due to the costs and complexity of running a family office.[xxiv] Multifamily offices and the largest family offices can have as much as $10 billion or more in assets under management. Ultra-high-net-worth individuals usually have at least $30 million of investable assets, excluding their home, personal assets, and collectibles.[xxv] Wealth managers, who provide wealthy individuals with investment advice, financial planning, and risk management services, can invest their clients' capital gains into QOFs. These three types of investors have the ability and desire to invest capital gains in QOFs that align with their specific niche and regional focus.

QOFs are the conduit to funnel investor capital into poor communities through investments in start-ups, businesses, and real estate. Businesses, start-ups, existing buildings, and undeveloped land across these communities are all eligible for investment. This scenario creates virtually limitless possibility for the transformation of these distressed communities into vibrant cities where residents can work in careers offering sustainable income. Even more importantly, there's the potential for every OZ stakeholder to build wealth. Several factors contribute to inequality, including an abundance of low paying jobs and the lack of opportunity for the bottom 60 percent of Americans to build wealth by either starting businesses or building equity through an employee stock ownership plan (ESOP). Through OZs, residents of distressed communities can not only get better jobs but also the chance to start their own businesses and participate in the wealth-building process.

Investors can profit through successful investments in QOFs, while QOFs can profit from successful investments in OZ real estate, businesses, and start-ups. OZs themselves benefit from successful OZ investments, which create lasting jobs, businesses, affordable housing, and dynamic communities.

Eager to drive investment to their communities, cities such as Erie PA, Birmingham AL and many other communities created economic development groups to work with QOFs, investors, and OZ businesses. They built websites, attended conferences, identified promising areas for investment, and then waited for the capital floodgates to open.

However, instead of capital arriving to rescue distressed communities across the country, premium developments in top-tier cities have reaped much of the media coverage. Well-connected and well-funded interests have used OZ tax benefits to attract funding for luxury developments. Some of these developments were actually underway before the OZ legislation was passed specifically in New Orleans, Louisiana, and Miami—as well as a few other cities. In these cities, early OZ development focused on high-end hotels, restaurants, office towers, apartment buildings, student housing, and storage facilities employing just a few low wage workers.[xxvi] This situation developed for a number of reasons. Many of the political insiders who deployed capital in these luxury developments had large sums of capital already raised. As soon as OZ developments were identified, these fund managers invested that capital quickly. Why? Because it is easier to deploy large sums of capital into one large project, which is a major reason why the earliest OZ projects tended to be large real estate developments.

Clearly, a major constituency in early OZ investing are these well-funded interests focused on large property developments in Tier-1 markets. While these investors have received a significant amount of media attention, they aren't the only investor constituency in the OZ universe. As I attended OZ conferences across the country, I encountered many investors who want to invest for social impact through the medium of QOFs. These are investors who shun the type of OZ development that has gotten so much publicity—major hotel and property developments in large cities. This large contingent of social impact investors is holding back from OZ investment because they don't want to be branded for taking advantage of the law or see their investments result in gentrification that pushes low-income residents out of their communities.

I realized that a major reason that OZ investing hasn't taken off is because professional investors can't find deals that further their social impact investing goals. Those big developments initially occurred—at least in part—because of the pressure that investment managers face to invest capital quickly, a pressure that is magnified because of the tight timelines imposed by OZ legislation. This pressure occurs because their investors want to see proven results. That means fund managers need to have deals available for investment. It is much easier for fund managers to deploy capital into one large deal, rather than spending time waiting for multiple small investment deals to materialize. For example, if a QOF manager has $100 million to invest and can choose from investing the entire amount in one large luxury development or in a number of smaller $10 to $20 million projects, then that fund manager will invariably choose the $100 million project. The fund manager will choose that option because one large project will put all that capital to work immediately to make money as opposed to sitting on the sidelines doing nothing. While it would have been better for the OZs in question to have gained from investments designed for real community impact, large real estate developments tend to be the easiest and fastest option to deploy capital in a hurry. It's also not easy to line up lots of small deals, which is one reason why OZ investment is getting off the ground slowly.

Investors gain substantial tax benefits—a 15 percent step-up in basis or a 15 percent tax exemption on their original capital gains after investing in a QOF for at least seven years. In addition, investors also benefit from tax deferrals of capital gains that they invest into QOFs. To obtain that benefit, investors can defer tax on any prior gains invested in a QOF until the earlier of the date on which the investment in a QOF is sold or exchanged, or December 31, 2026. Tax benefits continue through 2046 for the 10 percent step-up in basis or 10 percent tax exemption on their original capital gains when held for a minimum of five years.[xxvii] The third and most appealing tax incentive offers a permanent exclusion from taxable income of capital gains that stem from the appreciation of the new gains in a QOF investment, provided the investment is held for a minimum of ten years and the law stipulates that this permanent exclusion exclusively applies to gains that are accrued after an investment has been made into a QOF.[xxviii]

This pressure is especially difficult for QOF managers to deal with because of the lack of deal flow. Deal flow describes the amount of investment opportunities available to investment managers at a given time. The OZ deal market is very fragmented because of the large number of opportunity zones and the lack of a platform where QOFs, investors, entrepreneurs, and OZ communities can come together, network, and collaborate. Instead of selecting from a variety of attractive OZ deals, QOF managers have to attend conferences, talk to officials in individual OZs, and network to find any deals. What's occurring is that many of the deals that QOF managers are pitching do not match investors' exact investment filters. I call this the last mile of OZ investing. This is why I created DealConnect Hub—to bring efficiency to the last mile of OZ investing by connecting family offices, wealth managers, and private equity investors with high-quality investment deals.

In the world of capital raising, investment fund managers act as middlemen between investors and investment deals. This role is complex because there is rarely a balance between the amount of capital raised and the amount of deals available. For example, an investment manager may have raised $50 million, but may only have $30 million in investment deals or opportunities. In that case, the manager has to scramble to find additional attractive deal opportunities so that they can deploy that capital as efficiently as possible. Investors are eager for their investment managers to deploy their capital quickly so that they can begin profiting off of investment deals instead of having their investment sit around earning an approximate 2 percent return on cash.[xxix] In the traditional world of investing, it's challenging, but not difficult, to find investment deal flow. For example, mutual fund managers investing in small cap technology companies can run a screen for small cap technology companies that meet their investment requirements. However, for OZ investors, there is no centralized platform where they can find significant deal flow so that they can locate deals that fit into their regional and sector niche focus.

Most OZ stakeholders are frustrated because the market has been so slow to move.

Aside from those initial luxury deals—and plenty of conferences touting the tax breaks involved in OZ investing—surprisingly little investment has actually occurred. According to a CoStar analysis, QOFs are raising about 10 cents on the dollar of the amounts they hope to raise.[xxx] At the time of CoStar's analysis, they identified 160 QOFs targeting commercial real estate that were registered with the federal Securities and Exchange Commission through July 2019.[xxxi] These funds had raised $1.59 billion, but collectively targeted more than $15.46 billion, CoStar noted.

An article published on Primior.com, a real estate development and investment management firm in Diamond Bar, California, noted that "the funds with the most success meeting their targets are smaller funds focused on single property investments, according to the reports." On the other hand, funds that are trying to blindly raise money while identifying suitable projects later are struggling, the article stated.[xxxii]

Some funds have reported that they have yet to raise capital. Many investors are hesitant because they want to invest in specific deals and have yet to find a QOF with investments that meet their criteria.[xxxiii] Also, the U.S. Treasury and Internal Revenue Service were delayed in releasing rules due to the government shutdown earlier in 2019.[xxxiv] There is optimism that the market will pick up toward the end of the year as the deadline for 15 percent step-up in basis occurs on December 31, 2019.[xxxv]

"Opportunity zones are like high school sex," Brett Messing, president of hedge fund Skybridge Capital, told *Institutional Investor* Magazine in May 2019. "Everyone is talking about it, but nobody is doing it."[xxxvi] After attending many OZ conferences and meeting with America's wealthiest investors, family offices, QOF managers, and developers, I realized there were several key components missing:

Education: While conferences and networking are necessary, those seeking to raise capital first have to educate themselves on what professional investors seek in an investment deal and then learn the intricacies of how to attract investors to invest in their deals. Capital raising is a long and involved process that requires a sophisticated approach as well as discipline and perseverance. Investors with significant capital gains have a multitude of investment options where they can invest their capital aside from OZs. An investor with $10 million in capital gains to invest will likely diversify their investments, so only a small portion of that capital is likely to end up in a QOF. That means QOF managers need to persuade investors that their OZ deal is the best option among all the competing alternatives. These fund managers also need to possess a demonstrable track record through investment or development in distressed communities. That's why QOFs must define their niche, publish content, understand their target investor, and analyze their competition. Avoiding these necessary steps will not work, which is why so many QOF managers have little to show for all the networking they've done and conferences they've attended. When QOF managers master the basics, they will begin to attract experienced investors.

"The vast majority of QOFs are 'blind pools' that raise money first and hope to identify projects later," said Johnney Zhang, chief executive of Primior in an article on the company's website.[xxxvii] "The best way to make sure the firm meets Internal Revenue Service requirements and our investors' expectations is to create a fund for each development project individually. With fully entitled, single-asset funds, our clients can be confident that their investment will provide the targeted returns they are seeking." In addition, QOF investments are competing against other types of tax advantaged investments such as 1031 exchanges, which involve investors reinvesting capital gains in a similar investment property with the profits from the sale of a prior investment property.

QOF managers who avoid this type of blind pool approach by specifically positioning their QOF by sector niche and geographical area stand a much better chance of attracting investors. Once these QOF managers begin to attract capital, they will be able to develop a track record and build credibility. That will, in turn, attract more investors to invest in more deals. This is why a methodical approach to capital raising is so necessary. As more QOF managers master this process and attract more capital, they will be in search of more deals. As I noted earlier, QOF managers need to create as much balance between the capital they've raised and the deals they want to invest in. This balance is currently out of sync in OZs, which are in need of sustainable deal flow.

Deal flow: Deal flow refers to the quantity of investment opportunities available to investors at a particular moment in time. Deal flow is critical because it ensures that investors can find multiple suitable investment opportunities. To optimize OZ deal flow, QOF deals in thousands of OZs across the country need to be transparently available to investors. Because investors lack access to the specific types of deals that fit their investment filters, OZs suffer from a lack of deal flow. While some Tier-1 OZ communities have been proactive in identifying real estate, business, and start-up projects suitable for investing, more communities need to focus on identifying these types of deals too. OZ communities need deals to materialize to create better outcomes for the people that this legislation was designed to help.

Impact focus: Because early investors have focused on high-end developments, there's been very little consideration of impact investing, which can act as the seeds to create high paying jobs that will essentially enable people to afford better housing, healthcare, and an investment force multiplier for distressed communities. "Impact investing is defined as investing in something that reflects your social values," said Morgan Simon, author of *Real Impact*, on my podcast. Simon divided impact investing into two categories. The first is transformative, which addresses underlying structural problems in society or the environment. It is this type of transformative investing that is the core function of impact investing. The second is palliative, which doesn't make a sustainable difference and therefore is not true impact investing. An example of palliative impact investing might involve decelerating climate change or providing minor relief for the poor. When QOFs and OZ start-ups focus on social impact, there's the potential to optimize investment so that the investment has a chance to make a profit and make a difference. If OZ stakeholders focus on social impact first, OZ investments will provide the poor or economically struggling with the income they need to afford housing, decent food, healthcare, and better schools. Leading with impact must focus on jobs first—well-paying jobs—so that individuals gain the opportunity to create wealth for themselves. Real estate deals only benefit developers and investors because residents of OZs typically lack the higher amounts of capital needed and credit ratings to participate in real estate investment deals.

Connect: With no centralized location where OZ community leaders, QOFs, investors, and OZ businesses can connect and actually visualize and track where deals are getting funded, progress will be slow. That's why I created DealConnect Hub—to efficiently connect investors to high-quality investment deals. With an Airbnb-like platform, DealConnect Hub matches family offices and wealth managers with experienced and highly qualified QOF and direct deals. OZ deal flow is scarce because investors aren't aware of what QOFs are out there to invest in, just as QOFs aren't aware of all of the real estate, start-up, and business investment opportunities that exist in OZs. DealConnect Hub is designed to completely change the status quo, by providing education for all parties as well as data visualization designed to facilitate deal flow. All stakeholders can use the platform to filter OZs and deals to achieve their specific investment objectives. They can also see what communities are attracting capital and what specific types of deals are getting done. DealConnect Hub fills the current deal flow gap by connecting all stakeholders so that high-quality deal flow can occur.

I wrote Opportunity Zone Millionaire and created DealConnect Hub to educate, support, and connect OZ stakeholders for the largest possible social impact attainable. Each of these components is a critical building block in the success of OZs. Without education in the capital raising process, OZ leaders and new QOF managers won't be able to effectively attract and connect with investors to raise capital. Without an impact investing focus, capital can't be leveraged as a transformative force to reimagine and rebuild these communities. Without deal flow, investors can't deploy capital to the communities where it is desperately needed. Without connection, deal flow is impossible. Therefore, all these missing pieces need to be put into place for OZ investing to be fully impactful and flourish.

If you're a leader in an OZ, you need to know how to go about positioning your community's OZs to attract QOFs, investors, developers, and start-ups. If you're an investor, you need to know how to evaluate QOFs and OZ start-ups. If you're a QOF manager or developer, you need to know how to connect with investors, successfully pitch your fund and identify promising investments. Many of these stakeholders are frustrated, because the success they anticipated isn't materializing quickly enough.

Newer QOF managers are among the most frustrated, because the OZ incentives seemed like an easy sell to investors. However, investing is a long-term, relationship-building process. That's why it's a major focus of this book. With a step-by-step approach, I offer a practical framework for achieving success for OZ communities, OZ investors, QOFs, and OZ entrepreneurs. I share capital raising and marketing strategies that really work as well as stories of successful entrepreneurs, investors, and OZs. I describe virtually all QOF managers as inexperienced because QOFs are a completely new type of investment class. Unless you are an extremely well-connected capital raiser with lots of experience and a phenomenal track record, you need to spend your time building and refining your strategies, learning effective capital raising techniques and deciding on a niche focus. Yes, there are a few super experienced capital raisers out there who built impressive track records with investors who are eager to put money into their funds. Then there's the rest of us—those who have to keep working at it, building our funds one investor and one deal at a time. I've spent most of my life grappling with the very issues that OZ stakeholders face today. There's no shame in that—capital raising is hard. I wrote this book to help the vast majority of OZ officials, QOF managers, developers, and entrepreneurs who need to get better at focusing on how to attract investors.

I started Rocco Forino Capital to privately manage my own capital and investments. As I began to diversify across different asset classes

I was attracted to OZs. I liked the idea of OZ investing because it had the potential to create positive social impact and potentially create massive exits with both tax exemptions and capital gains exclusions. A double bottom line outcome to create both profit and impact. As I attended conferences and family office events, it was clear that a lack of quality and diversified deal flow was hindering OZ investment. Inspired by similar functionality that launched my previous startup AlphaBrand (A proprietary matching platform that solves my customer's most logistically complex interior design projects), I developed DealConnect Hub to create data visualization and solve the challenge of a lack of deal flow for my investment company and as well as others. Over the course of my life, my experiences have provided me with a unique perspective on OZs and OZ investing. In effect, I've occupied the position of every stakeholder at the OZ table. I've been the resident of an OZ, an OZ entrepreneur, an OZ investor as well as an OZ stakeholder for my own hometown of Waterbury, Connecticut.

In chapter 2 I describe America's growing wealth gap. By 2016, the richest 1 percent of Americans owned more than half of the overall wealth invested in stocks, mutual funds, and bonds.[xxxviii] This is significant because without the ability to invest and grow savings through compounding and price appreciation, most Americans will never be able to achieve financial security. Because of this gap, most Americans are unable—not unwilling to save—which has created a savings and retirement crisis. Many are trapped in a cycle of debt that they can't get out of. Many people haven't yet recovered from the Great Recession, which took a toll on all three of their income, savings, and property values. As you will learn from this chapter, none of these are investments—and investments are what create wealth. The vast majority of residents in OZs lack even $400 in liquid cash to pay for a car repair. Their 401(k) balances are also abysmally low—less than $40,000 on average—meaning that they have virtually no cash safety net to meaningfully create a better future for themselves and their families.

As the longest economic expansion in history nears its end, major questions exist as to how the government and the Federal Reserve Board will manage the next recession. Chapter 2 also takes a close look at the theories of billionaire hedge fund manager Ray Dalio, who believes that lowering interest rates and buying debt through quantitative easing (QE) will be insufficient to jumpstart the economy in the next recession. Instead, Dalio believes that when the government puts money directly into the hands of spenders, the economy will benefit, sparking recovery. I concur. To me, it only makes sense to use OZs, OZ businesses, and QOFs in conjunction with Dalio's theory on Modern Monetary policy to help America grow itself out of the next recession. There's no need to test the limits of the Fed's ability to manage future recessions when we can proactively employ spending to lift the incomes and prospects of Americans living on the economic edge.

Chapter 3 covers the nuts and bolts of OZs and QOFs, explaining the basics of the law and how to create a QOF. I explain the different corporate structures that entrepreneurs, investment managers and developers can use to create QOFs. OZs were founded on the premise that deal sponsors, investors and residents of distressed communities can collectively benefit from the potential to build wealth. The passage of the landmark 2017 TCJA also provides entrepreneurs and developers the option of founding, locating or moving a business to a qualified opportunity zone so that they can take advantage of the OZ tax incentives to enhance the likelihood of attracting investors to their investment deals.

Once you understand why opportunity zones were created and how various corporate structures can be used to start a QOF, you're now ready to learn more about the tax benefits of investing in QOFs in

Chapter 4. In the first part of the chapter, I quantify the benefits and review the final regulations, which the IRS issued in December 2019. I also explore the differences between QOFs and 1031 exchanges and discuss QOF risks and why it's critical to perform due diligence to ensure that a QOF is meeting its compliance obligations. An in-depth tax treatment is beyond the scope of the book. Fortunately, there are many experienced CPAs and attorneys located throughout the country that you can consult who are well versed on opportunity zone laws and the tax code.

Chapter 5 focuses on actionable, step-by-step strategies that OZ leaders can use to attract investors, QOFs, developers, start-ups, and entrepreneurs to their OZ communities. Communities that fail to act to attract OZ capital are depriving their citizens and communities of a significant economic development tool. In the two years since OZs were created by the 2017 TCJA, many communities have done little or nothing to identify attractive OZ projects or promote themselves to QOFs and investors. Community leaders who do nothing to take advantage of this legislation will guarantee that their residents are left behind when money does flow into active and competing OZs across the country. Residents in these communities should support candidates who will actively market their OZ communities and withhold support from those who are inactive, ineffective, and already late in the process. If you are an economic development official in an OZ, start by creating a positioning statement, then add professional marketing materials, a prospectus, and a web page with information about available deals as well as the contact information for economic development officials. This will ensure that your community has the tools to connect with QOFs and investors through the DealConnect Hub platform. Chapter 5 offers specific advice on how OZ leaders can gain a competitive advantage in the race to attract start-ups, developers, QOFs and capital to the community.

Chapter 6 is essential reading for QOF managers. In this chapter, I dispel the myth that capital raising is easy and provide hands-on strategies on how to position your QOF to attract investors. Professional investors are highly discriminating and unlikely to invest without first building long-term relationships. To succeed, you must differentiate your QOF from the competition by specializing in a specific niche and geographic area. Painting an in-depth portrait of your investor by creating an investor avatar is a very helpful step in understanding what your investors want to see before they invest. You must be aware of your competition, ensure your QOF's materials are professional, cultivate long-term relationships, and promote your expertise at every point of contact from social media to email marketing.

Chapter 7 covers the ABCs of capital raising for entrepreneurs, start-ups, and developers. This isn't your average entrepreneurial spiel. Instead, it's aimed at start-up founders from a similar background that I came from—those who lack access to investors, mentors, accelerators, and incubators. If you have access to those advantages, you've got a head start in the race for capital. Consider Boston, which has an ecosystem of investors and technology entrepreneurs connected to Massachusetts Institute of Technology and multiple other universities, as well as a variety of incubators and accelerators. My goal is to educate entrepreneurs who lack these connections so that they can have an equal chance to start businesses, raise capital, and change their own futures and the futures of their communities. This chapter helps you:

- Assess your strengths
- Leverage an immigrant mind-set
- Understand how to create a minimum viable product
- Avoid common mistakes
- Attract investors

Chapter 8, the final chapter, introduces the concept of impact investing, which uses investor capital to create social or environmental change. Impact investing offers the opportunity to not only make a profit on investments but also achieve positive social or environmental change. OZs and impact investing are a perfect match, because they combine capital, distressed communities, and the potential for desperately needed social change. In this chapter, investors, entrepreneurs, QOFs, and OZ leaders can learn about the benefits of impact investing and how to integrate an impact investing approach into their redevelopment efforts. When successfully combined, impact investing and OZs can build sustainable communities, provide well-paying jobs, create affordable housing, support equitable education, and offer the opportunities for advancement for all. Think about it this way—investing with impact means that you leave more value in a community than you take back out, as Simon put it on my podcast. You want to make sure that the community you invest in is a primary beneficiary of that investment and that everyone who is involved in that investment is treated fairly, she added. "It's not just about making a community better than it is right now—it's figuring out what is fundamentally fair and structuring an investment from that place," she said.

Over the past several decades, America has become more divided politically, economically, and socially. These divisions have become greater over time in virtually every facet of society. The purpose of *Opportunity Zone Millionaire* is to motivate all OZ stakeholders to step out of their comfort zone to repair broken connections and restore America to its former preeminence. This country was built on opportunity for all, a promise that we need to restore for a just and equitable society.

I invite and challenge all OZ stakeholders to use this book to consider how you can achieve your objectives to improve your community, growing your wealth, and building your business while also working toward making measurable change, improving the lives of others, and creating real impact. America was founded on principals of equality and opportunity. During the past half century, there hasn't been a lot of equality and most of the opportunity has gone to those who already had a lengthy head start.

If you're seeking to start a QOF in an OZ community, what steps can you take to not just raise capital, but also ensure that everyone in your community greatly benefits from the capital that is raised? How can you be as inclusive as possible so that the residents of your community have a say in where, when, and how development takes place?

If you're an OZ investor, how can you realize the returns you'd like to achieve while making positive social impact in the community in which you're investing? How can you best invest so that the community reaps sustainable benefits now and in the future?

If you're an OZ entrepreneur, what pressing needs have you identified in your community that need to be solved? How can you solve them? And how can you scale your solution so that you build a sustainable business while making an impact in communities across the country?

When you ask yourself these questions now and deeply consider your answers, you'll start on a path that will create a sustainable future for yourself and others. We are at a pivotal point in America's history. Citizens throughout this country have the opportunity to work together to collectively earn profits, make positive social impact, and continue to maintain America's role as the number one economy in the world for decades to come. It's my hope that this book and DealConnect Hub will become the catalyst to build a better future for all Americans.

Chapter 2

AMERICA'S GROWING WEALTH GAP

During the past 30 years, the United States has morphed into two unequal socioeconomic societies—the upper class and the middle and lower classes. Research reveals that a large gap exists between the upper class, which is composed of the top 40 percent of individuals, and the middle and lower class, which is composed of the remaining 60 percent. Since the 1980s, The income and net wealth of the bottom 60 percent has remain unchanged, while the income and net wealth of the top 40 percent exceeds that of the other group by a factor of ten, according to Ray Dalio in his book, *Principles for Navigating Big Debt Crises*.[39] It is my conviction that OZ investing offers the potential to bridge that gap for reasons that I'll explain later in this chapter.

First, it's important to understand why this gap exists, how it hurts America and how OZs can operate as a catalyst. For households in the bottom 60 percent, the lack of income also means a lack of extra money to put into savings, Dalio notes. More than half of those in the bottom 60 percent cannot save a portion of their income in case of emergencies.[40] According to a recent Federal Reserve study, 39 percent of Americans would struggle to raise even $400 in emergency funds.[41] As for retirement savings, the bottom 60 percent don't have enough. Only a third of households in the bottom 60 percent have retirement savings that average less than $20,000.[42]

While some may have some savings, most of it is in less liquid forms of wealth such as real estate and vehicles typically financed by debt. Only a quarter of their savings are in cash or some financial asset.[43]

Though most of the bottom 60 percent spend their extra income to pay bills and pay off their debt, according to Dalio. For the bottom 60 percent, 63 percent of their total debt comprise mortgage payments followed by student loans, auto loans, and credit card bills.[44] Student loans and credit card payments are especially devastating because of higher interest rates. The bottom 60 percent use most of their paycheck to pay off debt, whereas the top 40 percent have plenty additional income to save or invest, Dalio notes. According to a recent study by Bridgewater Associates, Dalio's hedge fund, assets of the top 40 percent are more focused on appreciable liquid assets like real estate, stocks, and business equities.[45] Unlike those with lower incomes, the wealthiest are less likely to spend their money on consumer products or other depreciable assets that require debt financing.

There's no doubt that most Americans operate with little financial cushion and too much debt, two factors that are caused by the meager salaries offered by American businesses. Low-paying jobs force Americans to take on debt and offer no spare cash for anything else but the bare necessities of life. They have no mechanism to save for retirement, build wealth, pay off debt, save for their children's college education or build an emergency fund, which is why so many live on the edge. "Compared to the previous decade, Americans are working much more for much less pay and they're paying substantially more for the basic necessities," writes Serbulent Turan of the University of British Columbia in an article entitled "Is the United States on the brink of a revolution?"[46] On the surface, it seems like there shouldn't be a problem—unemployment hit 50-year lows recently and consumers are spending. However, low wage growth, the prevalence of low-wage jobs and higher costs of living translate to most Americans falling behind financially. Between 2015 and 2018, the cost of living rose by 14 percent, according to an analysis by GOBankingRates.[47] This state of affairs comes on top of the fact that most Americans have yet to recover from the 2008 financial crisis. A rise in protests during the past decade, including Occupy Wall Street, the Women's March, and Black Lives Matter, hasn't changed the system. Not only have the situations gotten worse, but they've also been poorly covered by the mainstream media. Many Americans feel alienated from the political system on both the right and the left. The 2020 Presidential election reflects this, with President Donald Trump on the right and Democratic candidates on the left, including Elizabeth Warren and Bernie Sanders who profess that capitalism is broken.

The largest corporate tax cut in history, enacted in the 2017 TCJA that created OZs, was touted as an action to boost employment, raise wages, and encourage corporate investment.[48] Sure, some companies raised wages or provided bonuses initially. However, although the tax savings continue to flow, companies have used the vast majority of the savings to buy back stock, which can have the effect of increasing stock prices for the benefit of executives and stockholders.[49] While corporations spent a record $720 billion in 2018 repurchasing stock, wages barely budged in the wake of the tax cut. An International Monetary Fund analysis found that growth in business investment between the end of 2017 and the third quarter of 2019 was due to strong domestic demand and the rising market power of large corporations, rather than the tax cut.[50] Record profits also tend not to be invested in human capital; instead, they accrue to shareholders and company executives, who use increased stock prices and stock options to build wealth.

The toxic combination of low wages and lack of investment in employees, entrepreneurs, and education leads to generations trapped in distressed communities. The ongoing lack of investment in future entrepreneurs and future business leaders by businesses, successful entrepreneurs and communities maintains the status quo, keep rich people rich and the poor people poor. When Americans in OZs create an innovative product, there are no mentors, accelerators, or incubators, or business leaders to support them. This lack of support dooms these ideas and these would-be entrepreneurs to failure. It's a collective, nationwide failure. The opportunity cost of leaving all the potential start-ups and start-up founders out of a potential brighter future is not just a personal tragedy—it's a tragedy for America as a whole.

These young people can't escape their situation by starting a business or by going to college, which might seem the next logical destination to break out of poverty. However, because of their lack of family style wealth and lack of sophistication about the college admissions process, many fail to either gain a degree or maximize the degree that they've earned. Not so for those at the top of the income curve, the top 40 percent of the population spend four times more on education—a valuable asset—than the bottom 60 percent.[51] However, there is one fundamental difference between public and private education: wealthy students have access to better resources and opportunities. Naturally, the top 40 percent have access to top-tier schools, better paying careers, and other connections that leads to better opportunities unlike those in the bottom 60 percent.[52] Private schools provide more resources and world-class educational facilities whereas public schools often lack these essential resources, meaning their students aren't connected to the networks that their private school peers tap through their school and family relationships. Also, low-income students must borrow to finance their education, a situation which means that they are trapped in debt whether they obtain a college education or not. Even those who do graduate are anchored by mortgage-sized student loan burdens. "African American borrowers, students who are parents and low-income students have higher-than-average default rates, in some cases topping 50 percent," according to the Center for American Progress.[53] In contrast, students from the wealthiest families never have to borrow, so they enter the workforce free of the burden of paying back student loans. Poor students may be forced to take a low-paying job merely to repay their student loans. That career choice will likely trap them in an ongoing cycle of low-wage work that they can't escape. In fact, this outcome is more likely than not because they lack the access to the types of networks that can create a fast-track to a successful career.

The conventional wisdom states that higher education—especially at prestigious private high schools and universities—is the best way to restore equality in America. There are two problems with this conclusion. Number one is that the wealthy, as evidenced by recent higher education scandals, attempt to game the system to maintain higher educational privilege for their children and grandchildren through donations, the legacy system and other unknown manipulations to the system. Number two is that these private schools don't alleviate inequality, they actually perpetuate it. In *The Meritocracy Trap: How America's Foundational Myth Feeds Inequality, Dismantles the Middle Class and Devours the Elite* (Penguin Press, 2019), Daniel Markovits, a Yale Law School professor, believes that higher education has become a divisive force. At the top, higher education creates a system allegedly based on meritocracy—the idea that the best, most talented people should rise to the top—but instead perpetuates a class system based on advantage passed down from parent to child. He notes that the "academic gap between rich and poor students now exceeds the gap between white and black students in 1954, the year in which the Supreme Court decided

Brown v. Board of Education."[54] In this case, the Supreme Court finally ruled that "separate but equal" racially segregated schools were illegal.

It's not only higher education. There's the whole issue of rich kids getting ahead based on their parents' wealth and credentials. Consider how many children of the super wealthy ride on the coattails of their parents' privilege, accessing top-tier educations, prestigious internships, and investments by their parents and their family friends in their half-baked start-up ideas. This illustrates an important aspect of social mobility or lack thereof: not only is it harder for lower- and middle-class individuals to rise to the upper classes, it is getting almost impossible for the children of the upper classes to descent to a lower class. According to research conducted by Brookings Institution researcher Richard Reeves and others, it is more likely that the children of the rich will remain rich and the children of the poor will remain poor.[55] "One of the most striking social science findings of recent years is that only half of today's 30-year-olds earn more their parents," writes Reeves and Kathrine Guyot in *Fewer Americans Are Making More Than Their Parents Did—Especially if They Grew up in the Middle Class.*[56] "Raj Chetty and his coauthors showed that rates of absolute mobility—that is, the share of children with higher inflation-adjusted incomes than their parents—declined from around 90 percent for children born in 1940 to just 50 percent for those born in 1984."[57] article also agrees with the lack of downward mobility for the upper class, noting "the richer the parents, the larger the decline in mobility for their kids."

"There's a lot of talent being wasted because it's not able to rise, but there's also a lot of relatively untalented people who aren't falling and end up occupying positions they shouldn't," said Reeves, author of *Dream Hoarders: How the American Upper Middle Class is Leaving Everyone Else in the Dust, Why That is a Problem and What to Do*

About It (Brookings Institute Press, 2017). His study—along with the racial discrimination lawsuit that forced Harvard University to reveal its admissions data, showed how top universities amplify privilege that already exists amount their student body. Consider that a student from a wealthy family is 77 times more likely to gain admittance to an Ivy School than a student from a poor family. This reality shows how restrictive social mobility has become, in a higher educational environment where the University of Washington admitted more low-income students than the entire student bodies of Harvard, Stanford, Yale and Princeton. Selective colleges that rank just below the Ivy League show similar patterns of enrollment—many more students from the top 1 percent and many fewer from the lowest 20 percent. Mediocre students from wealthy families are also much more likely to be admitted to top schools than well-performing poor students, mainly because of legacy admissions. Joseph Fishkin, author of *Bottlenecks: A New Theory of Equal Opportunity* (Oxford University Press, 2016) said, "The greater the inequality, the greater the impact on opportunity. There's a self-fulfilling class anxiety among the middle and upper-middle class because they sense that the spaces are scarce now. There are fewer secure jobs. And the scarcer they are, the more valuable they are."

The implications of these findings are disturbing. The only conclusion that can be reasonably reached is that upward mobility has become much harder to achieve at the same time that downward mobility from the top has virtually disappeared. The isolation of the very top income cohorts from the rest of America has become entrenched at the same time that the lower income cohorts have become more disenfranchised from the hope or possibility of wealth and prosperity. The wealth gap, low wages and a lack of investment in distressed communities and their entrepreneurs creates more inequality and a bigger distance of the two major classes in America from each other, anchoring many people to debt and low income, while the elite few are encased in privilege and wealth.

The Middle-Class Consumer Debt Trap

Debt continues to rise faster than the income for households in the bottom 60 percent even during prosperous economic periods.[58] This occurs because of the factors I established earlier in this chapter—the prevalence of low-wage jobs, student loan debt, lack of opportunities to build wealth and lack of upward social mobility. Americans living in OZs have no choice but to take on debt because they have no other way to obtain cars to drive to their low wage jobs, pay for emergencies or pay for healthcare. Dalio further describes how as economies improve and unemployment rates decline, the bottom 60 percent rely on borrowing via the reliance on credit cards, mortgages, and car loans because their current income substantiates the ability to borrow, and this group assumes that their future self will have the same or higher income and extra money to pay off these accumulated debts in the future, which is often not the case.

The dynamics of borrowing work like this: When you borrow money, you need to spend less than you make in the future to make payments and eventually pay that debt off.[59] If you're like most people, you apply for loans when the economy is doing well and your income justifies borrowing. However, when the economy cools off, your income may take a hit or you may even lose your job. Then, you find yourself in a situation where you have to pay your debt with less income or maybe with no income. Like most people in the bottom 60 percent, your income has probably stagnated, which leaves you even less prepared to handle the next economic crisis when it comes, Dalio asserts.[60]

While the government was able to effectively lower interest rates and buy financial assets, which was the case during the Great Recession of 2008, these monetary policy tools won't be as fast-acting or as effective going into the next recession, Dalio believes.

Because of these factors, Dalio relates, the next economic crisis will require a different approach to prevent a long and severe recession comparable to that of the 1930s.[61] This approach will require the government to reconsider its approach to modern monetary policies and the wealthy top 40 percent of Americans will be required to do something radically different than in the past, by taking their capital gains and reinvest it back into distressed communities that exist in large numbers across this country as opposed to investing in debt and alternative currencies as I will explain below.[62] It is important to understand how financial crises occur and how the government responds to them so that we can determine the best investment alternatives to consider when the next recession ultimately occurs.

The Great Recession

In 2007, the United States entered one of the worst economic crises: the Great Recession. Those devastating impacts still linger in the economy— another reason to embrace investing in OZs. Prior to the financial crisis borrowers were approved for loans they could not afford to pay back. This was followed by flawed financial policies comprising of slashing interest rates. According to William J. O'Neil in his book *How to Make Money in Stocks*, the root of the Great Recession could be traced to 1995 when the Community Reinvestment Act (CRA) of 1997 was changed.[63] According to new regulations, banks had to give new subprime CRA loans to borrowers in lower income areas, even requiring no down payment. Otherwise, these banks would be penalized.[64]

Banks and government-sponsored enterprises such as Fannie Mae and Freddie Mac were buying a massive amount of subprime loans, which eventually led to government bailouts to save these entities from going bankrupt. While the original intention of helping lower-income people to borrow money to buy homes was good, it also ignited the house bubble, and it eventually burst with major consequences to the entire global economy.[65]

During the Great Recession, housing prices fell by more than 31.8 percent, after peaking nationally at $254,400 in January, 2007.[66] Homeowners could no longer sell their home or pay back loans they initially took out. Finding a job was near impossible and mass layoffs occurred across the country. Unemployment peaked at 10 percent in October 2009.[67]

Since the financial crisis ended in 2009, the country's economy has improved. The overall unemployment rate fell to 3.7 percent, down 63 percent from the height of 10 percent during the financial crisis. The stock market is steadily increasing, hitting its highest point during the second quarter of 2018.[68] However, the effects brought upon by the Great Recession remain. Despite the fact that corporations earn more profits than ever before, the country's poorest communities have not shared in this prosperity. All economic booms are followed by busts. It is the natural economic cycle. The question is: will the United States be prepared for the next financial crisis? Possibly, but only if preemptive and appropriate action is taken.

The Role of Monetary Policy during Recessions and Financial Crises

Monetary policy can seem obscure and opaque. However, to understand the impact that OZs can have in distressed communities and across the American economy, it's important to understand how short-term debt cycles work and how monetary policy affects the economy. Also, these policies deeply impact anyone who holds debt without much wealth to offset that debt. Many people in that situation were foreclosed on during the financial crisis and/or lost their jobs.

The government uses two types of economic policy to influence the economy: monetary and fiscal policy. Monetary policy, which is controlled by the U.S. Federal Reserve Board, determines the amount of credit and money released into the economy. Fiscal policy, which is controlled by Congress, influences where money and credit will come from and where it goes in the form of spending.

The Role of Debt Cycles

Typically, a short-term debt cycle lasts from five to ten years. The length varies depending on the monetary policies implemented during this period and the demand for credit. According to Dalio, America is currently "in the late-stages of both the short-term and long-term debt cycles."[69]

While short-term debt cycles last between five and ten years, long-term debt cycles occur every fifty to seventy-five years. Short-term debt cycles cause long-term debt cycles through a compounding effect of higher debt and debt service. In an effort to neutralize the impact of these factors on the economy, central banks first try to lower interest rates and then print money and buy debt, Dalio notes.[70]

The impact of this situation is two-fold. Profits and earnings growth are still strong while tightening of credit causes asset prices to decline. Asset prices and economies are sensitive to tightening, meaning central banks don't have much more power to ease credit because rates are already close to zero.

The economy will eventually start to falter as we exit the bubble phase and enter into another recession. As the rate of inflation and debt rises, it begins to put pressure on the value of assets causing them to fall, which is likely to eventually lead to another financial crisis. Nobel Laureate Robert Shiller, an economics professor at Yale University and author of *Irrational Exuberance* (Princeton University

Press, 2016) fears that a convergence of bubbles will burst precipitating the next financial crisis. He says the CAPE Ratio on U.S. stocks is at an elevated level of 29. The CAPE Ratio, also known as the Cyclically Adjusted Price-Earnings ratio, is defined as the ratio the S&P 500's current price divided by the ten-year moving average of inflation-adjusted earnings. Shiller says, "We got to the mid 30s in 1929. So that was a record." Markets subsequently crashed in 1929 and set off the Great Depression. He adds, though, the CAPE ratio can still go higher until an irrational exuberance bubble is deflated. "(The CAPE Ratio) went up to 45 in the year 2000 (prior to the 49 percent bear market decline from 2000 to 2002)," he said. But the CAPE Ratio is slightly higher now than it was in 1987, before the market's biggest one-day drop of 23 percent on October 19, 1987.

In an interview with *Investor's Business Daily*, he predicts that a bursting of bubbles in the real estate, stock and bond markets will lead to a long period of anemic stock returns, which he estimates running at an average of 4.4 percent during the next thirty years.[71] Shiller predicted both the 2000 technology stock market crash and the 2007 housing market implosion. He foresees a long run of consistently low stock market returns. This is likely to occur due to the stock market hitting multiple highs recently, creating extended valuations. Shiller also believes that the bond market is in for a major correction due to investors' appetite for interest income. "It (the bond bubble) seems to be related to people not paying enough attention thinking through the simple logic…this can't keep going and it's going to end badly," he said. "These things may sink at some point." The last of the bubbles Shiller predicts is in the real estate market, which he believes is in a bubble period similar to what occurred in 2005, right before prices leapt. "San Francisco and LA are already slowing down," he noted, which is a "bad sign."[72]

Even if the next recession or financial crisis isn't as bad as the last one, millions of Americans will lose their jobs and their financial security. That's why it's important to understand how and why debt crises and recessions happen and what can be done to prevent them in the future.

During a financial crisis, central bankers and fiscal policymakers rely on three monetary policies to stimulate the economy:

1. Lowering interest rates

2. Quantitative easing (Top 40 percent)

3. Distributing money to the spenders (Bottom 60 percent)

Monetary Policy 1: An Interest-Rate-Driven Policy

When an economy falters, central banks typically respond by lowering interest rates. That's the first tool in their toolbox. For those in debt, high interest rates can devastate borrowers because more income is required to pay down debt, making it more difficult to stay financially afloat. By slashing interest rates, central banks stimulate the economy through lowering borrowers' debt and debt service payments. The result? Borrowers can keep more of their income to either invest or spend, because they have lower monthly debt service payments. However, in a low interest rate environment as we are in now, when interest rates are already close to zero this monetary policy tool no longer becomes effective so central banks must roll onto the next monetary policy tool called QE, Dalio notes.

Monetary Policy 2: Quantitative Easing

In his book *A Template for Understanding Big Debt Crisis,* Dalio defines QE as the "printing of money" and buying of financial assets such as debt assets.[73] QE typically benefits the top 40 percent because when central banks buy debt assets such as bonds, it provides the top 40 percent "savers and investors" with funds that they can use to purchase more attractive financial assets.

Unlike lowering interest rates, this tool is directed at savers and investors. It relies on these two demographics to put more money into circulation by spending some of the money they have saved on debt service and use it for consumption as well as purchasing financial assets with growth potential. However, this monetary policy tool becomes ineffective with overuse as it pushes risk premiums down and asset prices are pushed up to levels that make holding cash "a terrible returning asset" a more appealing option. And with substantial overuse of this monetary policy option, people will begin to question the currency's stability as a store hold of value and eventually lead people to start moving to alternative currencies such as gold, Dalio writes. Many investors flee to gold when economic recessions are on the horizon due to gold's reputation for safety. While gold offers potential capital protection with limited appreciation, those returns can trail the combined wealth that can be generated through successfully investing in OZs. Investing in OZs can substitute gold as the new asset class for safety by allowing all parties, including the investors, the community, the beneficiaries and the residents, the chance to build wealth together. In fact, investing in OZs represent a new, attractive asset class where investors can channel their capital gains for potentially significant capital appreciation compounded with impressive tax saving incentives.

As with lowering rates, central banks have already gone on an asset-buying binge leaving little cash—or fuel in the tank—to make QE an effective option during the next financial crisis, according to Dalio.

Monetary Policy 3: Putting Money into the Hands of the Spenders

Unlike the previous two monetary policies, putting money directly into the hands of the spenders with the incentive to spend it or lose it can be more effective since it offers an immediate boost to the economy. Targeting spenders is effective since the savers typically invest/save money rather than spend the money into the economy, Dalio believes.

Dalio, who Forbes listed as the third richest hedge fund manager in the world, states that targeting monetary policy 3 policies toward the private sector could be an effective strategy to accelerate an economic recovery.[74] Unlike most economists, who write and teach about the economy in academia, Dalio has employed his investment strategies to great effect with Bridgewater, which serves institutional investors and has $150 billion in assets under management.[75]

When policy makers react to debt crises and recessions, they don't always use an exclusive version of the three monetary policy options. They may develop a hybrid of two or more of the three monetary policies listed above. The OZ program is the most recent government program that provides investors with substantial tax incentives to invest in America's high-poverty communities as designated by the United States Treasury. QOF investing serves as a preemptive supplement to the government's monetary and fiscal policy tools specifically monetary policy 3. Combining monetary policy 3—putting money in the hands of spenders—in conjunction with investing in OZs—investing in America's poorest communities—will be an important and effective solution to prevent another severe recession.

The greatest asset to the economy right now is that investing in OZs is preemptive pre-recession investment option that can be deployed immediately, which is better than waiting for a recession to happen first and then waiting on policy makers to agree on a solution and reacting to a financial crisis later, when at that point…will already be too late. Investing in OZs can happen immediately and if the investments can be deployed efficiently into these communities, the U.S. economy can avoid a potentially severe and drawn out recession.

Policymakers have preemptively signed into law the 2017 TCJA, a significant tax incentive for private money to flow into OZs through investing in real estate, direct businesses, and start-ups. This investment option has the potential to be more effective and more profitable than investing in debt or alternative currencies by providing wealthy investors with the chance to take an equity stake in OZ communities, creating a powerful incentive for all to profit and build wealth and begin closing the wealth gap that has divided this country over the past 30 years.

Chapter 3

Introducing Opportunity Zones and Qualified Opportunity Funds

As you'll learn in this and subsequent chapters, opportunity zones offer many benefits to start-up founders, local developers and existing businesses seeking to raise capital for their investment deals. Locating or starting a business in one of the 8,762 OZs across American offers unprecedented access to investors who seek to invest for social impact. For local developer, money manager, venture capitalist or wealth manager, setting up an investment fund as a QOF provides potential investors with access to impactful investment deals as well as impressive OZ tax incentives. OZs, QOFs and qualified OZ businesses directly benefit from legislation included in the 2017 TCJA that provides impressive tax incentives for investors to use their capital gains to invest in distressed communities identified as opportunity zones.

Entrepreneurs who leverage OZs, QOFs and the OZ tax incentives to their advantage will have a higher chance of attracting private equity investors to their investment deals. Raising capital is difficult, which is why it is important to take advantage of OZ tax incentives to increase the attractiveness of investing in start-ups and impactful development projects. While investors are unlikely to invest in OZ businesses or QOFs merely because of the lucrative tax benefits, those benefits combined with an attractive high-quality investment deal can make a good investment even more attractive to investors.

The intent of OZ legislation is that investments made in these areas must improve the community and the lives of the residents living in it. How does investment in OZs achieve this goal? Investment will create new jobs and improves the availability, value and access to housing, medical care, education and enable community members the opportunity to build wealth within those communities. That means the assets that already exist in an OZ must be substantially improved. To qualify for OZ tax incentives, investors must invest in new assets that cannot have been previously placed into service in an opportunity zone. I'll elaborate on these rules in much more detail below as I dig into the technical aspects of the law. It's important to understand that Congress had a very specific mandate in mind when writing this legislation, as investment in OZs must be faithfully carried out with the intent to produce positive social impact.

What are Opportunity Zones?

Opportunity zones are census tracts identified as high poverty communities, representing roughly 12 percent of the entire landmass of the United States.[76] Chosen by governors of the 50 states and representatives of Puerto Rico, Washington, DC and other U.S. territories, OZs are special areas where investments may be eligible for special tax treatment. To see exactly where these census tracts are located, go to www.dealconnecthub.com and either search by city and state or zoom into any of the 8762 shaded OZs across the United States. Due to their distressed economies and low-income, poorly educated workforces, many of these communities haven't experienced any type of sustained investment in decades. Now, through the federal OZ program, there is a chance to improve these areas through capital investment.

To channel investment into OZs, deal sponsors must form entities known as qualified opportunity funds (QOFs). These funds must invest the vast majority of their assets in businesses or property located in OZs. Within these criteria, there's a wide variety of potential investment opportunities in these distressed areas that can provide residents with the well-paying jobs and affordable housing they need to achieve the American Dream.

The objective behind OZs is to unleash as much as possible of the $6.1 trillion of potential capital gain investment from the recent long bull market.[77] Many successful investors are sitting on realized and unrealized capital gains. The tax incentives available for OZ investing provides investors a triple benefit of deferring capital gains tax, taking advantage of tax exclusions and potentially avoiding paying any capital gains tax on successful OZ investments held for 10 years.

Background on Opportunity Zones

Shawn Parker, founder of Napster and an early Facebook executive, realized the difference that investing capital gains could make for distressed communities after a visit to Africa. His friend and fellow venture capitalist, Peter Thiel, founder of PayPal and Palantir Technologies, liked the idea, but bet him $1 million that he wouldn't be able to pull it off. However, he did—with the help of his think tank, the Economic Innovation Group and other influential Washington, DC insiders.[78]

The Economic Innovation Group proposed the idea of strengthening underdeveloped communities through investments by the wealthy for tax breaks. Prior to the 2017 TCJA, Jared Bernstein, the former chief economist to former vice president Joe Biden, and Kevin Hassett, one of the current economic advisors to President Donald Trump, introduced the idea in a report, *Unlocking Private Capital to Facilitate Economic Growth in Distressed Areas*. According to Bernstein and Hassett, despite economic growth in the aftermath of the 2008 financial crisis, there are still many communities who are still affected by the devastation: "However, while certain areas of the country are doing remarkably well and nearing or exceeding their pre-recession economic states, the recovery has been profoundly uneven, with large swaths of the country facing chronic rates of long-term unemployment and historically low levels of new investment. Nationally, we see historically low numbers of new business ventures being established. Besides the unevenness of the recovery geographically, the unevenness within different income groups has been a growing concern for many policymakers."[79]

In the following year, several measures to create opportunity zones were introduced to both the House and Senate during the Obama administration but to no avail. In 2017, the federal program was implemented under the Trump administration as part of the Tax Cuts and Jobs Act in an effort to strengthen economically distressed areas while attracting the attention of investors with the promise of preferential federal tax incentives.

You might have heard of opportunity zones in connection with Amazon's attempt to build a second headquarters in Long Island City, which is only a stone's throw away from the saturated Manhattan and gentrified Brooklyn neighborhoods such as Greenpoint and Williamsburg.[80] With Amazon HQ2, Long Island City would have become gentrified. While new residential buildings were being built, it meant higher rent. While Amazon HQ2 promised more jobs, it meant a lack of jobs for the undereducated who did not fit the criteria. Residents had enough. They marched out to Long Island City, carrying boxes with the Amazon logo transformed into a frown. Strong local opposition led to Amazon pulling the plug on this HQ2.

Now, how does an area or a census tract becomes designated as an OZ? You might first picture a rundown urban areas like the Bronx designated as OZs. But these designations are not only found in urban areas like New York City and Los Angeles—it could even be some small town in the middle of Nebraska. OZs exist in underdeveloped and distressed small cities and towns across America. According to the Economics Innovation Group, one in six Americans live in these underdeveloped communities.[81]

There is a national guideline for a census tract to qualify as an OZ. In order for an area to be designated as an OZ, it either must possess a median income of 80 percent less than, or a poverty rate 20 percent higher than, the areas surrounding it.[82] According to recent data from the Economic Innovations Group, the typical OZ averages around a 29 percent poverty rate. The median income for OZs averages around $42,000 which is lower than the national average of $67,900.[83]

Despite the guidelines being set by the federal government, there are other, more flexible ways in which governors nominate certain areas to be designated as OZs. While the law sets the guidelines in terms of how many areas can be designated as OZs, governors were able to nominate fewer areas or add more criteria or shift their focus on specific areas.[84]

During the past two decades, a lack of investment in struggling urban and rural areas has led to the income disparities that I've previously noted. More and more politicians—as well as billionaires such as Warren Buffett—are sounding the theme that capitalism has only benefitted a select few. It's hard to argue with that thesis. I'm excited about OZs because they offer the potential to reverse and eventually close the wealth gap. I believe that we should use the information in the Bridgewater study to determine if this type of investment makes a significant difference in the wealth gap over the next five or ten years. Such a study would demonstrate how effective OZs have been in reducing the wealth gap and create a powerful argument for its continuation if successful. The OZ benefits are not eternal—whether you are an investor, a community stakeholder, or a business, the time is now to do whatever you can to ensure the OZs in your community are successful as possible.

Qualified Opportunity Funds

To encourage investors to invest in economically distressed communities, investors are required to invest through an investment vehicle called a qualified opportunity fund (QOF). Think of QOFs as a container that holds either one or multiple OZ investments. For example, *Shark Tank* investors can create a QOF to invest the fund's assets in either entrepreneurs, startups or real estate deals in designated high poverty OZ communities through the fund's investments. Also, you do not have to be a professional investor to set up a QOF. You can be a local developer looking to develop property, an oil and gas or mineral rights exploratory company, a women focused accelerator program or a cannabis entrepreneur to name a few of many examples. The goal is to understand how to set up a QOF as well as learn how to attract investors to invest in your QOF, which we will cover in detail in the chapters on capital raising.

QOFs must be certified by the U.S. Treasury Department and organized as a corporation or partnership for the purpose of investing in designated OZ property and/or businesses. The QOF must hold at least 90 percent of its assets in designated OZ property.

To become a QOF, an eligible corporation or partnership can self-certify by filing Form 8996 "Qualified Opportunity Fund" with its federal income tax return.

How to Set Up a Qualified Opportunity Fund

First, to set up a QOF, you must form an entity. This entity must be organized as either a corporation or a partnership. A number of different types of entities are acceptable, including a partnership, a limited liability company (LLC), C-corp, S-corp, Benefit Corporations or B Corps or another pass-through entity. Regardless of what type of entity you choose, the entity must self-certify as a QOF by filing Form 8996 with its tax return every year.

Fund Structures

A C-corp is a type of corporation in which profits and losses are taxed separately from its owners and shareholders. Any earnings and losses the company incurs are taxed on a corporate level for federal tax purposes. However, electing a pass-through entity is another structure that can be used.

C-corps offer a number of benefits, including:

• **Protecting shareholders from liability:** As stated above, owners and shareholders are not held liable for any of the QOF's legal or financial problems. For example, if an QOF has business debt, creditors cannot pursue a fund manager(s) or shareholder(s) personal assets.

• **Ability to quickly raise capital:** C-corps can quickly raise funds by selling shares. This allows even investors with a small amount of extra income to invest in a C-corp by purchasing a share.

Just as there are advantages to investing in a C-corp, there are also disadvantages. One disadvantage for all but the super wealthy is a lack of liquidity. If you invest in a QOF with a C-corp structure and need the funds back due to an emergency, you're in trouble because it will be nearly impossible to get that money out quickly.

Unfortunately, many inexperienced investors are being targeted to invest in C-corps to their detriment. Many C-corps target investors by offering shares to investors who may have capital gains in the $25,000 range—but for most inexperienced investors, that's all they have to invest. Experienced venture capitalists, fund managers, and others tend to steer clear of funds structured as C-corps due to the low barrier to entry and the high barrier to exit. An inexperienced investor who finds themselves in an illiquid investment may end up needing the funds they invested and then seek to sell quickly. In that case, there may be little to no market to sell those shares. So the investor may end up losing the tax advantages by exiting early and take a big hit on the value of the shares because of a lack of market for those shares. It pays to be wary of QOFs structured as C-corps. Another major disadvantage of organizing a QOF as a C-corp is the roadblocks that can be involved when selling an asset. Because the C-corp shares are widely distributed among small investors, it may be difficult to round up all the owners and get permission to sell. Interested buyers may get discouraged at the length of time that it takes to get permission from all the owners to sell, because they want to purchase the entire asset that is being sold, not 50 or 75 percent of it. Experienced investors understand these dynamics and will think twice before either investing in a QOF organized as a C Corp or purchasing assets from such entities.

In a C-corp, there are certain events that trigger inclusion of all or a portion of a deferred gain:

• A liquidation of a QOF or a reorganization through events such as a merger.

• A liquidation of the QOF investor (only a portion is deferred)

• Transfer of eligible interest in a partnership or stock in a C-corp.

By inclusion event, the U.S. Treasury Department means an event that disqualifies some or all of the qualified OZ investment for preferential tax treatment.

S-Corp

You might decide to elect your LLC as an S-corp for tax purposes. According to the IRS, S-corporations are defined as "corporations that elect to pass corporate income, losses, deductions, and credits through to their shareholders for federal tax purposes." This means that any corporate income is taxed at a personal level rather than at a corporate level thus avoiding corporate taxation. This type of tax structure must work for you if you elect S-corp status. S-corps must submit Form 2553, which must be signed by all shareholders.[85] The advantages of an S-corp include:

• **Protecting shareholders from liability:** Shareholders are not held responsible for any liabilities of the corporation. For example, if a corporation needs to pay business debts, creditors cannot pursue an QOF manager(s) or shareholder(s) personal assets.

• **Pass-through taxation:** S-corps are not required to pay taxes at the federal or state level, in most cases. Profits and losses are passed through to the shareholders and thus taxed at a personal level rather than a corporate level. Businesses—especially new businesses—will want to avoid double taxation.

Disadvantages of S-corps include:

• **Limitation on membership:** According to the IRS, S-corps can only have one hundred or fewer shareholders. This differs from other entities such as LLCs, where they can have an unlimited number of members.

- **Restricted ownership:** S-corps can only be owned by U.S. citizens or residents unlike other entities such as LLCs, which means that foreigners can't invest.

- **One class of stock:** IRS requires S-corps to be allocated to one class of stock (Class-A, Class-B, and Class-C shares).

In an S-corp or partnership, investors can choose to either allocate eligible gain through its owners or defer it at an entity level.

Certain events require inclusion of all or a portion of deferred gain such as:

- An election or termination of S-corp status.

- If an S-corp experiences changes in 25 percent of its ownership. All gain deferred must be recognized.

- Conversion of an S-corp investor to a partnership or another disregarded entity.

Limited Liability Companies and Limited Liability Partnerships

According to the IRS, a qualified opportunity fund can either be an LLCs or limited liability partnership (LLPs).[86] LLC is short for "limited liability company," whereas LLP is short for "limited liability partnership." While these two business structures share some similarities, there are also significant differences. Both types of business entities pass-through profits to owners directly and offer some liability protection. The differences between the two are complicated by the fact that states impose widely different requirements on LLCs and LLPs formed within their jurisdictions.

LLCs offer characteristics of both a partnership and a corporation. LLCs require little investment, even if it means a few hundred dollars. You can even form a single-person LLC, requiring no other investors or investments. For this reason, many small businesses are structured as limited liability corporations, which offer the following benefits:

- **Taxation:** The business itself isn't taxed. Instead, profits are declared in an owner's ("member's") personal tax income filing. An LLC can decide on "pass-through taxation."[87] LLCs can decide corporate-level taxation if forming a corporation. Most LLCs opt to be taxed as a partnership and all profits are taxed in a member's personal tax income filings.

- **Involvement in day-to-day operations:** Members retain the ability to provide input into operations whether the business is run by a professional manager or not.

- **Liability protection:** Members are protected from business debt and other obligations.

Disadvantages of limited liability corporations include:

- **Fees:** LLCs often have high renewal fees and high taxes depending on the states.

- **Taxation:** Unlike other entities such as C-corps unless electing to be taxed as a corporation, partners will have to face self-employment taxes. Though, many see this pass-through taxation as an advantage rather than a disadvantage.[88]

LLPs are general partnerships created by at least two partners. Many professional businesses, such as physician, accounting, and law practices are organized as LLPs. Advantages of LLPs include:

- **Limited personal liability protection:** General partners are protected from partnership liabilities, though that protection depends upon the state in which the partnership is formed.

- **Involvement in day-to-day operations**: General partners maintain a say in how the business is run.

- **Open-ended operations**: No end date is required when the partnership is formed.

Disadvantages of LLPs include:

- **Complicated tax filings**: Federal taxes pass-through to individual owners.

- **State restrictions**: Some states prohibit LLPs and others don't recognize them as legal entities.

- **Independent decision-making:** All partners can make decisions independently that are binding on all the other partners.

Most QOFs begin as LLCs due to the tax benefits and flexibility, especially in terms of real estate (e.g. hotels, condos and apartment complexes). But if your QOF is an LLC, remember that it will be taxed as a partnership or a corporation. There is no single-member LLCs unless it's taxed as a corporation. In a partnership, there must be more than one member whereas in a corporation, there must be an election. As for an exit strategy in an LLC, if an investor cannot hold that investment before the end of the ten-year period, they must sell their position to another investor.

Venture Capital

One of the best ways to start a QOF is as an LLC or an LLP through a VC firm.

VC firms provide funding for start-ups in exchange for equity stakes. For example, an investor might provide $700,000 to a new QOF. Then the QOF will invest in a business and its property located in an OZ or invest that money into a start-up operating in an OZ in exchange for 15 percent equity in that company. In 2026 or later, that VC firm should then receive their principal back plus any profit realized due to the investment. VC firms raise millions of dollars in funding from investors and then turn around and invest that money in start-ups, which allows them to grow faster than a normal business typically would. While there are inherent risks in VC investing, these investors are selective about their investments, and tend to fund businesses with long-term growth potential.

VC funding provides the following:

• **Resources:** Along with significant funding, VC firms can also provide support regarding operational, tax, and legal matters. This is especially important for start-ups which lack such expertise.

• **Advice:** VC firms can provide guidance on business management. Such advice is very valuable for start-ups as inexperience and bad decision making can be costly.

• **Connections:** Many investors involved in VC firms already have a large network. Tapping into their network and obtaining new connections can be vital in finding guidance, landing clients, or hiring professionals.

Venture funds, which can operate as an QOF, are a type of investment vehicle. Venture funds are typically structured with limited partners, a management company, a general partner, and portfolio companies. Limited partners are investors who invest in these funds and can be foundations, family offices, or wealthy individuals. Venture funds usually have a life cycle of seven to ten years.

Then, there is the management company within the venture fund that handles each fund or LLC. The management company handles the administration and back-office operations of the VC firm in exchange for a small management fee. Next, there is the general partner (GP). The GP manages the venture funds, making decisions on how the fund should operate and raise funds. The general partner managers also collaborate with portfolio companies who receive funding regarding how the VC firm will eventually exit from its ownership position.

Well-known VC firms include Accel, Sequoia Capital, and Andreessen Horowitz. With the boom of start-ups, VC funding has also grown. In fact, VC funding set an all-time record in 2018 and continued that momentum during the first quarter of 2019, according to PitchBook-NVCA Venture Monitor.[89]

Venture funds come in many different shapes and sizes with some funds specialize in specific sectors, geographic areas, or specific investment stages such as early stage (seed stage), mid stage (series A,B,C), and late stage.

Then, there is the exit strategy. Typically, in an exit, returns are generated through acquisition by another larger company, a buyout of an investor's ownership, or an initial public offering, or IPO.

While venture funds are enticing, they do not guarantee success. In fact, over 70 percent of start-ups fail despite the large amount of fundraising. In the last ten years, only 3 percent of start-ups exited above $100 million while only 0.7 percent of start-ups exited above $500 million.

VC firms tend to favor organizing as S-corps, LLPs, or LLCs. Most VC funds opt to start as an LLC, and the best way to start a QOF is through an LLC.

For example, if an LLC wanted to invest in my firm's QOF, AMERICA FUND 1 the limited partner would be shielded from any liabilities that AMERICA FUND 1 may get into. Also, limited partners can chip in funds from their LLCs when needed. Whenever AMERICA FUND I purchases an asset, it owns the whole asset. Whenever AMERICA FUND I sells an asset, each

LLC investor gets their respective portion. Since it is a pass-through entity, income from AMERICA FUND I passes to the limited partners and is then taxed as part of their personal tax income. Hence, this is usually the best way to start a QOF. Though investors, entrepreneurs, and businesses alike will need to do their own research and determine what investment vehicle works best for their unique situation.

Benefit Corporations

Traditional corporations are designed to maximize shareholder value. In contrast, Benefit Corporations (or B-Corps) focus on pursuing social impact through a distinct structure designed to broaden the scope of traditional corporate law.[20] These companies take an expansive view of their purpose, governance, transparency and accountability beyond the traditional goal of benefiting shareholders. Instead, they seek to benefit a wide range of stakeholders, including employees, the communities in which they operate and the environment.[21]

Benefit Corporations offer many advantages for start-ups focused on positive social impact, including:

• **Decreased director liability:** Because Benefit Corporations are designed to serve a wide variety of stakeholders beyond shareholders, their directors gain legal protection so that they can effectively balance financial and non-financial goals when making decisions. These protections extend to director actions in situations such as a potential sale of a Benefit Corporation or when a Benefit Corporation is publicly-traded.[22]

• **Expanded stockholder rights**: B Corps offer advantages to social impact investors because they are accountable for a specific social impact mission, unlike other types of corporations.

• **Access to social impact capital**: Companies organized as Benefit Corporations stand out for their commitment to social impact goals for family offices and other investors interested in the social impact niche. The annual benefit report, which B Corps must produce, provides valuable information for investor due diligence.[23]

• **Enhanced employee recruitment**: Millennials and many other professionals seek meaningful work and B Corporations are by definition focused on social impact. In a tight labor market, B Corporations may very well have an edge in recruitment over companies that are focused on profitability over social impact.[24]

• **Improved brand image**: More consumers than ever are interested in doing business with companies with legitimate sustainability goals. Organizing as a B Corp provides proof to skeptical consumers that your company is, in fact, dedicated to pursing social impact goals.[25]

Disadvantages:

• **Expanded reporting requirements**: Operating a B Corporation requires a significantly amount of transparency, including the issuance of a yearly annual report to shareholders and the public.[26] As part of this report, your company's Corporate Director must provide an opinion as to whether the B Corp. functioned within it's specific social impact purpose. If it did not, the specific reasons for the failure must be stated in the report.[27]

• **Must consider social impact**: Incorporating as a Benefit Corporation means that your company must maintain some type of social impact focus throughout the life of your start-up. That decision excludes a pivot to a focus that excludes social impact.

• **May constrain short-term profits**: A commitment to a specific social mission may mean choosing social impact over profitability.

That decision may further your company's social objectives while sacrificing profitability.

• **Future accountability**: Accountability can be a double-edged sword. As a start-up founder, you may have to make a tough decision that advances the survival and profitability of your company over it's social impact mission. Auditors and investors could call those decisions into question in the future, because B Corps must file annual reports.

• **Regulatory uncertainty**: Because B Corporations are fairly new with varied state requirements, there is a degree of uncertainty associated with how they will be regulated and how courts will interpret B corporation social mandates, according to CohnReznick.[28] The states that permit B corporations have varying requirements, which means that companies interested in organizing as B corporations should carefully evaluate jurisdictions before incorporating. In addition, not every state offers B Corporations.

As of December 2019, 36 states permit the formation of Benefit Corporations: Arizona, Arkansas, California, Colorado, Connecticut, Delaware, Florida, Hawaii, Idaho, Illinois, Indiana, Kansas, Kentucky, Louisiana, Maine, Maryland, Massachusetts, Minnesota, Montana, Nebraska, Nevada, New Hampshire, New Jersey, New York, Oklahoma, Oregon, Pennsylvania, Rhode Island, South Carolina, Texas, Utah, Vermont, Virginia, Washington, DC, West Virginia and Wisconsin.[29]

Several states have B Corporation legislation pending, including Georgia, Iowa, Mississippi, New Mexico and Alaska.

States that do not permit Benefit Corporations include Alabama, Michigan, North Carolina, North Dakota, South Dakota, Tennessee, Washington and West Virginia.

Certification as a B Corp.

To organize as a Benefit Corporation, you must fill out the appropriate paperwork in a state that allows this type of entity and pay the appropriate fees. In contrast, certifying as a B Corp. is a different matter. "Certified B Corporations are businesses that meet the highest standards of verified social and environmental performance, public transparency and legal accountability to balance profit and purpose," states B Lab, a non-profit organization that supports companies organized for social impact goals. [100] You can organize your start-up as a Benefit Corporation without certifying as a B Corp. Or, you could do both, or neither.

Well-known companies that are certified B Corps include Ben and Jerry's, Patagonia, Warby Parker and Etsy.[101] More than 3,000 companies in 71 countries seek to balance social impact and profit.[102] B Labs offers resources for companies seeking to certify and for companies that have already certified, all designed to facilitate businesses fulfilling social impact goals.

State Taxation Rules

All states have their own tax rules. Because state and federal tax laws cover many of the same issues, there are areas where state and federal tax laws agree on the treatment of specific issues and there are areas where they diverge. This agreement or lack of agreement between federal and state tax rules is known as conformity. Conformity is a highly complex issue, because each state has different ideas and principles regarding taxation and tax laws.[103] Those rules have evolved over time and are subject to change depending on which political party is in power.

Every time the federal tax code changes, as it did when the 2017 TCJA was passed and signed into law, states must decide individually how they will conform to the new law.[104] Since state decisions on these matters necessarily lag behind federal government rules, it can take months or years before individual states decide how to resolve their difference with federal tax rules when new laws pass. For the purposes of OZs, states can be divided into the follow categories:

Full conformity: The state conforms to the current Internal Revenue Code

Limited conformity: The state specifically conforms to Section 1400Z-C of the Internal Revenue Code, which are special rules for capital invested in OZs

No capital gains tax: The state has no income tax and generally does not tax capital gains, which means that capital gains are already exempt from tax

Non-conformity: The state conforms to an earlier version of the Internal Revenue Code or has specifically decoupled from the OZ portions of the Internal Revenue Code.[105]

Some states comply for the purpose of personal income taxes and corporate income taxes, while others comply for one or the other or neither. Other states automatically conform—known as automatic rolling conformity—while others exclude certain aspects of the tax code from conformity. State conformity to OZ provisions is in flux, so states that may not conform now, may change and conform in the future. Also, because states are highly individualistic in their treatment of taxation, there are no states that completely conform to the IRS tax code in every way.[106]

In some cases, even if an investor's home state conforms to the OZ personal income tax treatment, the state in which they invest may not.[107] That could disqualify the investor from receiving an income tax credit for the taxes paid in a state due to non-conformity on OZs. Whether a state has a personal or corporate capital gains tax also bears on OZ taxation; states that have neither personal nor corporate capital gains tax offer a favorable OZ investing environment because there are no concerns about conformity at least as far investing within that specific state goes. Before investing in a QOF, consult a tax advisor to determine whether state and local tax codes conform to Internal Revenue Code for the purposes of OZ investing and how that might impact an OZ investment for the perspective of state taxation. Because each state differs on how they tax personal income or corporate income and whether a state is conforming or is non-conforming, it can get quite cumbersome to unpack all this information when trying to evaluate investment deals on a state by state basis. You can stay up to date by subscribing to DealConnect Hub, which provides visualized and easy to follow color-coded maps on the status of each individual states' conformity to the Internal Revenue Code.

Recycling Capital

According to IRS regulations, QOFs have a one-year period of grace where they can sell their assets and reinvest the proceeds into another OZ investment. This provides QOFs with more leeway and flexibility.

A Note on Indian Tribes and Qualified Opportunity Funds

Indian tribal governments are permitted to set up entities that can become QOFs despite the fact that U.S. law regards them as self-governing. Although Indian tribal governments possess different powers than other individuals and businesses in the United States, they are subject to the same taxation and tax incentives that apply to other individuals and businesses.[108]

Qualified Opportunity Funds and Investors

For start-up founders, developers, business owners and investment managers, there are many strategies to structure a QOF to attract investors. But what if you're an investor with qualified capital gains who may not want to form a QOF and just wants to invest? Chapter 4 offers an overview of the many compelling tax advantages of investing in QOFs as well as how to conduct due diligence on QOFs to assure the QOF is in compliance with the rules and regulations of internal revenue code.

Chapter 4

TAX INCENTIVES FOR INVESTING IN QUALIFIED OPPORTUNITY FUNDS

Building on your knowledge of opportunity zones and QOFs, in this chapter you'll learn about the special tax incentives designed to facilitate investment in OZs as well as how to invest in QOFs and qualified OZ businesses. Like any other investment, investing in OZs, QOFs and OZ businesses carries potential rewards and risks, which this chapter explores.

Opportunity Zone Tax Benefits

QOFs will provide three kinds of tax benefits to its investors who have accumulated capital gains: deferral of capital gains taxes, a step-up in basis—another way of saying tax exemption—and a permanent elimination (exclusion). This can be done by reinvesting capital gains into a QOF. In Section 1400Z-2(d) (1), a qualified opportunity fund (QOF) is defined as "any investment vehicle which is organized as a corporation a partnership for the purpose of investing in qualified opportunity zone property... that holds at least ninety percent of its assets in qualified opportunity zone property, determined by the average of the percentage of qualified opportunity zone property held in the fund."[109]

A QOF can be a partnership or a corporation. This capital gain must be reinvested into a QOF within 180 days for an investor to receive these tax incentives.

Gain that is not derived from an exchange or sale with a related party though gain from the sale of a Section 1231 asset can be eligible gain. Under final IRS OZ rules, investors with Section 1231 gains can immediately contribute their Section 1231 gains into a QOF. That contribution can be made even if that taxpayer experiences other Section 1231 losses later in that same year.[110]

When investors invest in a QOF, they can defer tax payments on their capital gains until December 31, 2026 or earlier if they sell the investment. Investing in a QOF can offer more potential profit than other types of investments. If such investments are held in a QOF for at least five years investors receive the first tax incentive the 10 percent step up in basis, which allows investors to exclude 10 percent of their initial capital gain from being taxed. If the investor holds the investment in a QOF for an additional two years for a total of seven years investors get an additional step up in basis of 5 percent, which allows investors to exclude 15 percent of their initial capital gain from being taxed. December 31, 2019 is the last date for investors to enjoy the 15 percent step up in basis or tax exclusion. The final and most appealing tax incentive is if an investor holds an investment in a QOF for at least ten years the investor will receive a permanent tax exclusion on the new appreciation, meaning that if you invested $100,000 in a start-up and resulted in an appreciation of $1,000,000, you would pay zero federal taxes on that $1,000,000.[111]

In order to defer paying taxes on eligible gains, investors aren't required to reinvest all the proceeds from a sale or exchange. Instead, they must reinvest the gain into a QOF or qualified opportunity zone businesses (QOZB).

The final Opportunity zone rules made a significant change in reinvestment of gains. In the provisional rules, investors were required to sell their entire interest in a QOF to qualify for a second deferral. In a highly beneficial change for investors, the final rules provide that investors can defer gains related to a partial sale of a QOF investment by reinvesting in either the same or a different QOF within 180 days of the sale.[112]

If an investor invests in a QOF or a QOZB and doesn't qualify for the 10-year exclusion, gains will be taxed at whatever capital gains rate is in effect 2026 when deferred gains are recognized. If Congress changes the tax rates, capital gains rates could be higher than those in effect in late 2019, when the rules were finalized.[113]

While QOFs must invest within OZs or in QOZB, the QOF does not have to be physically located within an opportunity zone.[114]

Brownfield Sites

Investing in previously developed land that is not currently in use, known as brownfield sites, is a permitted use under the rules, satisfying the original use requirement. The final IRS regulations state that remediation of contaminated land counts towards qualified improvements. To satisfy IRS requirements, investors must improvement the safety and environment standards of such sites.[115]

Substantial Improvement

In order for buildings to qualify under the IRS's substantial improvement regulation, they must meet the following tests:

1. When occupying a single deeded property, buildings are treated as a single property, rather than multiple properties[116]

2. When occupying properties that are contiguous parcels of land, such buildings qualify for treatment as a single property provided

they are operated exclusively by a QOZB or QOF, share business functions such as back office or accounting functions or employees and conduct business in coordination with at least one trade or business.[117]

If two or more buildings qualify for treatment as one property, the IRS states that the aggregate basis of the building creates a baseline for future improvements.[118] Collective improvements on those buildings will be counted against that baseline amount.

In regard to operating assets, to meet the substantial improvement test they must be used by the QOZB or a contiguous property and improve the functionality of the assets.[119] For example, if a QOF purchases an existing hotel that is no original use, certain purchased original use items such as furniture apply to the substantial improvement of that property as do renovations to an existing in-hotel restaurant.[120] However, if a QOZB or fund also owns an adjacent apartment building that does not operate in conjunction with the hotel, improvements to that apartment building do not qualify as substantial improvement.[121]

As far as land is concerned, the IRS final regulations are vague. They stipulate that land does not have to meet a substantial improvement test to qualify for tax incentives. However, they do state that land must be improved by more than what they describe as an "insubstantial amount."[122] They do not specify exactly what percentage qualifies as an insubstantial amount. However, the final IRS rules did state that land improvements including remediation of contaminated land, clearing and grading will be taken into consideration in terms of this test. If an investor acquires related QOZB property that facilitates using the land in the business entity's trade or business, that will also be taken into consideration.[123]

Selling Assets to a Qualified Opportunity Fund

The final IRS Regulations, issued at the end of 2019, clarified an unresolved issue regarding tax treatment of proceeds gained from selling an asset to a QOF. Under these rules, an investor who sells an asset to a QOF cannot then invest the proceeds from that sale into the fund and receive preferential tax treatment on those proceeds. In other words, that investment of proceeds will not be treated as a gain eligible for capital gains benefits under opportunity zone rules.[124] Here's an example: an investor sells a building located in a qualified opportunity zone to a QOF for $100,000. That investor then cannot invest the proceeds of that sale — the $100,000 — into the QOF because there is no separate gain from the sale of the building to qualify for preferential tax treatment. The IRS does not allow such circular movement of cash to qualify as a capital gain; instead, it treats this transaction as an exchange of a building for an ownership interest in the QOF.[125]

Triggering Inclusions of Deferred Gains

There are certain situations in which deferred gains are triggered, known as "inclusion events." When these events occur, deferred gains are triggered — meaning, they become taxable for the investor. In general, when an investor either cashes out a portion of their investment in a QOF by receiving a distribution greater than the taxpayer's basis or a taxpayer reduces a direct equity investment in a QOF.[126] Specifically, inclusion gains occur when a QOF is decertified for example or when an interest in a QOF is transferred between spouses as part of a divorce.[127] In addition, a change in a QOF's entity status also qualifies as an inclusion event. For example, if a QOF changes it's tax status from a corporation to a partnership, an inclusion event is triggered.[128]

For investors in QOFs organized as C Corps, dividend-equivalent redemptions are classified as triggering events for the entire amount of the distribution. The only exceptions are for wholly owned corporations or if the corporation only maintains one class of stock.[129]

For investors in QOFs organized as partnerships, divisions of QOF partnerships are recognized as a triggering event.[130]

For investors in S Corps organized as QOFs, a triggering event does not occur when there is a greater than 25 percent change in the ownership of the S Corp, a change from the proposed regulations. The final regulations also clarified that conversion is within sub chapter S from a qualified sub chapter S trust to a small business trust are not treated as triggering events.[131]

Investors who have experienced triggering or inclusion events are still eligible for five or seven year basis increases providing that deferred gains are not yet recognized.[132]

180-Day Reinvestment Window

Investors have the ability to defer gains received from investments in QOFs into other QOFs or the original QOF they invested in. That reinvestment must occur within 180 days from the sale or exchange that created the gain.

For partnerships or S Corps that allocated realized gains to investors, the affected investors can choose when to start the 180-day investment period. For example, if a partner receives a gain in March 2020 but does not receive a Schedule K-1 reflecting that gain until a year later, that extends the starting time of the 180-day reinvestment period to Dec. 31, 2020. However, if the investors wishes to immediately reinvest following the distribution, that moves the 180-day window to start when the distribution was received. This flexible treatment of the 180-day window in IRS regulations provides investors with a great deal of latitude in regard to reinvesting gains.[133]

Finally, investors or partners in flow-through entities gained even more flexibility in the final IRS regulations published in December, 2019. These investors can decide to wait to start the 180-day period on the due date of the pass-through entity's tax return. However, this doesn't include any extensions the pass-through entity requests. This potentially allows investors to extend the 180-day window until six months follow the March 15th tax filing deadline for such entities.[134]

Original Use Test

Under IRS regulations, the original use of vacant property begins when an investor originally places that property into service for purposes of depreciation.[135] Under the final regulations, vacant property can be put into service and qualify for tax incentives if it meets two tests. Such property must have been vacant for one full year before the area was designed as a qualified OZ and continues to be vacant through the date of purchase by a QOF or QOZB.[136] Vacant property that was taken by local governments due to blight, non-payment of property taxes or other reasons is viewed as original use property when purchased by a QOZB or a QOF from a local government.

If an investor purchases vacant property that does not meet these criteria, then it must meet a three-year test before being put into use.[137] For the purpose of the regulations, vacant property is defined as less than 80 percent of the usable space in use prior to the purchase.[138]

Investments by International Investors

Non-American investors can invest in QOFs and QOZBs if they have capital gains subject to U.S. federal income taxes. Such gains can only be invested in QOFs and businesses if these non-U.S. investors waive any treaty benefits that would exempt those gains from U.S. federal taxes, according to the final IRS regulations. The IRS and U.S. Treasury have yet to clarify regulations regarding withholding under the Foreign Investment Real Property Act (FIRPTA), which are special rules for how U.S. tax regulations treat non-U.S. investors who invest in U.S. real property, in light of OZ regulations.

Installment Sale Gains

Final IRS regulations issued in December 2019 dispelled uncertainty around the investment of gains from installment sales. An investor with installment sale gains can either invest their gains in a QOF or business within 180 days of when the gain is received or within 180 days of the last day of the year the gain would be recognized under the installment method.[139] This means that an investor can defer gains from multiple installment sales, using either multiple 180-day periods or a single 180-day period that occurs at the end of that investor's taxable year.[140]

When a Qualified Opportunity Fund Experiences a Gain

Let's analyze the example of someone with a $250,000 capital gain from the initial investment who invests in a QOF. This investor was fortunate enough that their investment in a QOF appreciated after a holding period of ten years by $100,000. Let's walk through this example step-by-step:

1. Because this investor held the investment for the required seven years, 15 percent of the initial investment was tax-exempt ($250,000 × 15% = $37,500).

2. That left the taxable difference of $212,500 ($250,000 − $37,500 = $212,500) to be taxed at the 20 percent combined rate or $42,500 ($212,500 × 20% = $42,500). After tax proceeds from initial capital gains $170,000 ($212,500 − $42,500)

3. Even better after the ten-year hold, there is no tax on the $100,000 of appreciation from the QOF investment, leaving the investor with total after tax funds of $307,500 ($170,000 + $37,500 + $100,000), which represents a total net return of 23 percent.

When a Qualified Opportunity Fund Experiences a Loss

Unfortunately, not all QOFs will be successful. Even if a QOF experiences a loss, that investor is still eligible for this increase in basis if they hold their investment for the required five to seven years. For 2026 or the year of the exit from the QOF, their recognized gain will be less than the original deferral or the fair market value their interest in the QOF.

For example, let's say you created an QOF to purchase OZ property valued at $250,000 within an OZ. After seven years, the QOF sold the property for $200,000, a 20 percent loss. That means a capital loss of $50,000 was incurred. After the loss, the balance is $200,000—80 percent of the original investment. Despite the loss, the investment was held for the required seven years. That means the investor still receives the 15 percent increase in basis or a future tax exemption of $37,500. In this instance the 20 percent loss is negated by the 15 percent tax exemption from the seven-year hold.

When a Qualified Opportunity Fund Experiences an Early Exit

For example, let's say that you used your capital gains to invest $250,000 in an OZ business. After five years, the business is offered a lucrative buy-out, meaning your stake is now worth $750,000. That gives you a capital gain of $500,000. Because you held the investment for five years, you receive a 10 percent step-up in basis, meaning that 10 percent of your initial $250,000 gain isn't subject to capital gains tax.[141] However, because you didn't hold the investment for the required ten years, you don't get the capital gain exclusion on the new gain of $500,000. If you decide to roll the gains on the recent investment over into another QOF, the 10-year clock starts again. However, there is another provision in the tax law that could help in these situations. Section 1202, also known as the Small Business Stock Gains Exclusion, offers an exclusion of specific types of capital gains that occur from small business stock sales.[142] The stock sold must be issued by a U.S. C-corp, excluding hotels, restaurants, financial institutions, real estate companies, farms, mining company, or businesses relating to law, engineering, or architecture.[143] The stock must be held for at least five years and meet all the required guidelines to take advantage of the capital gains tax exclusion.

Qualified Opportunity Funds as an Alternative for 1031 Exchange

A 1031 tax exchange, also referred to as a "like-kind exchange" or a "Starker Exchange," is a deferred tax strategy under the Internal Revenue Code Section 1031.[144] It's an investment vehicle in which many investors, specifically real estate investors, used to defer paying capital gains taxes. According to the IRS, in a 1031 tax exchange, an investor can defer paying capital gains taxes as long as a "like-kind property" is exchanged.

As outlined by the IRS, properties that are of "like-kind" must possess the "same character" regardless of whether or not the property is improved. It cannot apply to properties located outside of the United States or properties still for sale. It also cannot apply to other assets such as vehicles, equipment, machinery, artwork, intellectual property, or other personal or tangible property.[145]

While a 1031 tax exchange is a great idea, QOFs are giving them a run for their money as providing another option for investors. According to Fundrise, in a QOF investors are responsible for "rolling over" capital gains by 180 days.[146] Only a portion rolled over can be eligible for tax advantages given in a QOF (deferral of capital tax gain).

Unlike a QOF, in a 1031 tax exchange, investors are required to reinvest capital gains within 180 days. It also requires an intermediary whereas a QOF doesn't require one.

Here are some of the differences between OZ and 1031 Exchanges:

• **Assets:** Only real estate can qualify in a 1031 exchange whereas in a QOFs any tangible property employed in a business that is located in an OZ qualifies.

• **Investment structure:** In a QOF, the pooled funds can be invested in virtually any type of asset within an OZ. However, in a 1031 exchange, the replacement property must be very similar to the original property. The IRS term is "like-kind," meaning that the replacement property must possess the "same nature, character or class." Because the rules don't discriminate based on quality or grade, most real estate will qualify as an exchange for other real estate.

• **Step-up in basis:** A "step-up in basis" is an accounting term used to refer to an increase of an asset for tax purposes. This frequently occurs when property or financial assets are inherited. In a QOF, you don't necessarily need to wait to inherit an asset to receive this tax benefit. Investors can receive capital gains through a step-up basis after five to seven years on the initial gain. After five years, they receive a step-up basis of 10 percent. After seven years, they receive a step-up basis of 5 percent thus receiving 15 percent.

• **Capital gains deferral:** In a QOF, capital gains can be deferred until December 2026 whereas in a 1031 exchange, there is no definite time period in which capital gains can be deferred. Though, this is also a benefit for some investors since in a 1031 exchange, an investor can continue deferring capital gains for years until the property is passed on through inheritance or sale.

Both 1031 exchanges and QOFs have their pros and cons. They also have their similarities and differences. Each one is suitable for a particular investor. For real estate investors, older investors planning on the inheritance route and investors who don't require access to their principal capital, 1031 exchanges are suitable. Though for other types of investors—especially investors looking to diversify their portfolio beyond real estate and require access to their principal capital—investing in an OZ is a great opportunity.

10-Year Exclusion of Gain

For investors, QOFs or businesses that sell assets after 10 years, capital gains from such a sale qualify for the 10-year exclusion. The IRS requires that the only ordinary income that must be recognized in this situation comes from the sale of inventory. The final rules specifically allow other types of ordinary income such as depreciation recapture to qualify for the 10-year exclusion. If a QOF or business disposes of assets over several years, investors can elect to exclude flow-through asset gains.

Risks Inherent in Opportunity Zone Investments

Any type of investing carries inherent risks. If you're an investor seeking gains through QOFs you must understand that investing in distressed communities is a high-risk investment alternative with an unproven track record and no history of success.

Additionally, there are potentially high barriers to entry when it comes to investing in QOF. Investment minimums typically start at $25,000 and upward, rising to six figures, depending on the specific QOF and its track record. Investors with moderate gains may want to think long and hard about the advantages of the tax deferral and step up in basis, as they require an investment of at least five years in duration.

Exiting a QOF in less than five years will trigger taxes owed on the original gains, which are then due immediately with no realization of a step up in basis. Leaving a QOF early may involve taking a loss because QOFs will take time to become profitable. A better alternative for an investor with smaller capital gains is to pay the capital gains, then reinvest the balance into a low-cost index fund so that those funds can be available in case of an emergency or unexpected life event. Deciding to invest in a QOF exclusively to receive the tax exclusions is not worth the risk. And because OZ investments require capital to be locked up from five to ten years to receive the tax benefit, there is a high probability for the United States to experience a recession during that time. When the inevitable recession occurs, that may trigger small investors to pull their money out, which would then require the payment of taxes on the original gain.

If you're an experienced investor with a surplus of wealth and six to seven figure capital gains—carefully evaluate any qualified OZ investments to ensure that the potential benefits outweigh the risks. While the true intention of the OZ program is to bring capital to high-poverty communities and create jobs—tax incentives are the vehicle of choice to accomplish this goal. Though these incentives are quite enticing, investors—especially investors just starting out— must consider a number of factors when assessing a QOFs, such as compliance, due diligence, fees, and track records in both communities and sectors.

Conducting Qualified Opportunity Fund Due Diligence

As part of the due diligence process, determine if the QOF manager possesses a successful track record in both the investment niche and geographical area they specialize in. The QOF fund management should also be very conversant with the geographical area in which the QOF will operate. Do some research to find out how much experience the manager has in this type of investing, what types of investment funds they have experience running and if they hold a degree from a respectable college or university.

Fees should be reflective of the fund manager's experience. If the fund manager does not have a proven track record then his fees should be strictly performance based, in addition to having his own capital at risk aka skin in the game. Some funds charge a variety of fees such as a management fee, project development fees, carried interest rates, acquisition fee, asset management fees, disposition fees, etc. If they do have skin in the game in terms of investing their own capital in their own QOF, that capital can be quickly recovered through acquisition fees, disposition fees and management fees. What are the implications of that type of approach? It means that the manager has zero risk with the investors taking on all the risk in the investment.

These fees have varying percentages (e.g. 20 percent carried interest and 2 percent management fee). Before you invest, consider the impact of these fees on the fund's projected returns. Otherwise, you may not benefit from the qualified OZ tax incentives because the fees you're paying may outweigh the projected returns and tax incentives.

Check Out Compliance Reporting

You should also examine the QOF's compliance, maintenance, and fund agreement. These aspects of fund operations are essential to maximizing tax incentives offered by QOFs because if a QOF falls out of compliance, the tax advantages won't exist.

Each year, qualified opportunity funds must conduct IRS compliance reporting. First, investors must examine the QOF self-certification. They can self-certify through Form 8996 annually, which must be filed with the rest of the income tax return.

The "90 percent test" is a critical part of QOF reporting. That's because the IRS requires all QOFs to hold at least 90 percent of their assets in qualified OZ property. The IRS measures this on the last day of the sixth month of the QOF's tax year or the last day of the last month of the QOF's tax year. For example, if a corporation self-certifies as a QOF on January 1, 2019, then the "90 percent test" will be measured on July 1, 2019. However, if they self-certify on October 1, 2019—then it will only be measured on December 31, 2019. If a QOF does not meet the 90 percent test, the IRS stipulates that it must pay a penalty for each month that it doesn't meet the requirement, unless the failure was due to a reasonable cause.[147] Regulations don't explain what consists of reasonable cause or describe what the penalties might be.

Next, investors must make sure the qualified opportunity fund's designation is maintained. This is essential since investors will want to realize tax benefits associated with the QOF. You should always request an updated and current copy of Form 8996 as proof of the QOF designation maintenance every year.

Finally, you should examine the QOF's fund agreement. The agreement should be clear about its structure, terms, fees, investment strategy, exit strategy, and return calculations. This is crucial so that you can position yourself receive all tax benefits that the OZ program offers.

Qualified Opportunity Zone Investments

Now that you know what a QOF is and the options for setting one up, the next step is to locate suitable OZ investments. A qualified OZ is defined as any business or real estate within an OZ. As I noted earlier, a QOF must hold 90 percent of its assets in qualified OZ business properties. In order to qualify as qualified OZ business properties, these properties must be tangible properties purchased or leased by a taxpayer operating within a QOF with at least 50 percent of their business's total gross income derived from its operation.

Not all investments qualify because assets owned or leased within QOFs must undergo substantial improvement. For leased property, the lease between a QOF or QOF business or other related parties can't include a prepayment made by the leased exceeding twelve months. Also, significant improvements must be made at a value equal to the value of the leased property within thirty months.

Definitions

Opportunity Zone (OZ): OZs are economically distressed census tracks, or areas contiguous to those census tracks, which qualify for the OZ program under guidelines set for by the 2017 Tax Cuts and Jobs Act.

Qualified Opportunity Zone Property: A qualified OZ properties may include partnership interests in businesses that operate within a qualified OZ; stock ownership in a business that conducts most or all of their operations within a qualified OZ or properties such as real estate located within a qualified OZ.

Qualified Opportunity Zone Business: A qualified OZ business must earn at least 50 percent of its gross income from the active conduct of business within a qualified OZ. In addition, a substantial portion of the intangible property of such an entity must also be used in the active conduct of business in the OZ.

Starker or 1031 Exchange: A Starker Exchange is essentially a 1031 exchange. It describes a like-kind exchange that is deferred. When an investor who wants to use gains earned through the sale of one property to invest in another like-kind property but is unable to find a suitable match at the time, those gains are placed in the care of a third-party middleman. That third party holds the gains after the sale of the first property and then buys the second property for the investor.

Becoming a Qualified Opportunity Zone Business

According to the IRS, a qualified OZ business is a trade or business operated by a taxpayer that owns or leases tangible property within an OZ.[148]

The QOF that acquires the qualified OZ business must newly construct or substantially improve the tangible business property. That business must also be operated within the designated OZ for the entire time the business is held by the QOF. Substantial improvement is defined as incurring capital expenditures on the property within 30 months of the property or business acquisition that equals or exceeds the purchase price of the property.[149]

QOFs can either directly invest in a qualified OZ business or channel investment through a subsidiary. When operating through a subsidiary, assets which a taxpayer owns or leases tangible property the tangible property owned or leased must adhere to the 90 percent test. For a subsidiary to become a qualified OZ business, they must satisfy certain requirements set by the IRS.

Ineligible Businesses

Similar to regulations set for eligible qualified OZ partnerships, the following types of businesses are ineligible to be considered qualified OZ businesses:

- Country clubs

- Tanning salons

- Gambling facilities (e.g. casinos and racetracks)

- Country clubs

- Golf courses (commercial and private)

- Liquor stores or any business that sells alcohol for consumption outside of the property

The 70% Test

According to the IRS, at least 70 percent of all tangible property leased or owned by a business of a subsidiary must meet the requirements of a qualified OZ property as shown previously.[150]

The Income-and-Assets Test

According to IRS regulations, all qualified OZ businesses must be involved in an active conduct of a business or trade within a qualified OZ.[151]

In order to retain the status as a qualified OZ business, each tax year, that business must:

- Receive at least 50 percent of gross income from active business conduct in the qualified OZ;

- Own a large amount of intangible property (e.g. branding, intellectual property) used in the conduct of this active business;

- Limit non-qualified financial property (e.g., debt, partnership interests, warrants, stock, etc.) to less than 5 percent of assets, excluding working capital.

The first rule—the 50 percent rule—may not apply to all businesses. In general, start-ups may not be considered engaged in the active conduct of business or trade until revenue is generated. Though, in this scenario, there are several proposed safe harbors for businesses such as start-ups to be engaged in the active conduct of business or trade. Of these safe harbors, a qualified OZ business must satisfy one of these to comply with the 50 percent gross income rule.[152] These safe harbors include:

- 50 percent of hourly services performed by employees and contractors must be performed within a qualified OZ

- At least 50 percent of amounts paid for by a business for services performed by employees and contractors must be performed within a qualified OZ

- At least 50 percent of gross income generated by a qualified opportunity zone business must be performed within the qualified OZ

Opportunity Zone Tiers

OZs can be divided into three tiers, labeled Tier-1, Tier-2, and Tier-3 cities. Tier-1 OZs are those that are located in top markets such as New York, San Francisco, Atlanta, Charlotte, Washington DC, and Chicago. Tier-2 OZs comprise middle market cities such as Austin, TX, and Nashville, TN, while Tier-3 OZs include small cities like Waterbury, CT where I grew up, and Erie, PA.

Many investors are attracted to investing in Tier-1 cities. However, before you commit to investing in OZs in specific geographic areas, you need to understand the importance of maintaining a significant margin of safety specifically with real estate. You don't want to find yourself overpaying or investing in overpriced markets because there will be little upside in the event of a recession, which is inevitable at some point.

That's why it is wise to think twice before purchasing property in tier 1 cities due to heavy development costs and extraordinarily high property valuations. For example, a 1,955 ft^2 run-down store front location in a Brooklyn OZ costs $3,500,000. Since the building is old, outdated and has the minimum square footage to sustain even moderate profitability, the best option would be to demolish the building and build a modern mixed use building with a much larger footprint. There's only one problem. This $3.5 million building is sandwiched between two equally old and run-down buildings with similar asking prices. For a developer considering a project like this, there must be a consideration to purchase the adjacent buildings, which basically triples the upfront cost. The developer must also factor in the cost of demolition. If the developer decides against purchasing the adjacent building, there's a good chance that those adjacent buildings will drag down the value of the new proposed development. This is how gentrification starts. When the cost of purchasing and then demolishing a property is already at $10.5 million and you haven't even broke ground yet, it is clear that whatever replaces those buildings will not be affordable for most people who live in the surrounding areas. While gentrification is a risk involved in OZ investing, it's not an ideal outcome because it displaces the residents and businesses that the OZ was originally designed to help.

Though, on the other hand, there are thousands of pieces of property and businesses located in the 8,762 OZs throughout the United States. Here's another example from my hometown, Waterbury, CT, with several large (15,012 ft^2) buildings. For the reasonable cost of $250,000, an investor could purchase one of these buildings, leaving much more margin for profit. Investing and developing in a cheaper but larger property in an OZ community like Waterbury provides safety, less risk, and more upside. This is especially true in the event of a severe economic recession were to occur upon completion of the property development, as the developer would have significantly less invested capital at risk. This risk mitigation tactic would protect the developer and investors, unlike an investment in the Brooklyn property. The costs and the margin of safety between these two properties are substantial. Investing in OZ communities has its benefits, one being that investors can get more for their money, make a significant impact on the community, and minimize the effects of gentrification all while making sizable returns for their investors.

Unfortunately for OZ communities, QOFs, OZ investors, and OZ businesses, "slumlord" type property owners may seek to take advantage of the potential for development within the OZ. These property owners typically are absentees and have let their properties seriously deteriorate into either blight or vacancy. In an effort to extract the maximum possible profit from their properties, many will only hold out and sell at inflated prices.

This holds down the potential for an entire OZ because no QOF or OZ business wants to redevelop a building next to blighted and vacant properties. For example, if my QOF saw potential in buying large buildings and rehabilitating them for mixed use space, but the building was next two blighted building that cost twice as much as the buildings I want to renovate, I wouldn't want to proceed. That's because the cost to acquire the blighted properties would make the rehabilitation much less financially attractive. Or if I do proceed with the renovation the blighted or vacant property will ultimately drag down the price of my proposed mixed-use space potentially making the project less profitable for my investors.

Greedy owners of blighted and vacant properties must be reined in by the cities in which they operate. The only way to stem blight and keep it from interfering with OZ development is for a city to take aggressive action to curb blight and demolish uninhabitable buildings that have been vacant for years. Cities need to be more proactive in quickly condemning blighted properties and either taking them by eminent domain or forcing the owner to accept a reasonable price to sell that property.

If you are operating a QOF in a specific area with some blight, be sure to check into local regulations and the reputation of zoning and planning officials regarding how quickly blighted properties are addressed. You don't want to find promising OZ business property or businesses and then get held back by adjacent blight and vacant properties.

Fortunately, there are plenty of potential projects that allow you to avoid blight and blighted areas. Investing in OZ businesses and start-ups for instance, mitigates blight risk. Collaborating with communities that have strong blight protection laws and proactively deal with blight is also a way to mitigate the risk of blight on your OZ investments. Finally, by becoming closely acquainted with the communities where you plan to invest, you can avoid blight and reap the opportunity offered through this once-in-a-lifetime opportunity to reinvest your capital gains, make a profit, and significantly reduce your basis and potential future capital gains taxes.

Many communities with OZs are capitalizing on this chance to channel investments into their areas. These communities can facilitate investments by making it as easy as possible for investors, developers, start-ups, and entrepreneurs to locate in their OZs. If you're interested in these communities, you can visit their websites and easily locate information about investment opportunities as well as contact information for local officials eager to help. It makes sense to choose to invest and do business with OZ communities that do whatever they can to make the investment process seamless.

Chapter 5

How Opportunity Zone Communities Can Attract Investors, QOFs, Entrepreneurs and Developers

Now that you understand the potential for OZs to create meaningful change and how the law works, it's time to address the issue of how OZ stakeholders can attract and raise capital to position themselves for success. I'm starting with OZ communities, because they are the lynchpin in the OZ ecosystem. Action or inaction on their part determines whether other stakeholders—investors and QOFs—will find and invest in deals in their individual communities.

There are 8,762 OZs competing and vying for investor capital. Those OZ communities that act first, start an effective marketing campaign, and clearly define their niche will be among the few communities that will realize the benefit of building successful OZs. The stakes are high—the potential to transform distressed areas of your community with well-paying jobs and affordable housing can reinvigorate, reimagine, and reinvent your region's footprint.

Imagine leveraging and redesigning your community's OZs to alleviate unnecessary vehicle traffic to create the walkable cities of the future and create real economic hubs that will transform communities. More than $6 trillion of investor and corporate capital remains available to invest in OZs.[153] Successfully attracting this capital, much of which is controlled by the professional investors that form QOFs, requires the right perspective and a commitment to building long-term relationships over time.

There is no shortcut to persuading QOFs, developers, start-ups, and entrepreneurs to invest in your community. Even if you've got terrific shovel-ready deals, the odds that an QOF, investor, or business will commit to investing in your community without conducting extensive due diligence and building a relationship with key stakeholders are quite slim. Trust must be earned, and trust is key in capital raising. Investors, QOFs, developers, and entrepreneurs want to know that the community is both serious and committed to fast track the changes needed to yield positive investment returns for all OZ stakeholders.

If your OZ follows the step-by-step process I've outlined below, you will maximize the potential to get deals flowing in your community.

Step 1: Develop a Positioning Statement

The first and most important task an OZ community must think about involves defining their core assets and developing a positioning statement around them. The positioning statement sets the community apart from the rest and quickly communicates its core strengths. If your community's OZ sits on waterfront property, use that to your advantage and build a solid positioning statement around it. If your community has the largest square footage of abandoned factory buildings in the state, create a positioning statement highlighting that these buildings can be updated and repurposed for modern factory usage or even a modern mixed-use walkable community.

Your community may be sitting on an ocean of oil or mineral rights or have the largest population of college educated millennials. Outside investors who are not familiar with your OZ community will not know about these potential assets, and the best way to highlight them is to build a positioning statement around your community's greatest assets. For example, Las Vegas' positioning statement is "What happens in Vegas Stays in Vegas." It clearly communicates that the city of Las Vegas is an adult playground for engaging in adult activities.

Through its national advertising campaign and backdrop in many movies like *The Hangover* and *Ocean's 11*, the entire country is attracted to the excitement built around bright lights, architecture, and adult themes. Who would have thought that millions of people would travel across the country every year to a city built in the middle of the desert because of a clever positioning statement and an effective marketing campaign? That's the power of being hyper focused and leveraging your core strengths with a well-thought out positioning statement. A positioning statement should be a crystal-clear one-sentence statement that accurately captures your community's differentiators. It should also clearly communicate your advantage in the market place. This isn't something you can toss off in an afternoon. It will go through many iterations. Carefully think it through and take time to draft and redraft that pitch sentence. Bounce your drafts off other stakeholders in your community. Keep working on it until it clearly and concisely communicates your community's strengths.

Step 2: Define Your Target Audience

Before you start churning out a website, prospectus, video, and other materials, get clear on exactly what market you're targeting. Because QOFs, investors, and businesses have different objectives and focuses, you need to define your target audience very specifically.

Targeting every QOF out there will be self-defeating, because you'll waste time engaging with QOFs with different sector and geographic focus.

This is why it's important to conduct a market analysis before you create marketing collateral to support your efforts. To conduct a customer analysis, follow these steps:

1. Set up investment groups: Encourage local wealthy community members to set up investment groups to create QOFs. In order to attract outside professional investor capital, your local business leaders need to invest in creating communities to show a commitment to professional outside investors who may want to invest in your community. These investment groups can take many forms. Teresa Esser, author of The Venture Café: Secrets, Strategies, and Stories from America's Entrepreneurs (Business Books, 2002)[154] and managing director of Silicon Pastures Angel Investment Fund, notes that even a local bar can become a gathering place around investment as long as there is an incentive, including free beer. "On the MIT campus, the Muddy Charles, a bar, is a place where many investors, entrepreneurs and grad students with bright ideas can meet to collaborate. That creates an environment with a really good vibe where you can talk about your project, build connections, lower risk and find business partners," she noted in a recent episode of my podcast, *The Rocco Forino Show*.

2. Define your target customer: Narrowly define exactly what types of investors and businesses you're seeking to attract to your QOF. If you're a tier three city, going after the largest investors located in New York and Los Angeles won't work. Instead define the types of investors, QOFs, and businesses that will find your specific OZs attractive.

3. Create a target avatar: A target avatar is a visual picture that represents your target investor. Consider potential roadblocks that

would discourage your investor avatar from investing in your community's OZ. These include their risk profile, their target profit margin, their lack of knowledge about your community, or a lack of alignment between your objectives and theirs. This avatar specifically defines your ideal target investor so that you can filter all of your marketing materials through the lens of whether that avatar would find them compelling or not.

4. Conduct a competitive analysis: Assess the strengths and weaknesses of what other OZs are doing to attract investment. Ensure that your materials exceed those efforts.

5. Develop a scalable solution: Determine the best ways to reach your target customer through web portal, social media, and marketing materials.

6. Implement your solution: Design an attractive web page and ensure that your materials are easily accessible. Place the contact information of knowledgeable economic development officials prominently so that potential investors can easily reach out and get their questions answered.

Step 3: Leverage Your Community's Strengths

Creating compelling marketing materials and video highlights requires precisely defining what your community and your OZs have to offer. Touting generic tax benefits won't cut it. Even listing all the shovel-ready projects isn't enough. Analyze your unique advantages from the standpoint of your investor avatar, which as I mentioned earlier in this chapter creates a well-defined picture of your ideal target audience. Once you've done that, promote the specific benefits that are most appealing to that ideal investor.

If your OZ is the entire island of Puerto Rico, for example, it can be leveraged as a safe tourist destination built with the latest renewable energy technology. That's a benefit that's very attractive to hospitality and tourism-oriented investors. Or, if your OZ sits within close proximity to STEM research universities, hospitals, corporations, and accelerators, that's interesting to OZs operating in STEM niches. STEM is defined as a focus on science, technology, engineering and math.

Understanding and quantifying your communities' core assets is critical. When you identify and capitalize on a specific niche with high-quality marketing materials and thought leadership, you'll attract investors, QOFs and businesses interested in your OZ community. Otherwise, you'll waste your time and energy targeting QOFs, investors, and businesses that aren't interested or do not exactly fit what your OZ community has to offer.

Step 4: Create Professional Marketing Materials

Now that you've defined your niche and identified your audience, your community is ready to build foundational marketing materials. This collateral will form a strong base for your marketing campaigns, providing your community with a solid start in the race to attract prospects.

Remember that the collateral your community is creating is just the start in a long-term marathon to attract QOFs, investors, and businesses into your community. In the twenty-first century, marketing is not a one-and-done. It's an integral part of the relationship-building equation. To stay in front of prospects, create thought leadership designed to stay connected to your prospects and attract new ones. Push that content out through social media channels and create hashtags around the community's greatest assets and encourage community members to do the same and share this information across social media channels such as Twitter, Instagram, Facebook, and LinkedIn. Create written, video, and audio content so that customers can consume your content in whatever way they prefer.

Integrate credible evidence, statistics, stories, and examples into your materials so that QOFs, investors, and businesses can more easily imagine and project how investment in your community's OZs will help them meet their objectives. All too often, marketers focus on the features of their offerings, rather than the benefits to potential investors. Don't make that mistake. Your job is to dig into your target audience—QOFs, entrepreneurs, and investors interested in your type of community—and understand exactly what they need. Then target all your marketing materials to that audience.

To impact interested investors, your community needs to craft a wide variety of marketing materials. These should include:

1. Prospectus: A solid prospectus showcases your community, highlights investor-ready projects, and details the organized, community-wide effort behind your OZs. The prospectus should include hard data about the commercial, industrial, retail, and residential aspects of your OZs, detailed information and maps covering each zone, market strengths, institutional capacity, inclusion strategy, adjacent areas, and information about the area's population, employment growth, largest employers, and educational profile. Adding your prospectus to OZ databases, platforms, and networks that connect communities with QOFs and investors helps you reach thousands of QOFs seeking to deploy capital.

2. Online portal: Through a professionally designed webpage, investors, business owners, and other stakeholders should be able to access professional OZ marketing materials, maps, and contact information for officials facilitating the investment process. Ensure your website's search engine optimization (SEO) is fully optimized and that you leverage offsite link building. Your city's website should offer click to chat software so that visitors can instantly interact with your website and get answers to questions in real time.

3. Pitch deck: A professional pitch deck that highlights statistics about your community, selected investment ready-projects, and a snapshot of the benefits of investing can help solidify your case with interested investors. This pitch deck should be a maximum of 20 to 30 pages long and visually communicate your unique value proposition and how investing in your community's OZs will benefit your target audience. Every pitch deck should include: your community's competitive advantage in the OZ space, specific information about shovel-ready projects, OZ team leaders and background on all team members, the process involved in investing the OZ, community and investment statistics, and contact details.

4. Video: U.S. adults, including your potential investors, spend an average of six hours a day watching videos.[155] Don't ignore the value of a well-produced, engaging, and short video that highlights the potential of your community as an OZ investment destination. Your video should feature the key attributes that will attract your target audiences and the people who can make your community's story come alive. Uploading your video to DealConnect Hub gains you broad access to thousands of QOFs and family office investors seeking to invest in OZ communities.

5. One-pager: In your initial contacts with investors, it's very useful to have a one-pager that summarizes the key benefits for investors in pursuing investment in your community's OZs. This document gives investors a quick rundown of all the key data points and visuals for quick and easy consumption. The one pager should be a teaser that gives the viewer just enough information that they will reach out and ask for further information. When QOFs express an initial interest in your OZs, they can either download the one-pager or you can email it to them or leave it with them after an initial meeting. This piece of collateral is highly effective, as many OZs haven't

taken the time to distill the benefits of investing in their community so concisely.

Consider what action you want investors to take as you craft your materials. What is your call to action? Do you want investors to pick up the phone and call your OZ team? Do you want them to visit your OZ dedicated webpage? Do you want them to download materials? Be very clear about what actions you want investors to take and how to move them along the process to engage with you more deeply and invest in your OZ.

As your materials are finalized, upload them to OZ platforms and databases where they are more likely to be noticed by QOFs, investors, businesses, and entrepreneurs seeking to deploy capital. Seek out platforms that provide exposure to the investors with interests that align with yours, such as family offices and wealth managers focusing on OZ investments. Check out how DealConnect Hub might benefit your community.

Step 5: Lead Community Development with Design

Opportunity zones present a one-time, unique opportunity to reposition cities through design and walkable communities. The walkable cities of the future will incorporate more coworking spaces and encourage the use of driverless car technology to eliminate excessive traffic and overdeveloped parking lots. Replacing old prison-like industrial buildings, soulless apartment complexes, and cookie-cutter shopping plazas with twenty-first-century developments designed by forward-thinking architects ensures that cities will stay relevant and continue to attract capital and residents.

As Winston Churchill said: "We shape our buildings and afterwards our buildings shape us."[156] Your community's buildings shape not only the perception of the residents, but also that of investors, entrepreneurs, tourists, and future residents. Research conducted in

Germany on cities that innovated through allowing star architects to create bold visions through buildings experienced not only economic resurgence, but also additional pride on behalf of residents as well as enhanced reputations. Other impacts, that were harder to quantify and not necessarily anticipated, occurred. "The architecture impacted the cities spatially by revitalizing neighborhoods and changing the way people moved through towns," *Architectural Digest* reports.[157]

In Atlanta, city planners are part of a new wave of design-conscious planners who are forcing developments to meet tough design standards.[158] These standards emphasize attractive design that promotes growth and tourism. This movement is driven by the idea that higher design standards attract businesses and residents to city centers.

Research reveals that high-quality architecture revitalizes cities, changing the way that residents view their cities and providing a domino effect that encourages developers to continue to employ innovative design techniques.[159] In Los Angeles, innovative design employed for low-income housing is changing public perception of such developments as being detrimental to property values.[160]

Affordable housing can not only utilize attractive designs, but also employ techniques that reduce crime rather than attracting it. In San Antonio, TX, environmental improvements such as additional lighting, secure entrances and spaces that encourage community involvement act as a deterrent to crime.[161] These examples show what's possible when stakeholders work together to reinvent communities and meet impact investing objectives. This potential can be super-sized when OZs are appropriately positioned to capture investor capital.

Step 6: Build Art, Music, and Food-Oriented Communities

Ensuring that your community is host to a vibrant art, music, and restaurant scene reaps many benefits for your region. More restaurants are designing specific experiences so that diners can post memorable moments to their Instagram feeds. With more than 1 billion people using this popular app every month, it's important to ensure that your community has its share of Instagram-able destinations. Some cities, such as my hometown of Waterbury, Connecticut have many beautiful buildings around town, including churches and an Italian clock tower that would make you think you were in Europe. These architectural assets can be leveraged as a destination for photographers and architectural tourism.

Miami, for example, was never a city known for its art scene—instead, it's bona fide rested on its beaches. However, a focus on art-related developments in the community has transformed the area into an artistic destination ripe with Instagram-able attractions. Beginning with the Art Basel Art Fair in 2002, the region blossomed with art museums, vibrant architectural styles, street art, and a strong push toward installing art in public places.[162] Artists such as Romero Britto, Mister E, and Lefty Out There are also creating amazing art that attracts tourists, investors, and others. Romero Britto is a Brazilian artist, sculptor and painter who combines pop art and cubist abstraction.[163] Mr. E creates colorful interpretations of American currency.[164] Lefty Out There constructs works of art based on intricate patterns and bold colors.[165] Our culture is immersed in photo platforms such as Instagram, as people search their local communities and travel long distances in search of the best art experiences and photo opportunities.

Then there's Greenville, South Carolina. For years a forgotten mill town in northwestern South Carolina, Greenville has blossomed as a foodie, music, and art destination. Greenville takes advantage of the early Spring and late Fall by hosting free, live music downtown every Thursday, Friday, and Saturday nights, paid for by corporate sponsors such as Duke Energy. Jam-packed weekend. Festivals featuring art, music, and food include Artisphere, Euphoria, and Fall for Greenville. www.VisitGreenvilleSC.com, the city's convention and visitor's bureau, cultivates media and social media attention by promoting Instagram-able destinations on their social media feeds and website. Greenville's attractions and successful promotions of those attractions landed the city on the New York Time's coveted "52 Places to Go" list in 2017.[166]

Don't forget Atlanta, which not only has a hit TV show named after it, but also boasts a thriving music, film, arts, and food scene. Movies ranging from *The Blind Side* to *The Hunger Games* were filmed here as well as hit TV shows including *The Walking Dead*. Artists such as OutKast, Usher, and Ludacris, and major labels such as Grand Hustle and So So Def are based in Atlanta.[167] The community food scene is thriving in Atlanta, as a hearty mix of cuisines from all over the south and all over the world emerge in restaurants and markets. Food Halls are big here, many carved out of restored industrial spaces, where visitors can try cuisine from a number of restaurants in the same locale.[168]

Step 7: Create Business Incubators

Cities that prioritize a start-up culture by facilitating business incubators and tech accelerators position themselves to jumpstart an innovative, entrepreneurial culture. Such a culture attracts investment, creativity, and a well-educated workforce. The more accelerators and incubators your community creates, the higher the probability these start-ups will become successful businesses employing thousands of people and careers with well-paying jobs.

Esser notes that there is much OZs can do to foster a culture of investment. They don't have to reinvent the wheel—instead they can leverage the Venture Café format to create space for local entrepreneurs to join in on the weekly Thursday gatherings between 3:00 and 8:00 p.m. Inspired by the book and the website www.venturecafeglobal.com, these weekly meeting offer the opportunity for informal networking, exchange of ideas, and programming that fosters innovation.

By adopting a format such as the Venture Café, your community can join communities such as Boston, St. Louis, Winston-Salem, Miami, Philadelphia, Tokyo, and Warsaw in supporting and attracting entrepreneurs, investors, and others. "Many investors and entrepreneurs with successful businesses and business exits show up at Thursday Night Venture Café gatherings to share their wisdom, make connections, and learn from others," she noted on my podcast.

Atlanta's TechSquare neighborhood acts as an innovation hub, where TechSquare Labs hosts a quarterly Atlanta Startup Battle pitch competition, where hundreds of start-up founders pitch their ideas to win a $100,000 prize and hands on-mentorship. The two-day competition pairs start-ups with seasoned mentors, who then present to active venture capitalists from Atlanta and Silicon Valley to build the next generation of tech giants.[169]

Small businesses are critical to successful OZs because they employ nearly half of all-American employees and created 1.8 million jobs in 2018.[170] Today's small businesses that are growing in your accelerators could be the tech giants of tomorrow.

Step 8: Build Investor Networks

Communities can further facilitate capital raising by creating investor networks. Esser, who has helped facilitate investor networks in Milwaukee, recommends that the community development corporations collaborate with regional OZs to support the creation of investor networks. Some type of low-stakes give-away can ease the way toward establishing an investor network as is the case with the Muddy Charles get-together on the MIT campus that Esser participated in.

There may be opportunities for businesses to find partners to invest in their businesses and for QOFs to locate suitable investments. Investor networks, in conjunction with business incubators and accelerators, offer your community more bang for the buck in terms of facilitating OZ investing.

In Atlanta, a growing network of entrepreneurs of color has created an informal investor network around the thriving technology scene. These include Paul Judge, founder of TechSquare Labs, Atlanta's leading seed-stage venture fund, Tristian Walker, founder of Walker & Company, Russell Stokes, president and CEO of GE's energy business, Tricky Stewart, hit record producer, and many others seeking to leverage Atlanta's growing tech, cultural, and entertainment scene.[171] Many of these African American entrepreneurs left Silicon Valley because of its lack of diversity and are committed to building a diverse and successful tech and innovation hub in the South.

Georgetown grads and classmates Ryan Wilson and T. K. Peterson hatched the idea for the Gathering Spot, a next generation private membership club, in their dorm rooms.[172] The first location? Atlanta, which had the type of atmosphere that the two sought to bring together people from diverse industries and backgrounds. It's been such a smashing success—hosting events for major brands such as Google, Coke, Netflix, and Spotify—that the partners are opening a second location in Los Angeles. They plan to further expand on their model, which disrupts the private club ethos of exclusion by ensuring that their membership represents people of color and women, which is the future of America.[173]

Jewel Burks Solomon, who sold her visual-recognition tech start-up Partpic to Amazon in 2016, partnered with other influential black entrepreneurs to form Collab, an investment firm that facilitates connections between black entrepreneurs and investors, partners, and resources. Solomon, along with Justin Dawkins and Barry Givens, is dedicated to foster wealth building and economic mobility in the African American community, which is historically underserved by traditional capital raising.[174]

Amanda Sabreah, founder and CEO of Partnr, a digital platform for creatives, to the list of black entrepreneurs determined to turn Atlanta into a start-up Mecca where entrepreneurship and creativity flourish side-by-side.[175] Sabreah rejected a VC deal that would have required her to move her start-up to the Bay Area. Although she remains tuned into the scene in Silicon Valley and values the deep advisory start-up network there, she's fully committed to Atlanta.

What's transforming Atlanta isn't unique to that city. Atlanta's journey from a sleepy Southern capital to a cultural, music, food, arts, and start-up Mecca didn't happen overnight either. It took a commitment by community leaders, business executives, and successful start-up founders to create the infrastructure that made it all possible.

Step 9: Shake Out Slumlords

In a large percentage of OZ communities, slumlords typically occupy large real estate holdings, which are frequently decrepit buildings operated with minimal maintenance and upkeep. These slumlords maintain these holdings with the hope of eventually benefitting from their key locations in major cities and programs such as OZs. Many of these slumlords are also politically connected and know how to work inside the grey areas of the zoning laws. And now that the real estate that they own and adjacent properties fall into OZ designations; slumlords can benefit by holding out and selling these now potentially hot property locations to the highest QOF bidders.

This is a problem, because it will cause QOFs to look elsewhere if they are smart, or purchase these properties above market rate. If they purchase the properties above market rate, the higher price per square foot that they pay will ultimately be passed onto future renters of the property, which is how gentrification starts. OZ community leaders at the state and local level have to create policies and laws that favor QOFs that state if slumlords are not willing to sell their property located in OZs at a fair market rate, they either have to upgrade the property to the same standards that QOFs and developers are willing to invest or be forced to sell at market rate less demolition costs and related sunk costs if the property does not make economic sense to renovate or repurpose.

Another scenario is if an QOF wants to invest millions of dollars into developing a property on one side of the street and across the street a slumlord is sitting on property that they are not willing to renovate. The slumlord property—if not updated or renovated will ultimately drag down the property value of the QOF property and those around it. Therefore, if an QOF is investing millions of dollars into a property then the owners of those neglected properties across the street should be required to sell or be forced to upgrade their property to the standards to the new QOF property. If slumlords can get away with manipulating real estate values to enrich themselves at the expense of OZ communities, QOFs, investors, residents, and businesses, it may create a situation where such investment is not worthwhile due to extremely thin potential return on investments.

When landlords invest in their properties on both the inside and the outside—as in Atlanta's mission to stop unattractive building construction—building owners, OZs, and the entire community benefits. Unfortunately, without prodding, it's unlikely that slumlords will voluntarily rehabilitate their properties. Cities like Mobile, AL, and Memphis, TN, are taking matters into their own hands and aggressively addressing blight. For decades, Mobile unsuccessfully struggled to address blight, as well as its residents' needs for affordable housing and decent paying jobs. The city also wanted to return land and buildings into service and meet the needs of businesses for an affordable, well-trained workforce and plenty of reasonable industrial, office, and warehouse space.

Mobile sought to transform blighted areas before OZ legislation by creating an agreed-upon definition for blight and streamlining the process for repairing and rehabilitating housing in blighted areas.[176] During a four-year period, Mobile reduced the number of blighted properties by 45 percent. By facilitating the rehabilitation process, Mobile can keep up with the workload necessary to ensure this trend continues, all without having to hire more staff. Many communities are adopting this cutting-edge approach to fighting blight. Memphis created a Blight Authority, which is charged with rehabilitating vacant, foreclosed, abandoned, or tax-delinquent properties.[177] Memphis attacked blight through a coordinated campaign designed to enforce codes, take possession of abandoned property, and return such buildings to useful purposes.[178]

Slumlords and blight are some of the biggest hurdles I see that will impede forward progress and could dissuade QOFs from putting time and energy into communities that will ultimately wind up working against them instead of with them. If OZ communities are committed to positive change and are serious about attracting and retaining investors, QOFs, start-ups, and entrepreneurs then they have to quickly take all the steps necessary to remove all barriers to stakeholders investing and willing to relocate to their community. Adopting the tactics used in Memphis can quickly get run-down buildings out of the hands of neglectful, absentee landlords. Community and business leaders can contribute to Blight Commissions and land banks so that these organizations have the resources to purchase abandoned and run-down buildings so that they can be re-developed. Finally, community leaders should work with state legislators to change the laws so to put more power in the hands of local communities to condemn or repossess buildings so that OZ investors aren't stymied by slumlords.

Step 10: Collaborate across Regions

To tap into investor capital, regions must band together so that all stakeholders are on the same page and present a unified front to the investors and businesses that will make or break your OZs. Cities and communities can't sit still waiting for investment to happen. As I've noted, proactively creating professional materials that paint a compelling picture for interested investors is critical.

It can't stop there—community officials and policy makers must streamline local and state policies and procedures to ensure that investors and businesses aren't sidetracked by time and energy intensive requirements to deploy their capital. That's because if OZs and their investors encounter high barriers to investment in the form of onerous rules and regulations, they will go elsewhere. Communities interested in facilitating investment should follow the example of Colorado Springs, Colorado, which created a rapid response team run by the city's Economic Development Division that fast tracks land use applications and building permits. Using this process allowed the city to cut the time for land use and building permits to get through the approval process by 50 percent.[179]

Once your community establishes momentum with investments, make sure to publicize your success stories. Leveraging established stakeholder relationships with the media—local and national—can be very helpful. The goal for OZ communities is to attract multiple investment stakeholders and leverage that growth and compound it.

Your community must demonstrate a track record of OZ investments to draw further investor attention. That's because QOFs and the family offices and VC firms who professionally invest will avoid communities that only show minimal investment momentum and minimal community effort, which is the same attitude and lack of effort that ultimately lead it to becoming an OZ in the first place.

That's why Tier-1 metros such as New York City and Washington DC are attracting capital—because those cities offer economic growth that investors can build on via profitable OZ investments. Tax incentives are all well and good, but to attract investors, you need to show them a well-rounded community plan demonstrating progress and compounding momentum. This type of activity demonstrates the potential for investors to create positive returns on investment and maintain those results ten years into the future.

Step 11: Design with Driverless Technology in Mind

The coming driverless car revolution will enable architects and planners to take this vision even further. The elimination of parking garages and lots will facilitate the construction of walkable communities around affordable housing and mixed-use developments. These will be replaced with drop off lanes and loops for ride-sharing and driverless cars.

While driverless car technology isn't ready for prime time, ride-sharing platforms are reshaping how Americans travel. By 2030, one in ten cars will be shared and 15 percent of new cars sold will be autonomous, using self-driving technology.[180] As driving habits change, there's an opportunity to get rid of the oversupply of parking garages and lots that dominate American cities, opening up real estate for walkable communities will lower carbon emissions, and substantially reduce traffic all while putting the focus on affordable housing and mixed used developments.[181]

Creating designs for walkable cities is easier now than ever with Urbano, a free software app that uses data, metrics and a user-friendly interface to facilitate the planning process. Built by developers at Cornell University,[182] Urbano assesses the walkability of cities based on three factors. The first factor determines how streets are used for specific purposes. The second factor assesses whether popular amenities are within walkable distances of homes and workplaces. The third factor leverages demographics to estimate how useful various services are to community residents.

Step 12: Collaborate with Surrounding Communities

Within municipalities, stakeholders inside and outside local and state governments must collaborate to ensure OZ priorities align. In many communities, OZs cluster inside and outside of municipal borders, providing the potential for officials to collaborate to maximize the appeal of geographically-adjacent OZs.

In Charleston and Huntington, West Virginia, economic development leaders created Advantage Valley, a collaborative economic development organization. They produced a regional pitch book designed to promote 13 area OZs and 20 specific investments within those areas.[183] Cleveland, Ohio, offers 64 census tracks in Cuyahoga County designated as OZs. A diverse group of economic development groups founded Opportunity CLE to attract capital into projects designed for social impact across this region of 1.25 million.[184]

Communities most likely to succeed possess the following qualities:

• Providing easy access to OZ officials

- Creating specific OZ investment strategies

- Updating investors with targeted regional OZ investments

Step 13: Build Relationships

There is no silver bullet when it comes to attracting investment into your community. Capital raising is hard work that requires a long-term perspective. That's because investors with capital to invest are more interested in making the *right* deal than a quick deal so time is on the side of the investor. That may seem counterintuitive, but professional investors are not in a hurry to invest just because there is tax incentives involved. Investors still seek quality deals from trusted sources and OZ investing is now just another investment option among many alternatives.

Their experience has shown that the most profitable deals come after a significant period of due diligence and relationship building. QOFs and their investors want to be sure that your OZ investments fall into their area of expertise while providing an appropriate return-on-investment. The best capital raising leads occur when a prospect approaches your community based on information that they've seen and read about your OZs. The barriers to converting these leads are much lower than cold campaigns, where the prospects don't know anything about you at all.

To get these leads, your community needs to repeatedly demonstrate your value-add through credible content. Such content builds credibility over time, as you corner your own niche and demonstrate expertise. That shouldn't be a problem, since your community is by nature an expert about the potential of your own OZs. If you consistently execute over time, many valuable relationships can come your community's way based on the materials you publish about the unique qualities of your OZs and how they can create long-term profit from your target investors and their QOFs.

Step 14: Remove Barriers to Investment

When I sought to take advantage of incentives to start a technology business in my hometown of Waterbury, Connecticut more than two decades ago, the barriers to accessing those incentives were high although the city specifically created an ITZ to attract and fund start-ups. Because these incentives seemed so compelling, I thought this development agency was on our side and we put too much energy into raising capital from this single source, a quasi-government agency, instead of seeking capital through a broad range of sources, such as angel or VC investors. However, these alternative investors like angels and venture capitalists were not setup in or around the greater Waterbury area at the time. Waterbury still lacks investment networks, angel and venture capitalists, incubators and accelerators, creating an unnecessarily high barrier to entry for start-ups and start-up founders. This is why OZ communities need to have accelerators, incubators and investor networks already set up in order to leverage the energy and interest of local entrepreneurs. Otherwise, entrepreneurs will take their start-ups to competing OZ communities with better incentives. Encouraging local entrepreneurs is critical to OZ success because capital raising is difficult, especially at the end of a long bull market.

With the exception of a stock market downturn in late 2018, the market and economy have experienced more than ten years of growth. That's highly unusual and indicates that the odds of a recession occurring in the next year are rising. In fact, 60 percent of economists surveyed by the National Association of Business economists believe that America will enter a recession by the end of 2020.[185] An analysis of past economic expansions and recessions reveals that the economy is overdue for a recession. Between 1945 and 2009, recessions lasted an average of 11 months and expansions an average of four years and eight months.[186]

There's no way to know exactly what impact a recession will have on OZ capital raising. It might dampen investment or it might encourage investment as investors move their capital gains from the stock market into other investment opportunities. However, the window for OZ investment is limited. If you miss the opportunity created by your community's OZ and an economic expansion, your community may miss out entirely on the chance to build a walkable city, create affordable housing and bring in well-paying jobs. Too much is at stake—I don't have to tell you what a lack of investment, blight and poverty does to a community, because most of you already see and experience it.

If you're serious about luring investor capital into your community, you need to do whatever is in your power to create investor-friendly policies, procedures and regulations. Collaborate with your state legislators to rework or revise regulations and laws that might impede investment. Write new laws and regulations while the economy is booming to expedite as many processes as possible so that when the economy begins to slow investment can get off the ground and proceed as rapidly as possible.

Investors do want to deploy their capital. But most are quite savvy and QOFs aren't going to take a flyer on projects that won't meet their return on investment criteria. Even with the tax incentives, projects still have to be profitable and fairly quick to launch, which means that they can't languish in a bureaucratic hell for months or even years, waiting for permits and approvals.

I'm not saying that anything goes because obviously structures have to be safe and legitimate rules must be followed. But all too often, there's a lot of unnecessary time wasted in navigating various bureaucratic requirements. Optimizing processes for investment is in everyone's best interest.

Step 15: Publicize Success Stories

Media and social media attention are critical to getting your message out there. This not only includes OZ success stories but also all the aspects of your community that make it a desirable place to invest.

Make sure that you have active social media accounts associated with your OZ team. Consider what social media channels are most likely to influence your audience of QOFs, investors, and businesses. Actively engage with your followers by posting updates and information about every aspect of your OZ. Follow and engage with QOFs, investors, business media, and bloggers within your chosen channels.

With the current limited window of OZ tax write offs, the time to spotlight your OZ and the benefits it brings to potential investors is now. There's billions of dollars of capital out there that can transform your community with impactful housing, employment, and business opportunities. It's those OZ communities who act quickly and decisively that will benefit and gain from all potential benefits from this investment initiative.

Your OZ machine needs to fire on all cylinders to capture investor interest. Only by leveraging all the tools available to you, including community collaboration, marketing, streamlining regulations, and engaging with investors and stakeholders will your operation have the chance for OZ success.

Step 16: Embrace the Benefits beyond Opportunity Zone Communities

OZ stakeholders include communities that are adjacent, but not actually within, designated OZs. It's important for those communities to understand that development within OZs won't leave them behind. When investments are made into OZ communities, those investments will ultimately raise living standards and property values within the surrounding areas as well.

Rising property values and living standards within OZs will create a domino effect that will spill over to neighboring communities. There are clear benefits from being near redevelopment, especially when that development replaces blight. And because the living standards and property values will essentially rise in the OZ community, it will increase property values more quickly in surrounding towns because these towns will now be close to a growing economic hub versus the former distressed community. Once people in these surrounding communities realize that this program has the capacity to transform property values and economic climates around them, they may be incentivized or motivated to invest and contribute to the process from the start.

Kamil Homsi, founder and CEO of Global Realty Capital, notes that OZs are designed very specifically to economically assist distressed areas by providing tax incentives that help encourage affordable housing and well-paying jobs. "Opportunity zones are a start on providing a solution to gentrification that we didn't have until Senator Booker and Senator Scott sponsored the legislation to make opportunity zones," he said in an episode of *The Rocco Forino Show* podcast. "Many local communities lack emergency facilities, healthcare, schools, treatment for cancer and playgrounds for the children. People need the dignity of having a job for the economics of their lives to change. OZs offer the chance to touch the lives of low-income people in many ways."

Step 17: Connect with QOFs and Investors through the DealConnect Hub Platform

When you've completed the abovementioned steps, it's time to build your OZ community's presence on the DealConnect Hub platform to raise your profile with family office and private equity managers seeking to deploy a substantial portion of the $1 trillion of their privately managed capital. DealConnect Hub offers an Airbnb-style interface designed to facilitate connection between family offices and wealth managers that seek to invest in OZs and its stakeholders. DealConnect Hub proprietary algorithm has identified the Top 400 OZs in the United States, if your OZ community made the list, your community should advertise this distinction on your community's website and in its marketing materials. This prominent badge signifies that your OZ community is a low-risk, high-quality investment option for investors and QOFs and a great place to build a business for developers, entrepreneurs, and start-ups.

Other advantages to joining this platform include:

1. Creating community engagement: Build or request DealConnect Hub to create a video profile of your community's greatest needs so investors and QOF managers can become familiar with the community and build solutions to solve those needs.

2. Gaining transparency: Track who is investing in your OZ community and the types of investments being planned, including new business starts, businesses receiving funding, new property developments, number of full-time non-construction jobs created, and total investment to date.

3. Tracking the bottom line: Monitor investments by dollar value and percentage assigned to each asset class.

4. Visualizing data: Leverage heat mapping and analytical tools to track and measure investment impact across your community's OZs

Nowhere else can you find the type of data that DealConnect Hub offers. Data that identifies and measures actual OZ investment in your community can be added to your marketing efforts, enhancing your OZs in the eyes of funds and investors and facilitating further investment.

QOFs are the primary vehicle for investing in OZs. Without QOFs, OZs don't have a chance. Raising capital for a QOF is a complex endeavor that requires discipline and commitment. QOF managers that get it right will have the chance to make a real difference in distressed communities across the country.

Chapter 6

Capital Raising for Qualified Opportunity Funds

To succeed in the race to attract investor capital, QOFs must clearly define their investment niche, create attractive marketing materials, distinguish themselves as experts and know their audiences. That's because capital raising isn't easy.

Professional investors are highly discriminating and willing to wait to find the right deal. They won't be pushed into a relationship that they are not ready for and are not likely to act quickly.

However, professional investors are much more likely to build relationships with established QOFs that have demonstrated expertise in their specific investment niche. If you are new to capital raising, your Fund I should start small and stay hyper focused on a specific investment niche within a highly targeted geographical area. Fully defining and communicating the purpose and intent of your fund is critical to professional investors and to the OZ community.

Evaluate your position so that you understand where you are and where you need to go to attract the capital your fund needs to succeed. Creating professional marketing materials, establishing a strong local presence, and executing a consistent thought leadership and social media engagement strategy are critical to success in OZ investing.

Differentiating your QOF from the competition is critical. Analyze what competition is in or near your investment niche and find out what you can do better to attract investor interest. Cultivate relationships over the long term by positioning your QOF within the community to maximize your proximity to the investors that you want to get to know. Because the investors you want to reach have a long-term mind-set, consistent execution of your engagement and marketing strategies is the key to success. Remember that success doesn't happen overnight. Focus on owning your investment niche through ongoing, engaging thought leadership. Make sure your fund managers are out there, taking face-to-face meetings. Fire up your marketing machine to create ongoing engagement through automated email marketing, consistent web and social media postings and regular appearances in the local and national media.

As you ramp up your QOF, don't forget that OZs were created to bring capital into parts of the country that lack the benefits that a start-up culture, business accelerators and incubators and a robust capital raising culture provides.

To position your QOF for success, follow these steps as you start on your fund's capital raising journey:

Step 1: Define Your Investment Niche

Because the OZ space is wide open, hundreds of QOFs have opened for business. Without an established niche, most of those QOFs will go nowhere. Why? Because professional investors are not looking to throw money into a QOF because of favorable tax incentives, the tax incentives are just a deal sweetener. Instead, investors seek to build relationships with OZ experts in specific sectors and geographic areas.

That's because such experts, when they corner a market and own it, obtain a competitive advantage that typically result in higher returns on capital than funds that try to be everything to everybody with a self-defeating generic strategy. For example, it's better to position your QOF as a healthcare tech fund specializing in OZs in Pittsburgh, Pennsylvania, than trying to own the healthcare tech space in the entire state of Pennsylvania. Being hyper focused communicates two key characteristics about your QOF: 1. You plan on taking investors capital seriously. 2. You are a master of your space.

Or perhaps your QOF has a method for building mixed-use developments with an affordable housing component. Narrow your focus from the entire West Coast to Portland, Oregon, where more expats from expensive California cities are relocating. If you're a real estate developer, specializing in self-storage exclusively in Atlanta, Georgia that will place you at the top of mind for self-storage investors in that specific geographic market.

When Facebook launched it was initially exclusive only to Harvard students.[187] Once Facebook owned all of the Harvard market, it then opened the platform to other Ivy League colleges and universities. When it dominated the Ivy League, it then opened the platform to the rest of the colleges and universities throughout the United States. And now Facebook is the largest social media platform on Earth all because it had a hyper-focused and methodical approach that began with local domination and then replicating that strategy at each stage of growth.

Amazon also launched as a hyper focused online book retailer.[188] As Amazon grew it expanded to include a multitude of products categories, order fulfillment, and one-day shipping. As retailers became overly focused on increasing store locations, Amazon built an addictive platform where customers could order nearly any product you can think of from the convenience of their smartphones.

Amazon launched as a small start-up book seller and morphed into one of the most fierce and valuable businesses on the planet.

Once you decide on a niche, you can focus on creating marketing and thought leadership materials designed to attract investors to you. Consistently creating and pushing out insightful, interesting content on your niche will attract investors, who tend to pay close attention to their news and social media feeds, focusing in on the areas where they invest. If you consistently publish engaging and relevant content that meets their needs, professional investors will find you and your QOF.

Step 2: Know Your Investor

By understanding exactly who your target investor is, you can position your QOF to concentrate on their needs and concerns. A particularly effective strategy is to create an investor avatar for each investor type you plan to attract. An investor avatar is a fictional description of your ideal investor.

That avatar should precisely describe the type of investor who will be most interested in your QOF. For example, if you are a commercial real estate QOF focusing on Reno, Nevada, make sure you're clear on what investors are going to be interested in this type of opportunity. Do not pursue VC firms in New York City as your first investor targets; rather, find family offices and high-net-worth individuals located in or near Reno because these investors have a stake in that community and want it to succeed. The more specific your description, the more precisely you can target your pitch materials and content.

As you create content, filter it through your investor avatars to make sure you are staying on target. When you're talking to or meeting with your target investors, always listen to what they need and ask a lot of questions. In order to become influential and successfully raise capital, you need to know how to solve pain points for those investors.

When building relationships with investors, space out your communications so that you appear professional but not desperate. If you're successfully positioning your QOF within your niche, investors will seek you out provided you're clear about who you serve and what value you provide to those investors.

Step 3: Allocate Time and Energy to Raise Capital

If you are a new fund manager, trying to raise capital for your QOF will take more time than you think. And because the investment clock to deploy capital into OZs has already begun, many new QOF managers may have a sense of urgency to raise capital immediately. It doesn't help to read news stories featuring established funds that have closed more than $100 million funds already.

Slow and steady will win the race for OZ capital because there are plenty of investors looking for the right deal. If your QOF carefully follows the approach laid out in this chapter, your QOF will succeed because you will have a built-in competitive advantage. Even though the OZ clock is running, there is no need to rush, because the entire OZ program is slowly rolling out.

While there are a few high-profile cities moving at a faster pace and some experienced funds have already raised millions, they are the exception rather than the rule. There is the possibility that the initial OZ time frame could be extended by legislation. In fact, the original authors of the legislation, Senator Cory Booker and Senator Tim Scott have introduced legislation extending incentives that would expire at the end of 2019 into future years.[189]

Step 4: Carefully Consider Fund Size and Fee Structure

Professional investors are incredibly detail-oriented, meaning they will thoroughly review your QOF's structure, terms, fees, investment strategy, exit strategy, and return calculations. Investors are highly cognizant of the standard fees that traditional and experienced fund charge and will not pay the industry standard fees to newly established funds with limited to no track record.

One of the biggest mistakes new funds make is focusing exclusively on the total capital raise amount. This may be because they hear and read about fund managers closing large rounds in the $25–$100 million range and believe that these are standard raises for new fund managers. That is not the case. Experienced fund managers can close larger dollar raises because they have built a track record with smaller initial funds. Then, they built up to raising larger amounts successfully because they have proven themselves trustworthy and capable of positive return on investments. For inexperienced fund managers, it will take longer to close large capital raises because you have to build trust and build a track record with a smaller raises first before investors will trust you with more of their money.

Another mistake new fund managers make is choosing a capital raising target based on the potential fees they will reap. For example, a prospective fund manager may want to raise $50 million and charge a 2 percent management fee to pull in $1 million. The larger the capital raise amount the more appealing the management fee becomes, but professional investors will not risk their capital or pay industry standard fees with an unproven fund manager. Doing a top-down fee structure clearly screams inexperience and will quickly make your capital raising efforts difficult to achieve.

A more impressive approach is to base your fee structure on the initial capital raise strictly performance based with no management fee. So if you start with a smaller capital raise and are seeking to raise

$2 million, try a 50 percent performance fee with an 8 percent hurdle rate for example. This will communicate to prospective investors that you are willing to sacrifice fees to build trust and a track record by putting your own skin in the game until the QOF starts generating positive returns. If you think in terms of the investor's needs and requirements, the capital raising process will be much more successful and productive. Focusing on a smaller initial capital raise with a well-structured performance fee structure will communicate to investors that you are focused and will prove you are willing to work hard first to demonstrate results.

If your QOF is new and lacks experienced management, focus on performance fees and hurdle rates while avoiding management fees, leasing fees, financing fees, acquisition fees, and disposition fees. The hurdle rate is a minimum rate of return on a specific investment or project by a specific manager. In other words, the hurdle rate defines what each manager determines as appropriate compensation given the project or investment-specific level of risk. That's because funds and managers earn the right to charge those fees based on a long-term successful track record. New QOFs with inexperienced managers need to demonstrate that they have skin in the game, which is what performance-oriented fees demonstrate.

Step 5: Create Professional Marketing Materials

If you want investors to take your fund seriously, you must take capital raising seriously first. That starts with professional marketing materials. Hire professional graphic designers and writers—to get the job done right so that your QOF appears professional from the start.

Branding is the foundation of your marketing materials. Your objective is to create a brand that causes prospects to lean forward and want to learn more about your fund. Positioning your brand effectively excludes anyone outside of your niche, which avoids wasting your time and the time of prospects who aren't interested in that niche. This is in contrast to a generic brand that does not concisely communicate the firm's specialty. Never be afraid to reposition your brand to gain better traction.

Your QOF needs a variety of foundational materials to begin building relationships with prospects. These include:

1. Business cards: Your business card should contain your name, title, email ID, cell phone number, website address, LinkedIn handle, and a concise positioning statement that clearly sets you apart from the competition. If you attend an investor conference the positioning statement will make you memorable and stand out.

2. One-pager: You must be able to concisely summarize your value proposition, investment process, team, strategy, and what differentiates you from the competition so that potential investors can quickly scan it. Include pictures of your top two to three team members and include flow charts and infographics to quickly demonstrate your investment process. The one-pager should be compelling enough for the investor to reach out and request more information.

3. One-liner or positioning statement: Your positioning statement defines what your QOF is and what unique differentiators you offer to your investors. Spending time up front condensing your value proposition down to a one-line or 160-character positioning statement forces you to really understand what you offer to your target market. Expect to go through at least twenty drafts with your team because this isn't something that you can just fire off in a day, as it will take time to build and retool.

4. One-liner Fee Structure and ROI time frame statement: QOF managers should develop a one-liner of 160-characters or less to describe their fees and the timeframe to return investor's capital.

This will be useful on DealConnect Hub because investors will quickly get a feel for how you will return their capital and what fees you will be charging.

5. Pitch deck: The ideal pitch deck presentation runs between twenty-five and thirty slides which should cover, in this order, your competitive advantage in the marketplace, your QOF's background and focus, your team, your investment process, how you manage risk, and contact information. A truly attention-getting pitch deck ideally includes an impactful two-minute video from your CEO that details your investment value-add. The first page should have the name of your firm and your one-liner that makes them lean forward and want to learn more. Focus on impactful pictures and graphics that capture your points rather than pages and pages of bullet points and text. Visuals allow you to focus on the value-add you offer in the industry. Include a unique value-process diagram as well as details of the opportunity you are offering. Selected case studies and examples demonstrate your QOF's experience in your selected niche. Include professionally taken photos of team members with consistent backdrops. A timeline that shows when your firm was founded and major projects that you've undertaken demonstrates relevant experience. Highlight your QOF's track record near the beginning of the pitch deck. Include specific information about your QOF's structure and fees. Every page should include a page number and the final page should include phone numbers, email addresses, contact names, and website URL. At the end of the pitch deck is where to place the legal disclaimers and summary of risks.

6. FAQ pages: Be prepared to answer frequently asked questions about your team, strategies, operations, and fees as well as any specific questions that might be awkward, such as a past investment that didn't work out or a change in leadership in your fund. Back up your answers with precise data and figures. Being completely up

front about mistakes that you've made builds trust and creates transparency because no firm is perfect. Even better, create a document that details the experience and what you've learned, get it approved by your compliance attorney and then make it available to prospects when the issue surfaces.

7. Master Due Diligence Questionnaire (DDQ): Investors want to gain a comprehensive understanding of how your QOF operates, who is on your team, and its investment strategies, which they do through the DDQ. These questionnaires range anywhere from five to 50 pages. Get ahead of the curve by creating a model DDQ so that answers to these questions are already prepared professionally and thoughtfully in advance. Then you can harvest the answers you need from that document to put into the various DDQ forms that you'll receive. While you want to be forthcoming and answer investor questions, you should not provide information that isn't asked for as that could potentially complicate the case for investing in your QOF. [Members of DealConnect Hub will have access to a free DDQ template]

8. Form 8996: Make sure your tax filings are accurate and you have fully self-certify your QOF status. Investors need to be assured that your QOF is compliant so that they can potentially reap the substantial tax benefits associated with OZs.

9. Prospectus: A prospectus is a legal business and disclosure document that must be supplied to potential investors. The prospectus usually includes an executive summary, offering terms, specific jurisdictional language, investor suitability, risk factors, team, capital deployment, fees, capital return schedule, tax issues, and subscription agreement.

Your QOF's website is your calling card to the investor community. That's why it's vital to build a mobile-responsive, search engine optimized website with a premium domain name. A website with click-to-chat software brings an interactive component to your site. Use tools like Screaming Frog to continuously audit your site to analyze page titles and metadata, integrate with Google analytics, and perform other functions to optimize user engagement and measure key performance indicators. Likes and follows are useless vanity metrics that hold little to no key performance indicator (KPI) weight. Instead, track metrics that tell you *why* visitors come to your site instead of *who* visits.

What matters is why visitors are visiting your site, how long they stay on your site, which pages they visit, what content they download, and what call to actions they follow. You want to understand the path that visitors take when they visit your site, where they come from, how effective your content is, and how long they engage with video. Google Analytics and Google Webmaster tools are a good start to measuring and analyzing this data. Use Google AdWords, to create a variety of search engine ads to drive traffic to your site.

Leverage your website with email opt-in and follow-up strategies to ensure that prospects receive a regular stream of content from you once they've opted in. Your emails should include an email signature with your photo, your firm's logo, and a personalized opening. By adding a photo to your email signature, you are making your digital communications more personable and building personal branding and a visual connection with your potential prospects.

The goal of creating marketing materials and thought leadership engagement is to build a sales funnel that will attract investors directly to you. There's a big difference between chasing prospects through tactics such as cold emails and cold calling versus attracting them through thought leadership. Prospects are attracted to you when you consistently publish highly targeted and credible thought leadership in their niche. Giving valuable content away builds trust so that by the time they get in touch—and they will get in touch—they've developed some trust in you and your expertise.

"You want to reverse the flow of how sales typically occur," says Richard Wilson, author of *Capital Raising: The Proven 5-Step System for Raising Capital from Private Investors.* "You don't want to chase, target or hunt down customers. You want them to come to you and find you over and over again. Google says that the best way to find customers is to have them find you when they are looking to solve a problem by searching online for a solution. In other words, position yourself to solve a problem that is unique to the individual so your target audience will find you, instead of having to hunt down your prospects."[190]

To encourage this type of attraction, remember that content is king. Produce written content for websites and newspapers. Produce long videos for YouTube and local TV and break down the long content into microcontent that can be produced into short videos for social media platforms.

Writing a book and getting it published is a great way to stand out as a thought leader, positioning you and your QOF as a credible expert on your niche and industry. Leverage platforms such as Kindle Direct Publishing to streamline the publishing process to get your ebook and book in front of your target audience as quickly as possible.

Step 6: Build a Professional Presence

Part of cultivating relationships involves building a professional presence in the community that you're focused on. If you're interested in OZs in Greater Los Angeles, California, it makes no sense to be headquartered in Arizona, for example, or even in another California locale.

Before you open an office, find out where the investor community you're targeting is located. Frequently, investors cluster in specific areas for work, home, and leisure. To make the best connections, that's where you need to be. If investors are located in Beverly Hills, then that is where your fund managers need to be building face-to-face meetings and networking with investors.

When you golf at the same clubs as your target audience, send your kids to the same private schools, and lease offices in the same buildings, it is much easier to strike up friendly acquaintances with members of your target audience. Joining professional associations favored by investors in your area will also provide opportunities to cultivate relationships.

While no investor is going to hand you a bag of cash based on the fact that you both have office space in the same complex, locating in close proximity to potential investors will give you a leg up. It will be much easier for them to find investors in this community who share a similar niche with you and who might be interested in investing in your QOF.

Your professional presence must include a professionally designed logo, an attractive headshot, and business cards, along with a LinkedIn link. The logo can be displayed on your pitch deck, stationary, website, and social media profiles.

You can streamline getting a new office set up and the relationship building process by following these processes:

- Rent an affordable coworking space.

- Subscribe to Grasshopper for local numbers and scalable phone lines.

- Hire a virtual assistant for administrative tasks.

- Acquire qualified lead lists.

- Create professional phone scripts.

- Write effective press releases.

- Get out and network.

Always check with a legal professional in your jurisdiction to ensure you are complying with state and federal laws when soliciting prospects for investment in your QOF.

Step 7: Evaluate Your Position

Whether your QOF is new to raising investor capital, or whether you've been doing it for decades, it is vital to evaluate your position in the OZ universe. As you assess your qualified opportunity fund, ask yourself and your team the following questions to get an idea of where you need to improve:

- Do you have a team member dedicated exclusively to raising capital?

- Is your QOF actively developing investor relationships?

- Does your QOF have marketing materials, strategic assets, and secret sauce all lined up to present to investors?

- Is your QOF aware that it takes at least one to two years of building credibility, integrity and transparency before professional investors will consider even investing in a deal?

- Does your QOF have a multi-modal marketing plan to reach out to investors?

- Is the QOF's CRM up-to-date?

- Does your QOF have key documents, such as pitch decks and a website that professional investors seek?

- Are your QOF managers creating sufficient face-to-face engagement?

- Is your QOF overly focused on raising capital in a short period of time?

- Is your QOF manager out there in your niche establishing themselves as a thought leader?

- Is your QOF manager using the trifecta of writing, speaking, and proactively selling to build authority and an unfair competitive advantage in your Unicode?

- Does your QOF have an established track record?

- Does your QOF specialize in a niche investment strategy?

- If your QOF real estate related, or is it focused on a hyper-local geographical area?

Step 8: Analyze the Competition

With more QOFs opening to take advantage of the thousands of OZs across the country, you need to stay on top of the competition. But before you can do that, you need to know *who* you're competing against.

Start off by studying the competition and copying their best strategies. Analyze their strengths and weaknesses and get strong where they are weak. Understand which stage the industry is in so that your QOF can create a strategy that suits the current market's needs.

As you analyze the competition, if you find that the funds you are competing against dominate a broad investment area, then position your QOF as highly focused on a certain niche. Never chase the latest trends—instead, concentrate on what you're passionate about. Chasing trends is self-defeating—it doesn't work. Instead play to your strengths and focus on the investment niche that you are knowledgeable in and passionate about.

Never forget that your potential investors constantly evaluate your QOF against the competition. To investors, your fund is just one of many investment opportunities they've encountered. These investors want to know why you deserve their money more than other investors. You need to be able to explain to them:

• How your QOF compares to the competition?

• What your QOF offers that the competition does not?

• What advantages does your investment strategy offers over others'?

• How your performance compares to the competition?

That's why you need to be an expert on your competition, understanding their value proposition, their strengths and weaknesses, branding, marketing, market position, and investor avatar. Keeping tabs on the competition helps you position your QOF more appropriately and continue to fine-tune your positioning over time.

Step 9: Assess Your Advantages

Because investors seek to invest in QOFs that align with their investing objectives, it's important to clearly and tightly define your niche and your value proposition. Consider these questions as your QOF clarifies its differentiators:

• What is your QOF's mission and investment thesis?

• What is the size of your QOF in U.S. dollars?

• What type of investors do you seek?

• Is your QOF single asset or multi-asset?

- Are 90 percent of your assets currently deployed in qualified OZ investments?

- Does your QOF intend to publish a social impact report?

- What—if any—diversity and inclusion considerations does your QOF management team practice?

- Did your QOF engage with economic development and/or elected officials prior to investing in OZs?

- What form has your QOF's engagement taken and how has that engagement shaped your investments?

- Is your QOF engaged with community members? Describe that engagement.

- Does your QOF select partners—including developers and business owners—who are members of the local community?

- What proportion of your QOF's investments include partners who are local community members?

- How does your QOF select local partners for your investment projects?

- What proportion of your QOF investments is aligned with local priorities?

- Provide examples of how your QOF has identified and incorporated community priorities in your QOF's investment.

- Is your QOF committed to prioritizing business investments that will employ mostly local community members?

- Provide examples of how your QOF's investments will create local jobs.

- Does your QOF prioritize investments with developers with local construction hiring practices?

- What percentage of your QOF's investments collaborates with developers that utilize local construction hiring practices?

- Provide examples of how your QOF investments created construction jobs within the local community.

- What percentage of your QOF investments includes a locally owned developer or business?

- Does your QOF prioritize investment in developers and businesses that are minority or female-owned?

- Give examples of how your QOF's investments include minority and/or female-owned businesses or developers.

- What percentage of your investments includes developers and businesses that are minority or female-owned?

- Does your QOF prioritize investments that build wealth in the local community?

- Provide an example of how your QOF investment intends to build wealth in the local community.

- What proportion of your QOF investments includes additional wealth-building components?

- Is your QOF committed to exiting investment by finding a buyer that is committed to a community-based strategy?

- What percentage of your investments includes an existing responsible exit strategy?

- Provide an example of a responsible exit strategy planned for one of your QOF investments.

- How does your QOF prioritize investments that include a social impact component?

- What proportion of your QOF's investments includes social impact components?

- How does your QOF prioritize investments that are environmentally friendly?

- What percentage of your QOF's investments is environmentally friendly?

- Does your QOF collect information on key outcome measures from your investments?

- Approximately how many outcome metrics does your QOF track for each investment?

- What key outcome measures does your QOF track across your entire investment portfolio?

- Does your QOF build measurement and reporting components into investment contracts?

- What percentage of your investments builds measurement and reporting covenants into contracts?

- Provide an example of one or more of your QOF's measurement and reporting covenants.

- Does your QOF use a standardized measurement system to evaluate investment decisions?

- How does your QOF plan to use information gathered about current investments to inform future investment decisions?

Step 10: Cultivate Relationships

With your local professional position established and your marketing materials created, you can now focus on cultivating relationships. Rather than engaging via cold calls or emails, put yourself, your QOF, and your platform out there in as many different ways as you can. There's no shortcut to meeting people, engaging with them, and understanding their needs.

"…The truth is, sales is about people. You have to build relationships first. You have to put yourself in the customer's shoes and empathize with their position. No app is going to teach you that," says marketing expert, best-selling author, and serial entrepreneur Gary Vaynerchuk. "Real relationships take time. You're going to have to spend hours trying to interact, engage and provide value in order to win."[191]

Be as visible as possible on social media platforms, in your local community, and in investor professional organizations that cover your niche. Speak at conferences and seminars and attend relevant events.

Take a careful look at all the organizations in your community before you decide which are worthy of your time and attention. Professional organizations, such as local manufacturing associations, can be a great place to meet many local business owners, executives, and entrepreneurs. The Chamber of Commerce is another local organization that tends to have many influential members. Toastmaster's chapters usually consist of a cross-section of business owners, executives, and managers who join to take advantage of the opportunity to hone their speaking and leadership skills.

Meetup.com offers many special interest groups where you can meet a variety of individuals. Some have a specific focus—such as business owners, hikers, parents, or kayakers—while others are focused on socialization. Input your zip code on the website or app to access a list of local meetups and the events they sponsor.

A group of passionate LinkedIn users founded LinkedIn Local two years ago, which has sponsored meetings of local LinkedIn users across the country from Washington, DC to Seattle. Although the organization is not as active as it was, some groups are still meeting. If there's no LinkedIn Local in your area, consider starting your own group. If you already have LinkedIn Sales Navigator, it's easy to search your connections by geographical region and send out in-mails and make announcements about your upcoming event. If you don't have Sales Navigator, planning a LinkedIn Local event is a great way to jump into a 30-day free trial and check out the benefits.

Joining affinity groups or professional organizations is key to building your investor network. Joining and attending meetings of these groups can place you in a favorable position, being the only QOF manager in a vast supply of potential investor with limited to no competition. Consider checking out national organizations with local chapters such as:

- The American Dental Association

- The American Orthodontic Association

- Financial Planning Association

- Healthcare Financial Management Agency

- The National Association of Personal Financial Advisors

- Association of Fundraising Professionals

- American Academy of Dermatology

- American Academy of Ophthalmology

- American Academy of Pediatrics

- American Association of Oral and Maxillofacial Surgeons
- American College of Surgeons
- American Urological Association
- American Society of Clinical Oncology
- National Association of Insurance & Financial Advisors
- American Association of Professional Landmen
- American Optometric Association
- American Society of Plumbing Engineers
- American Pharmacy Association
- American Planning Association
- Association for Talent Development
- American Association of University Women
- American Medical Women's Association
- American Business Women's Associations
- National Association of Women Business Owners
- Business Network International
- Minority Chapter of Commerce
- Public Relations Society of America
- American Marketing Association
- Association of Information Technology Professionals
- BDPA (formerly Black Data Processing Associates)
- Association for Women in Computing

- Network Professional Association

- American Chemical Society

- American Medical Association

- American Osteopathic Association

- Association for Computing Machinery

- Association of Fundraising Professionals

- American Society of Association Executives

- American Bar Association

- American Institute of Architects

- American Healthcare Association

Understand the types of charitable events that your target audience focuses on and ensure that you're there. Join a country club and participate in activities where you can meet as many investors as possible. As you engage with investors, be as authentic as possible. Relationship building takes time and not every contact will result in a relationship that's worth pursuing. Build up enough face-to-face engagement with enough investors over time and you'll obtain plenty of leads. Just understand that you're not likely to get those leads sitting in your office building spreadsheets formulas and chatting on LinkedIn.

Step 11: Promote Consistently

There's no need to constantly reinvent the wheel when it comes to creating content. This barrier is what might be keeping you from jumping into content creation. Vaynerchuk pioneered the "reverse pyramid approach," in which one central piece of content is created, and then repurposed in bite-sized pieces in multiple formats on numerous platforms to gain search engine preeminence.[192] This central piece of content should be long form, while the bite size pieces that are easy for your audience to consume in social media.

For example, if you have a professional promotional video, you can excerpt multiple short clips from that video, each standing on their own and focusing an important component of your expertise in your QOF niche. Use different social media platforms for different types of content, depending on where your target audience spends its time and the orientation of the platform.

In this case, your promotional video should be uploaded to the DealConnect Hub platform. Then, distribute those clips over time on your social media platforms, with a call to action of driving traffic to your QOF's website. Of course, you don't want to only have one video. Keep creating videos—they don't have to be perfectly choreographed—and distribute clips.

Marketing, promotion, and social media do not always follow a one-size-fits-all approach. Pay attention to which content gets noticed and pattern future content on the most successful content. By "listening" to your audience in this way, you'll drive increased engagement. What you post on LinkedIn may not resonate with your followers on Instagram. Each social media platform has a specific focus, so tailor your content accordingly.

What social media channels should you invest in? It depends on your niche. Use a social media tool such as Hootsuite to manage social media content and schedule posts in advance across a variety of platforms. At a minimum, you should have a YouTube channel for long pillar video content, Apple, Castbox, Stitcher, SoundCloud, Spotify, Google, Tunein, Acat, and Otto Radio for podcasts and company and personal pages on Facebook, Instagram, Twitter, and LinkedIn for microcontent.

To connect as closely with your audience as possible, it's important to leverage your personal social media profiles. That's because you *are* your brand. Prospects today seek authenticity and personal insights into the entrepreneurs, managers, and brands that they buy from or seek to invest in.

Step 12: Reinforce Your Expertise

Establishing and maintaining your expertise takes time and energy. In addition to all of the techniques I've mentioned so far, you need to keep your content creation machine humming and stay visible within your target investor community.

To continue to stay top of mind with your prospects, build on your expertise by:

- Writing white papers and reports

- Creating consistent blog posts

- Writing a thought-leadership book

- Attending industry conferences

- Writing guest blog posts

- Writing columns for industry publications

- Creating infographics

- Publishing through Amazon's Kindle Direct Publishing

- Getting quoted in local and national media

- Speaking at conferences and seminars

Building a content map for the next six months helps you be as strategic as possible as you establish your expertise. That content map should include distributing at least two pieces of content daily across social media, local newspapers, television, and industry trade sites. When you create written content focus on headlines that attract reader attention.

To be acknowledged as an expert in your investment niche, you must lead as an expert locally before branching out regionally and nationally. Focusing on a specific region makes it much easier to stay in touch with and follow up with your investor contacts. A national focus requires you to spend a lot of time on the road with face-to-face meetings that may or may not pan out. Staying focused on a specific region enables you to manage your time more effectively and efficiently.

Leveraging DealConnect Hub will place your QOF directly in front of professional family office investors who manage a collective $1 trillion and are seeking to invest in OZs. Building on that opportunity, when investors search for you inside the DealConnect Hub network, they will find the content and marketing materials that you've created to establish your expertise, which will reinforce your brand and attract their interest.

Step 13: Execute Your Process

Once you've created the processes you need to continue to stay in front of your prospects, you need to ensure that they are consistently and continually executed so that you raise the necessary capital to invest in OZ projects and businesses. Hiring the right people who will ensure your processes are carried out is key—because it takes a team of specialists to effectively handle all components of the marketing machine.

You and your team need to continue to analyze, reposition, and adjust to the needs of the investors your QOF seeks to target. Be a formidable competitor in your space and corner off all angles to your market so that it is nearly impossible for others to compete with your QOF. Instead of relying on one type of marketing, employ all the techniques I've suggested above to attract prospects to your multifaceted marketing machine.

Step 14: Know How to Work with Family Offices

Family offices and private equity investors are a highly particular breed of investment managers. They seek long-term, high value-added relationships. Follow these ten strategies for working with family offices and private equity investors to secure deal flow:

1. No unsolicited contact: Your email or LinkedIn in-mail blast strategy won't get you anywhere because they won't respond.

2. Be transparent: Always answer every question in a DDQ—don't avoid answering questions as that will take you out of the running for capital.

3. Get referred by a trusted source: The best way to start a relationship with a family office is to get a referral from a source that they trust.

4. Leverage past relationships: If you previously worked with family offices at a past job, reach out, referencing your previous role.

5. Know what a family office invests in: Do some of your own due diligence so that you know what the family office invests in and whether your services are a good fit.

6. Deal flow sharing: Family offices will share deal flow with other related family offices, so if you bring a good deal, there is a chance you can get introduced to others in the sector.

7. Don't pitch a deal immediately upon an introduction: Take time to build a relationship before pitching. Think of it as if you were seeking to find your soulmate versus looking for random matches on Tinder. One strategy might have a quicker result, but the other has much more long-term potential.

8. Be the best of breed: Family offices are highly selective and only want to work with the best funds in each niche.

9. Establish a clear path to profitability: Any deals you bring must demonstrate a clear path to profitability.

10. Establish a clear path to exit: Deals must also have a path to liquidity realization and exit so that investors can extract their profits

Step 15: Manage Compliance

Your investors will want to see your compliance materials and understand your fee structure. Compliance is critical because your QOF must maintain all the compliance standards so that investors can take advantage of the significant tax benefits advantages associated with OZ investments.

Compliance materials include QOF self-certification, the 90 percent test and tax filings. To self-certify, QOFs must fill out and file IRS Form 8996. QOFs must invest 90 percent of their assets in qualified OZ properties or businesses. These properties and businesses must be located within qualified OZ.

That 90 percent can be measured in two different ways:

1. The last day of the first six-month period of the tax year of the QOF

2. The last day of the tax year of the QOF

Kamil Homsi expresses some concerns about the self-certification process from the investor point of view. "Let's assume that the fund manager will goof, will for some reason commit a mistake, intentional or unintentional. So let's say the IRS comes back and says you didn't comply and because of that you are decertified. Does that mean that your investors lose the benefits and no longer qualify for tax deductions?" This means that your QOF must be very diligent in following IRS guidelines and ensuring that you file all required paperwork correctly and on time.

Because the OZ program is so new, it's inevitable that the IRS will continue to add to regulations and clarify current regulations. Your QOF must stay on top of developments in reporting requirements and make sure you remain compliant.

Step 16: Get in Front of Family Office and Private Equity Investors

Becoming a member and showcasing your QOF on DealConnect Hub will precisely match and connect your QOF to an exclusive network of the top professional family offices and private equity investors seeking to invest in QOFs that specifically meet their investment filters. DealConnect Hub is the only private investor network that provides family offices and private equity investors with data visualization and deal flow to quickly and efficiently move investors and QOFs from deal sourcing to done deals. Family offices are the preferred investment vehicle of high–net-worth and ultra-high-net-worth individuals and families, who rely on DealConnect Hub for consistent and high-quality QOF flow. Because we thoroughly evaluate each QOF before we decide whether to list them, the investors on our platform know that if you meet our criteria, that your QOF is highly qualified.

Advantages of listing your QOF on the only comprehensive, holistic platform dedicated to facilitating expedited investment deals include:

1. Positioning your firm directly in front of an exclusive list of the top family offices and wealth managers seeking to invest directly in QOF deals.

2. Raising more capital from wealth managers and family offices than any other network.

3. Getting in front of investors who have a frequent minimum deal size between five hundred thousand and $5 million.

4. Gaining access to live investor events, conferences, and pitch events.

5. Building your QOF's brand by appearing on the DealConnect Hub and The Rocco Forino Show podcasts.

6. Data visualization to demonstrate and market to investors that your QOF is focused on an OZ positioned for explosive growth.

7. Accessing the top 400 OZs, as quantified by our proprietary ranking system.

8. Leveraging OZ heat maps that pinpoint where the most investments are taking place in real estate and business investments across the United States and its territories.

9. Using investment filters to scan for OZ businesses and real estate investment opportunities.

10. Visualizing what deals are getting funded by investment sector and geography.

While there are other basic OZ databases available, only the DealConnect Hub network offers an Airbnb-like user friendly data visualized interface that allows investors to quickly find your QOF and related deal flow. By successfully developing all the positioning and marketing strategies laid out in this chapter, you will position your QOF to capture the interest and attention from family offices and high net worth investors with total assets under management of $1 trillion.

Within OZs, there are many businesses, start-ups, and entrepreneurs seeking to connect with QOFs and OZ investors. These businesses and start-ups operate in a wide variety of business niches which match up with many of the niches pursued by QOFs. Diversifying your investment among different types and sizes of businesses spreads your capital across a variety of situations, mitigating your risk and offering the opportunity for significant gains.

Investing directly in businesses is one of the best ways to build wealth, with the potential to generate much higher returns than investing in real estate. Any gains your QOF receives from investing in businesses will also be eligible for OZ capital gain tax benefits.

Chapter 7

CAPITAL RAISING FOR ENTREPRENEURS, STARTUPS AND DEVELOPERS

Attracting capital for an OZ business poses major challenges for entrepreneurs from distressed backgrounds. That's because entrepreneurs who live in OZs generally lack the access to capital because those who became wealthy in these communities made their money and moved to the suburbs instead of first creating, venture capital funds, accelerators, and investor networks to invest in the next generation of entrepreneurs.

In fact, the evidence reveals that there are fewer entrepreneurs in low-income areas relative to wealthier areas. In addition, businesses that operate in low-income areas are less likely to incorporate and grow into larger businesses than those in other areas.[193]

What's stopping these would-be entrepreneurs? Insecurity, fear of failure, lack of self-esteem, or self-confidence? Vaynerchuk, a Russian immigrant, has this to say about insecurity: "Insecurity is a killer. I do believe the people that care less about what other people think tend to have a better life. Self-esteem is the ultimate drug in life."[194]

"The reality is that so many people are broken inside because they care about what their older brother or their husband thinks about their behavior or what their Mom said to them when they were growing up," Vaynerchuk continues. People are held back by others' opinions. Being self-promotional and putting yourself out there like I do—so many people have opinions about me. As long as I'm going with the opinions of the people who can look under the hood, the people who know me, then I will always win. As long as you feel good about who you actually are, you need to get loud."[195]

Vaynerchuk shares a technique for overcoming the fear of failing in front of others. That strategy involves talking to that family member, parent, spouse, or person and telling them that the only reason you haven't tried to do what you desperately want to do is the fear of letting you down. "Long term I'm going to succeed. Before I start, I want to make sure that if I fail at this at first, your response won't crush me and stop me from trying again,"[196] Vaynerchuk states.

Barbara Corcoran, a real estate mogul and expert on *Shark Tank*, has this to say about insecurity: "It's so hard to shake those things you carry with you from your childhood and past. But if you have something like that inside of you, wrap your arms around it and make it your friend. Find a way to use it. Insecurity makes you run. What's wrong with that?"[197]

To succeed, entrepreneurs from distressed communities need to adopt an immigrant approach to starting a business, embracing traits such as grit, resourcefulness, and determination. Raising capital takes tenacity; when you lack the advantages of your better-connected peers, it's an even steeper climb.

The journey begins by creating a minimum viable product, hyper focused on a single market. To sell that product, you need to know how to value your product, understand business valuation metrics, and create a two-minute pitch video.

To attract investors, make sure you understand the objectives of investors and build a presence through marketing, social media, and SEO. If your product or service has potential to scale and grow into something big, it's important to maximize your capital raising efforts as well, rather than spending too much time perfecting your product, because as Vaynerchuk puts it, "If you're not putting yourself and your product out there, there is a deeper reason. Either you don't believe in yourself or your product or you are making up perfection. Perfection is a disguise for insecurity and the bigger reason that you aren't confident."[198]

As you run your business, never forget that cash flow is king—no matter how well your product or service is selling, you can't stay in business without cash. The ability to pivot is one of the most important characteristics of successful business owners as longevity in business consists of developing an instinct for which trends you should follow.

Step 1: Assess Your Strengths

Because entrepreneurship is a tough—but ultimately a rewarding—road, it's important to understand yourself and how your personality aligns with the traits that entrepreneurs possess.

To understand your own entrepreneurial psychology, ask yourself the following questions:

1. Do you live in a high-poverty community?

2. Do your parents work in low-wage jobs?

3. Are you the child of a single parent?

4. Are you the first in your family to attend college?

If you answered yes to most of these questions, it's helpful to realize that you have more disadvantages in starting a business than many others. Bob McKinnon, founder of MovingUpUSA.com, an initiative focused on inequality, poverty, and opportunity, created a quiz that takes this self-assessment process a step farther. This quiz quantifies what factors you've had in your favor and what you've had to overcome to achieve your present status. Go to https://movingupusa.com to get your score. The higher your score, the more disadvantages you labor under.

The point of taking this quiz is to help you understand the barriers that exist for people who grow up in OZ communities, which are low-income and disadvantaged by nature. If you were raised in a single-parent home, had a parent or parents with addiction problems, are a person of color and/or a woman, identify as LGBTQ, lacked mentors, or influential friends and relatives, or didn't go to college, your path to success starting a business is likely to be much more difficult than someone who has not endured these obstacles. That's because a more advantageous background that includes growing up in a home with parents who went to college, having influential friends and mentors, being male, going to college, and numerous other factors vastly increase the odds of succeeding in business.

Oscar-winning actor and script writer Matt Damon struggled early in his career, despite his hard work. In an article published in *Inc.* magazine, Damon said, "My one skill is that I'll outwork anyone. Especially at that age…Ben [Affleck] and I would go to auditions where kids would be there with their parents, like their mom was making them go because their mom has some unrealized fantasy about doing it and was trying to live through the kid."[122] Damon and Affleck both auditioned for a role in the movie *Dead Poets Society*. And ultimately got a call back, but did not get a role in the movie. However, that summer, Damon and Affleck took a job at a local movie theater tearing tickets, where at the time the only movie playing was the *Dead Poets Society*.[200] Damon and Affleck went from auditioning for a part in the movie to tearing tickets in a movie theater where Ethan Hawk ultimately was nominated for the Academy Award for his role in *Dead Poets Society*—a role in the movie that either actor could have had.[201] And that's how Hollywood works; you could be a waitress one day or starring in a movie the next. They did the math and concluded that competing with leading actors for a lead role in a movie as budding actors was a long shot. It wasn't self-doubt. It was frustration with the system. Because the system is not built for you to succeed: You have to break through it. In effect, Damon and Affleck stopped hoping, dreaming, and waiting for that one breakthrough role and decided to collaborate on writing the movie *Good Will Hunting*—because they both knew the odds were against them as actors. Instead of pinning their hopes on beating the long odds of success in acting auditions, they gambled on writing their own movie, which eventually won the Oscar for best screenplay in 1998.[202] Damon and Affleck forged their own path because they knew they couldn't count on Hollywood to discover them. It's no different in business—if you have a great idea, you can't sit back and wait to be discovered, you have to get out of your comfort zone, face your insecurities, and get exposed to rejection and the word "no", a lot. Hard work is often the "secret" to success. The extra mile is largely unpopulated because few people actually go there.

Many people from distressed backgrounds don't let their circumstances dictate their outcomes. Look at the story of Dre (short for Andre) who was born in Compton, California, to Verna Griffin, who was 16 when she had Dre. He had a father who was in and out of the picture and had exposed his family to verbal abuse, physical abuse, drugs, and violence.[203] At an early age Verna knew her son had a passion for music and one Christmas bought Dre a mixer which allowed him to make music tapes. After setting up at a block party in his friend Easy E's back yard, his friends began coming up to him and asking to make them mix tapes and that's how he started his side hustle DJing. From there Dre wanted to up his game so he linked up with Easy E, and Ice Cube to create a label called Ruthless Records. Ice Cube wrote the hit song *Boys In The Hood* and Easy E rapped it while Dre made the beats—it was an instant hit.

As they gained success from their unique style, Dre, Easy E, Ice Cube, and MC Ren created the Group N.W.A. As a side project, they produced a record for a female group JJ Fad, called *SuperSonic*, their first gold record under Ruthless Records. Dee Barnes, the American rapper and host of Fox's hip hop show *Pump It Up!* had this to say about the experience: "A female group opened the door for N.W.A."[204] Then Ice Cube wrote the song *Fuck the Police* which was controversial and attracted national attention, including attention from the FBI. According to Ice Cube, "We were more than a group we were a political statement, it just knocked us into that position."[205]

Shortly after their rise to fame, Dre's brother and best friend Tyree was killed in a street fight. Then while N.W.A had a number one hit, the group broke up due to differences over Easy E's manager who managed the groups grossly unfair revenue split between the group members, ultimately forcing Dre to start over.[206] Soon thereafter, Dre discovered Snoop Dogg. At the time there were riots and the *Los Angeles Times* poll stated that the breakdown of moral values and the lack of economic opportunity were the two leading causes of the LA riots back in the early 90s. As the riots were going on, Dre and Snoop were finishing up an album called *The Chronic*. Dre mixed it, mastered it, and did all the artwork. Dre would shop it around and went to every record company in LA, New York, and everyone turned him down because they did not want anything to do with the gangster rap scene or deal with Death Row Records. At the time the police were sensitive to what was going on and this music was seen as a catalyst for the violence and mayhem in LA.[207]

While this was all going on, Jimmy Lovine, another hard worker and industry game changer, took on Dre. "I said wow these guys remind me of when I first saw the Rolling Stones and Megan Keith, they scare you but their music brings you in," Lovine said. He cleared up a bunch of lawsuits that Dre was tied up in and then signed them to Interscope Records.[208]

As the gangster rap scene started to heat up, Dre left Death Row Records after people were targeted and either getting beat up or shot due to the heated rivalry between East coast and West Coast rap. Dre had to start over once again as he left everything behind including his rights to all the music he made under the Death Row label since people were receiving death threats and needing to wear bulletproof vests at red carpet events. Dre then started a new label called Aftermath with a 50-50 partnership with Interscope Records.[209] However, his first album flopped, followed by another flop on album two. Then he discovered Eminem and took him in. Eminem told Dre that he was the most influential person in his life and together they created the hit album *My Name Is*. This was despite many executives trying to talk Dre out of getting involved with Eminem and literally risking everything by signing him to Aftermath. However, signing Eminem was the best thing that happed to Dre because soon after, Dre and Interscope attracted artists like Gwen Stefani, Black Eyed Peas, Nelly Furtado, Justin Timberlake, and the Pussy Cat Dolls turning Interscope into the biggest label on the planet. Then the Internet took over and artists were losing hundreds of millions of dollars in sales to Internet music piracy.[210]

Jimmy and Dre's next move was to do something big. They launched a headphone speaker line, Beats by Dre, selling 1.6 million headphones in just the first year. Then they built Beats Music, a music streaming platform. In 2014, Apple purchased Beats Music for $3.2 billion.[211]

After starting over numerous times and being hit with every obstacle possible, Dre never gave up and followed his passion. Forbes estimated Dre's net worth at around $770 million in June 2019 Forbes.[212] Over the course of his career, he discovered and invested in numerous artists and donated to numerous causes. Jimmy and Dre, neither of whom graduated from college, donated $70 million to the University of Southern California to build the Lovine Young Academy to foster entrepreneurship with entertainment so that students can build upon their technology and business skills.[213] The combination of hardworking beat maker Dre, hardworking producer Jimmy Lovine, and hardworking tech entrepreneur Steve Jobs were three titans who were impossible to hold back. A clear example of how entrepreneurs who work hard ultimately attract other hard working entrepreneurs who cross paths to create amazing things together.[214]

The traditional route of going to college, doing internships, sending out resumes, and getting a job isn't built for everyone. Dre shows how following your passion and learning from your experience creates its own opportunities. Along the way, people recognized his talent, work ethic, and passion, which positioned him to take advantage of opportunities that arose, allowing him not just to get ahead but to become fabulously wealthy, successful, and influential.

This is just one example of a bunch of kids who were raised in one of the most dangerous cities in the United States, Compton, California, where everything was literally stacked against them. Rebelling against the establishment, they created a billion-dollar industry with just beats and lyrics. In OZs across America, there will be more industries that will be created from literally nothing and I hope this book serves as the catalyst that inspires the next entrepreneur and next start-up to create big things.

While many entrepreneurs are succeeding—and some like Dre enjoy immense success—most face an uphill climb, according to the Economic Growth Business Incubator, a non-profit that supports entrepreneurs who face barriers.[215]

The challenges correlate strongly to the score you received when you took the American Dream quiz and include:

- No access to start-up capital

- Poor credit

- Limited connections

- Lack of role models and mentors

- Lack of basic financial literacy

Because many individuals from distressed communities don't know successful business owners, it can be hard for them to imagine themselves as business owners or understand the benefits of entrepreneurship.

It is precisely because of all these factors that you need to step back and evaluate whether you can endure the additional struggles and grind necessary to become a successful entrepreneur. As an entrepreneur from a distressed community, I can tell you it is twice as hard to become successful than for those from wealthier socioeconomic areas. Why? Because while you are grinding from your impoverished situation, trying to get your initial customers and prove that your business is viable, in the beginning your start-up won't bring in enough cash for you to pay your bills. You'll have to have a source of back-up income—a job. Starting a business doesn't immediately make your life better. In fact, it may take five or six years to make it work. Prepare for that reality, because there will likely be many obstacles and it will be tempting to quit.

Step 2: Adopt an Immigrant Mind-Set

Although distressed entrepreneurs may lack the advantages of their more privileged counterparts in wealthier areas of the country, they can compensate to a degree by adopting an immigrant work ethic when building a business. This psychology is embodied by Vaynerchuk, who says, "… I believe that I win because I out-work people. And I'm not sure that, if my Dad hadn't shown me the way, that I'd even think anybody was capable of working that hard. Working 19 hours a day for the last 20 years has been easy for me because it's the only gear I ever knew. I sucked at school so it was my only option."[216]

When you acknowledge and accept that fact—and you're ready to bring everything you have to the endeavor of starting a business—it's time to adopt the immigrant approach to entrepreneurship. This involves:

• Adopting a mind-set of grit, which involves displaying courage, determination, and strength of character and plowing through every obstacle that will be thrown at you without quitting

• Understanding that you're going it alone

• Employing resourcefulness with money and time

• Overcoming obstacles

The immigrant work ethic is neither an urban legend nor isolated to a few successful individuals. Researchers at the National Foundation for American Policy, a non-partisan think tank, found that more than 50 percent of 87 privately held U.S. start-ups valued $1 billion or more were founded by one or more person born outside the United States.[217] In addition:

- More than 40 percent of Fortune 500 companies were founded by immigrants or the children of immigrants

- Immigrants are twice as likely as native born Americans to start a business

In fact, more than 40 percent of companies in the Fortune 500 were founded by immigrants or the children of immigrants.

"I think immigrants have it better than ever—no matter where you emigrate—because it's not about the establishment giving them a chance," Vaynerchuk told CNBC. "The internet gives them a chance. The biggest change is opportunity has grown, not decreased. And what immigrants have is humility and work ethic because they are often starting from the bottom. And I think that's their biggest advantage."[218]

What key characteristics separate the immigrant work ethic from an everyday work ethic?

1. Having self-confidence and overcoming insecurity by not caring about what others think of you, especially those whom you don't care about. Don't view your reality through the lens of your peers and friends. Immigrants don't have to impress anyone, which is a mind-set you should adopt.

2. Leaning into discomfort: We're hard-wired to shy away from discomfort because, well, it's not comfortable. But for immigrants for whom English isn't their first language, discomfort is inevitable as they acclimate to a new country and a new language. When you realize this is a necessary step in growth, you'll understand the tradeoff for short-term discomfort is long-term success.

3. Building your identity around hard work: You may not succeed at your first, second, or third business venture. That's because you have no control over the economy, business conditions, or your future customers. But if you bring hard work to the table, success will follow.

4. Dropping your ego: A sensitive ego impedes learning as much as you can from each experience. Be willing to work from the ground up and experience failure. Humility and learning from all your experiences will get you much farther than indulging your ego.

"You have to have the mentality to show up every day of your life no matter what happens," says the Roc. "It's your responsibility to find your 100 percent."[219]

Immigrants don't have friends and aren't judged because they are working all the time. Too many people get addicted to easy likes that come from posting "booty pics," which takes them away from a laser focus on their start-up, Vaynerchuk says. "People start creative on Instagram, win, people start following them, and then they become a robot of the machine. You know how many attractive young women ask me: 'I really know a lot about health and wellness but when I post that, I get 4,000 likes but when I post my ass or my boobs, I get 15,000 likes and I can't stop.' I say: 'Ok, how about not having your self-esteem wrapped in how many likes you get on Instagram?'"[220]

Hard work wins, not popularity. In fact, a study published in the *American Affairs* journal reveals that more employers prefer to hire immigrants due to this type of work ethic. "Immigrants are judged to have a better work ethic and to work harder. They are more diligent, punctual, persistent, reliable, respectful and cooperative," according to the report.[221]

Daniel Alarik, an Army combat veteran, exemplifies this work ethic. Starting out with $1,200, he created a $100-million lifestyle brand, Grunt Style. Alarik's brand celebrates the military values of patriotism, self-reliance, independence, and toughness.[222]

Alarik doesn't just sell clothing—he's created a lifestyle movement with Grunt Fests that create community around food, music, beer, flag-waving, and motorsports, events that draw thousands. His career as a non-commissioned officer in the Army gave him leadership skills, insight into his target customers, and a sense of humor.

Because Alarik shares the values of his community, he engages with his customers authentically, a key ingredient of success in a lifestyle brand. His brand logo features identifiers well known to his customers, including a forward-facing flag, and 1776 designed to honor America's independence.

Just like many entrepreneurs with an immigrant work ethic, success didn't come easily or naturally to Alarik. He started out printing his own tee shirts and selling them out of the trunk of his car. He and his wife suffered through multiple setbacks, including having their entire company's cash balance stolen, blowing their marketing budget on a billboard that didn't sell any tee shirts and his wife's stage 3 breast cancer diagnosis. But they kept going and over time, with lots of grit and hard work, built the incredibly successful lifestyle business they have today.[223]

Entrepreneur Joy Mangano, the inspiration behind the 2015 movie *Joy* starring Jennifer Lawrence, experienced many similar setbacks. A divorced Long Island, New York Mom, Mangano, invented a detachable, self-wringing mop that formed the basis of her business, succeeding first on QVC and then on the Home Shopping Network.[224]

However, the mop wasn't her first invention. She actually invented a glow in the dark flea collar that made it easier for cars to see cats and dogs at night. She didn't patent the invention and Hartz Mountain brought a similar product to market. When she thought up the Miracle Mop in 1989, she used her life savings to initially develop and manufacture the product in a corner of her Dad's auto body shop.[225]

Before she struck it big with her self-wringing mop, Mangano struggled through a series of low-paying jobs as a waitress and airline reservations manager. Today, Mangano's net worth is approximately $50 million and she has more than 100 patents to her name, including one for Huggable Hangers, one of HSN's best-selling products.[226]

In addition to qualities associated with immigrants, entrepreneurs also need self-awareness to stay in touch with themselves, their employees, their investors, and other stakeholders. Remaining self-aware leads to better decision-making, better decisions, better relationships, and continuous improvement.[227]

Adding empathy to your daily interactions creates a warm and compassionate environment for your team, which helps motivate them and create space for honesty and the type of feedback that will help you, your products, and your start-up improve. Seek feedback that is authentic and truthful because eventually you will need to hear potentially difficult feedback that you need to embrace with an open mind and heart. That's the key to improving yourself, your business, and your products and services.

Consider building a regular meditation practice into your daily routine to help manage the stress that is inevitable when building a start-up and to help you make progress toward your goals. Settle your mind and imagine what in your life you'd like to change. Visualize the best possible outcome, the steps that you need to take to achieve that outcome and imagine what your life will be like when you've achieved the success of your dreams. Before you end your meditation, consider what action step you will take in the next week to move closer to your goal. Mindfulness practices such as meditation are proven to reduce stress, increase your ability to focus, and create more space in your mind for creativity.[228]

The bottom line is hard work, as widely successful entrepreneurs testify: "Work like hell," says Elon Musk, founder of PayPal, Tesla, SpaceX, and other start-ups. "I mean you just have to put in 80 to 100 hour weeks every week. This improves the odds of success. If other people are putting in 40 hour workweeks and you're putting in 100 hour workweeks then even if you're doing the same thing, you know that you will achieve in four months what it take them a year to achieve."[229]

"The mind is the limit. As long as the mind can envision the fact that you can do something, you can do it, as long as you really believe 100 percent," says Arnold Schwarzenegger, former Governor of California, actor, and bodybuilder. "If you want to turn a vision into a reality, you have to give 100 percent and never stop believing in your dream."[230]

"Where I excel is a ridiculous, sickening work ethic," says actor Will Smith. "While the other guy is sleeping, I'm working. While the other guy is eating, I'm working."[231]

"So keep working, keep striving, never give up, fall down seven times, get up eight," says actor Denzel Washington. "Ease is a greater threat to progress than hardship. So keep on living, keep growing, keep learning."[232]

"Nobody you know has become successful outside of it being given to them from their family, nobody actually created their success without hard work. That doesn't exist," says Vaynerchuk.[233]

Step 3: Create a Minimum Viable Product

The concept of a minimum viable product was born from lean start-up and agile design principles. The idea is to create a product that offers very basic features that you can enhance as you get feedback from your target audience.

Before you create a MVP, you have to decide who your audience is—and hyper focus on that audience. It takes courage to drive a stake in the ground around a highly specific audience. But anything less is very likely to fail because it won't strongly appeal to a core audience of buyers—instead it will be kind of appealing to lots of different people.

Operating with MVP principles allows you to avoid investing too much time, energy, and money in a product that isn't viable. You can also get your product to market quickly, learn what features customers prefer and get a sense of customer demand for your product.[234]

A minimum viable product mind-set means that you continually iterate your product. Eric Ries, who initially proposed the concept, identifies a minimum viable product as "that version of a new product which allows a team to collect the maximum amount of validated learning about customers with the least effort."[235]

While a minimum viable product avoids over-investment, it can't be too skimpy, or customers won't be interested. That's why your first step—before you create anything—must involve a thorough investigation of the problem you are seeking to solve with your product. As part of this endeavor, you must understand how your future customers use technology, whether they can afford your solution and whether they constitute a large enough market.

Key to the minimum viable product approach is a hyper-focused mind-set that seeks to solve one problem experienced by one audience. Trying to offer too much too soon has doomed more businesses than can be counted. In today's fast-moving world full of millions of websites and web-based products, all your product has to do is solve the problem of one target segment very effectively.

Essentially, creating a minimum viable product is like solving a hypothesis in a science experiment—you're trying to learn whether your product has a viable customer base and who is willing to pay for your product. "The willing to pay for your product" is key because investors need to see a road to profitability before they will invest. Even the most patient Venture Capitalist won't wait forever to realize a return on their investment—and patient VCs are few and far between.

Data analytics is the key to understanding what your MVP should focus on. In the absence of hard data, it's too easy to bake too many features into your product in an effort to meet the needs of the world. That's a recipe for failure. Mine your data to determine the common problems that can be solved by adding a feature, what features users are requesting, and what the most popular features desired are.

Once you've got a minimum viable product, sell it directly. Create a website and go directly to consumers, using social media to connect with your target audience. All too often, inventors or creators want to head straight to large retail brands such as Walmart or Home Depot.

Unfortunately, big box retailers require you to jump through lots of hoops to get your product on their shelves with no guarantee of success. Many entrepreneurs are willing to blow all their cash flow on stocking up on inventory just to say their product is sold in a big box store without any proof of the product will sell, which is the ultimate business killer. Always lead with sales first and replenish inventories as sales prove the product is viable.

You're much better off selling your product yourself on your own website or platform like Shopify and using Amazon to fulfill order once fulfilment is beyond your control. This type of approach will allow you to continue to iterate your product without investing too much time and energy until it proves itself successful.

You also need to stay extremely focused on your core audience. It's all too easy to get distracted if a big customer offers a gigantic revenue opportunity. If that revenue opportunity isn't in alignment with your core business and your core audience, it's not worth the distraction. Perhaps the revenue opportunity comes with huge string that will crimp your cash flow due to a 90- or 120-day payment cycle. Or it will require you to jump through so many hoops that you won't have the opportunity to pursue any other business opportunities. Staying focused on your core business and what is best for the company in the long-term will ultimately pay off.

Staying connected with your customer is critical because if you aren't customer-centric, your business won't survive. That involves getting out of your cubicle, garage, bedroom, office, or wherever you do business and talking to at least five current and five potential customers to understand:

- Who they are

- What they care about

- What they need[236]

Equally important to success in your business is a reliable team that can execute the solution you've created. That solution must offer a significant upgrade—like ten times better—than one aspect of your competitor's products. If your team doesn't have the skillset to consistently execute and iterate product development, you must find people who can. Otherwise, neither your product nor your business will survive.

Step 4: Learn Business Valuation

If you want to start a business, you probably already watch *Shark Tank*. If you don't, start watching because this show offers a valuable lesson in capital raising, business valuation, and what it takes to acquire investor capital.

As entrepreneurs come and go through *Shark Tank*, presenting their ideas, they have all sorts of ideas on how their businesses and business ideas should be valued. But the Sharks—the investors tasked with valuing their ideas—understand the brutal truth about business and ideas. That quite a bit can go wrong, which is why they aren't willing to overpay for ideas.

Investor Kevin Harrington puts it this way: "Nothing turns off an investor more than when an entrepreneur comes in with a ridiculous valuation."[237]

That's why when discussing your business with investors, you've got to have a grip on the language of business investment. You probably already know that when an entrepreneur seeks $50,000 for a 10 percent equity stake in their company, that they believe their company should be valued at $500,000. If investors don't agree— and rarely will an investor agree to the business valuation you set— they will counter back with a larger stake in the company, say 30 percent for the same $50,000—for example.

Where do investors obtain these numbers from? They have to come from somewhere. While they want to know how the business is performing today, their actual focus is on how the business will do in the future. They also want to know how your business compares other, similar companies, usually what other businesses sold for, or even publicly traded companies with a demonstrated track record of success.[238]

To determine how much they would invest in your business today, they need to get a sense of what it will earn in the future and how much risk their investment might be subject to.[239]

Why do the sharks put so much weight on risk in calculating what a business is worth? That's because small businesses with new products are risky. Unlike publicly traded companies where an investor can simply sell their shares on the open market, privately-held companies are difficult to exit from. In fact, far more privately held businesses fail in their early years, which means that potential investors have lots of reasons to carefully evaluate investing in start-ups. The Small Business Administration notes that 20 percent of small businesses fail in the first year, 30 percent in the second year, 50 percent after five years, and 70 percent by their tenth year in business.[240]

This is summed up in a type of analysis known as net present value analysis, which discounts the value of all future cash flows that a business is expected to generate back to the present value which compensates investors for the risk they would be taking in a specific investment by adjusting future earnings for risk. Investors will also need to evaluate what earnings might look like during the next five, ten, and twenty years, given the competitive threats that the investment may face in the future.

As an entrepreneur, you need to be conversant with and realistic about the terms that you hope to discuss with angel investors, venture capitalists, and other investors in the future. Terms that you need to be familiar with include:

• Capitalization table (aka cap tables): A spreadsheet that shows how equity capitalization is divided in a company. Types of equity typically shown are equity shares, preferred equity shares, warrants, and convertible equity. This includes all ownership shares, including those of founders, any reserved for future employees and investors.

- Term sheets: A written non-binding agreement displaying terms and conditions under which an investment will be made.

- Pro-rata investment rights: The right of an early investor to participate in subsequent rounds of funding so that they can maintain a specific percentage of equity ownership.

As an entrepreneur, how do you ensure that you walk the middle road between over-valuing your company and undervaluing it? Here are some rules of thumb:[241]

1. Find comps: Look for publicly traded companies, or companies that recently were acquired that you share characteristics with and check out their valuations.

Forecast revenue: Create projections around how your start-up's revenue will grow.

2. Forecast profitability: Create solid financial projections that predict when your company will reach profitability.

3. Determine your assets: Add up the value of your company's assets, including proprietary software, branding, patents, cash flow, users, and partnerships.

4. Define KPIs: Decide which KPIs you'll use to assess progress. Potential KPIs include user growth rate, customer success rate, burn rate, activation rate, customer acquisition costs, daily active users to monthly active users rate, customer churn rate, and revenue growth rate.

5. Select a model: Use the pre-revenue model if you're not earning revenue and the post-revenue model if you are.[242]

Before you engage in conversations with potential investors, you need to understand the difference between pre-money and post-money valuations. Pre-money valuations is the valuation of your company at the current moment before you accept any investment proceeds. Post-money valuation includes the pre-money valuation plus the investment proceeds.

Post-money valuations are important going forward because they establish a foundation for your start-ups' current valuation, which affects any stock options as well as the paper value of existing shares outstanding. In addition, post-money value impacts the way in which future pre-money valuations are calculated. You and your existing shareholders will want as high a valuation as possible so that you experience less dilution after an investment round. Pre-money valuation refers to the value of your business *before* an investment round. Pre-money valuations tend to be more complex because they might include factors such as employee share open plan expansion, debt-to-equity conversions, and pro-rate participation rights. The price per share that an investor will pay for shares in your company is directly proportional to the pre-money valuation. That means if the pre-money valuation increases, the price per share increases, which benefits you and your current or pre-money shareholders.[243]

While you and your current investors have a vested interest in maximizing the pre-money valuation of your start-up, future investors have the opposite mind-set, preferring a lower valuation. Why? They want to maximize the ownership percentage they receive in return for their investment.

Things get complicated as your start-up needs more funding and seeks subsequent rounds of investment. Each round begins with a new post-money and pre-money based on what has happened with the business and the market environment since the last funding round. Startups that flourish, meeting their KPIs, tend to see an expansion of valuation between earlier post-money and new pre-money. If a start-up fails to meet expectations, it can experience a situation in which valuations stay flat or shrink, known as a flat or down round, when trying to raise money in future investing rounds.[244] This can occur when valuations in initial rounds were too high, market conditions have changed or a start-up hasn't performed as expected. Down rounds can make it tougher for employees and founders, whose stakes typically are worth less along with less general upside potential and typically causes founders to bail at this point and leave for another venture.

Step 5: Create a Two-Minute Pitch Video

Creating an engaging pitch video that gets investors to lean forward and want to know more is critical to raising capital. You don't have long to capture attention, so you have to dive right in and make your point.

Start off by introducing yourself, where you are from, your business name, and how much you are seeking to raise in exchange for how much equity. Then describe the problem and how your company is the solution to that problem. Demonstrate the product or service so investors can see how it works and what problem it solves.[245]

After the opening shot, provide a short, ten-second, overview of the problem your product is designed to solve. Don't linger too long on problems because investors are interested in your solutions. Don't focus on yourself or your own bio because there isn't time and investors don't care about this either. Do focus on the benefits of your product to your target audience and support those benefits with the features of your product.[246]

From the technical standpoint, before you start your video, understand the time commitment that shooting and editing video requires. Unless you are an experienced video editor, editing a minute of video can take ten hours or more. You'll need lots of footage to work with as video can drag if you linger on the same shot for too long.

Record your audio in a quiet place and use subtitles. Make sure that you don't speak too quickly. Wrap up your video with a clear call to action.

Step 6: Build a Presence

While it doesn't pay to spend all your time and money on building a website and social media presence—your product and customers should be your number one priorities—your online presence and your overall marketing plan is important.

Your well-designed website must showcase a memorable brand and logo. Ensure your search optimization is fully optimized. Set up Google Analytics to track many important metrics, like the effectiveness of your online marketing strategies, onsite content, user experience, and device functionality as well as track new versus returning customers. Setup Google webmaster tools to get a glance about all important SEO aspects of your site, such as keywords, links, and possible crawl errors. Employ Screaming Frog for your website's technical SEO and leverage Ahrefs for keyword research and offsite link building. Ensure that your company name and brand are reflected in a premium dot com domain name.

In your email, make sure your email addresses are connected to your premium domain name rather than using something generic like Gmail. Employ a consistent approach that allows for expansion such as firstname.lastname@yourdomain.com. Include a photo with your email signature line, set up email auto follow up software and leverage email opt-in and marketing to grow your email list for marketing campaigns.

Measure engagement and key performance indicators rather than relying on likes and follows, which are useless vanity metrics. Never use services to purchase likes or followers because these are only shortcuts to nowhere and will never benefit your business in the long run. It may take months to build a following of ten followers. But at least you will know that these ten followers actually like what you are selling and these are the people you should focus all your efforts and attention on. If you are looking for fast results, purchasing followers and likes is going to lead to frustration and dead ends because you are not speaking to an authentic audience. So enjoy the grind, start slow, and be authentic.

As the social media landscape grows and becomes more fragmented, there are too many platforms for you to be everywhere. Instead, target your social media efforts toward the platforms where your audience spends most of their time. Major platforms and strategies you should consider include:

• YouTube corporate page and long content

• Facebook company page, geo-targeting, microvideo, and lead generation

• Instagram page, lead generation, microvideo content, and IGTV

• LinkedIn company page, personal page, microvideo content, and group development

• Twitter profile and microvideo content

Podcasts are another great marketing tool and should be broadcast over the following platforms: Apple, Castbox, Stitcher, SoundCloud, Spotify, Google Tunein, Acat, and Otto Radio.

Implementing the right tools to support your online efforts will streamline your online marketing and sales efforts. Based on my own experience starting and running several successful businesses, I recommend the following tools:

• Squadhelp.com for naming your company or product.

- Streak: Email scheduler great for dripping information on prospects

- Kindle Direct Publishing: Ebooks and print-on-demand publisher

- CreateSpace: Book publishing and formatting

- Aweber: Email marketing

- Screaming Frog spider tool: Spider tool to analyze and audit SEO

- Hootsuite: Managing and planning social media content for multiple platforms

- Facebook and Instagram: Advertising and email retargeting

- Ahrefs: Keyword research, backlink research, and content planning

- Retargeting cookies: Retargeting prospects after they leave your site

- Click-to-chat function: Engaging interactively with prospects visiting your site

- LinkedIn marketing: For targeting by profession

- Google AdWords: Reinforcing marketing efforts when combined with the above efforts

- Facebook geo-targeting: Dropping a pin where you know an event is happening and targeting ads to prospects attending the event during a specific time frame

Create an execution plan that ensures that all of the above tools are implemented and maximized for success. Continue to iterate the process as you gain feedback as to which strategies are the most successful.

Continue to analyze, reposition, and adjust the needs of your start-up and product/service. Be a formidable competitor and corner off all angles to your market so that it is nearly impossible to compete with your products and services in your specific niche.

Do not rely on only one type of marketing to attract prospects—instead, be a multi-faceted marketing machine.

Step 7: Check Out Crowdfunding as an Alternative

Crowdfunding is a legitimate alternative for entrepreneurs needing capital. Through major crowdfunding platforms such as Kickstarter, Indiegogo, and many others, you can access capital and position your start-up for future acquisition.

Most crowdfunding platforms connect business owners and product creators with consumers interested in their products. In exchange for a small amount of funding—$50, $100 or more—consumers receive special rewards. These rewards can include actual product samples or access to products as well as the opportunity to participate in the development of the product.

LendingClub, a lending platform, facilitates direct member investment in other members' businesses. While different from more traditional crowdfunding platforms, Lending Club also promises to cut out the middleman and traditional banks.

MVMT, a start-up that designs and manufactures fashionable, affordable watches, leveraged Indiegogo for $300,000 in start-up funding from 3,000 investors. Founders Jake Kansan and Kramer LaPlante were unable to secure funding from banks or venture capitalists, so they turned to crowdfunding.[247]

"With crowdfunding, there's nothing stopping you from turning your ideas into something big," Kassan told Indiegogo.com. "Almost every day, I see people walking down the street wearing products we built from nothing. It's completely unreal, and it's the most fulfilling thing in the world."[248]

Ultimately, MVMT's hot start on crowdfunding resulted in a $100 million acquisition by Movado Group. And since they did not rely on investor equity, the money from the Movado acquisition was equally split between the founders. Along the way, Forbes named MVMT the world's fastest growing watch company. The company was able to grow their initial base of 3,000 crowdfunding investors into $80 million of annual revenues.[249]

In retrospect, Kassan believes that the lack of initial funding from banks and VCs was a blessing in disguise. "Crowdfunding through Indiegogo allowed us to retain 100 percent independence and build the company we wanted, without being beholden to people who might not share the same vision," he told Indiegogo.com.[250]

Step 8: Avoid These Common Mistakes

Just as the arc of starting a business and raising capital has commonalities across businesses and sectors, so do the mistakes that start-up founders tend to make. Justin Kan, CEO of Atrium, a machine learning technology company serving the legal industry, outlines three common mistakes made by founders:

1. Offering an undeveloped narrative: The best start-ups lure investors and employees in with a compelling narrative. That narrative should present the current state of your market and your expertise in that market, the large problem that you want to solve and the changes in the market that create the ideal path for your product. Build the narrative first, then create your video, and pitch deck based on that narrative.

2. Trying to serve too large a customer base: If you try to serve too large of a customer base, you won't succeed because you'll be too busy trying to be everything to everybody. Instead, narrow down

your base by deciding who your primary customer is and sticking to it.

3. Failing to grow your team: In the furious pace typically followed by start-ups, it's easy to stick with the same team that you've had since the beginning. However, not every employee will grow with a start-up or want to stay in the same role indefinitely. Regular, candid conversation with your team members about the company's needs and what support those team members need from the start-up.[251]

Step 9: Understand Why Cash Flow is King

Sales and profits are great—every start-up needs them both. However, for start-ups, cash flow is king. What exactly is cash flow? Cash flow is how much money you have at the end of the week or month after all bills, expenses, and taxes are paid.

For example, if you have a weekly payroll of $10,000 to pay and you only have $500 left after paying it, your cash flow is extremely weak. If at the end of a month when you have payroll, rent, debt, and taxes to pay of $18,000 and you only have $2,000 left, your cash flow is also weak. These are examples of cash flow where a business is living from check to check. This is the result of having large accounts receivable balances owed to the company, expenses that are too high and pricing your product or service too low, leaving margins that are too thin. While there is a lot of money moving through the account, little of it is captured in the form of cash flow. If your company's cash flow operates like this during good economic times, it won't take long before some unforeseen event will put you out of business.

Prioritizing cash flow ensures sufficient liquidity to pay your employees, service your debt, pay your suppliers, pay your taxes, and invest in your business. Whether you're just starting your business or need advice on how to get back in a strong cash flow situation, here are some strategies for maximizing cash flow and liquidity:

1. Obtain upfront payment for services: Booking revenue is great, but actually getting paid is more important. Don't fall into the trap of doing too much work up front and chasing payment later. Collecting from delinquent customers is a huge hassle and distraction. If left unchecked, it can actually put you out of business.

2. Align your revenue with your expenses: Don't offer thirty-day terms until your prospective paying customers become good paying customers. Just because the industry standard is to automatically extend thirty-day terms, a smart business person will first request upfront payments from new customers that have not built a payment track record with your company. This will ensure positive cash flow and prevent entrepreneurs from being too reliant on accounts receivables which is doing work first and expecting payment much later.

3. Establish a strong invoicing process: All too often, bookkeeping and invoicing is a start-up afterthought. Invoices must be generated as soon as the product or service has been delivered. Automate the process through payment platforms and bookkeeping apps.

4. Keep expenses in check: Avoid unnecessary expenses by understanding what expenses are absolutely necessary and what expenses can be eliminated. Also, of the necessary expenses, make sure you are not overpaying and always keep searching for the best prices, because keeping expenses low will keep your profits high.

5. Correct pricing is the key to maintaining positive cash flow. Choose a pricing strategy that makes sense for your service or industry. If you do not price your product or service for profitability your margins will get crushed, and you will either be always extremely short on cash or worse be forced to go out of business.

So spend a good amount of time determining your business's pricing strategy while always searching for ways to keep expenses low.

Step 10: Learn How to Pivot

Pivoting is a valuable trait for start-up founders. Start-ups frequently need to pivot because their original business model isn't delivering the anticipated results. Or their initial model may be succeeding, but the market is changing and they need to pivot before sales start to drop.

Alan Spoon, general partner at Polaris Venture Partners, suggests in an Inc.com column that founders should regularly ask themselves two questions:

1. "What do we do—whether based on talent, technology or culture—that is distinctly valuable and defensible and might be extended to other customer needs?"

2. "How can our customer interactions be made more lasting and valuable? Are there recurring revenue services and products that can extend beyond the initial sale?"[252]

He describes these pivots as "pivoting for growth."

Highly successful companies such as Netflix, Slack, and Instagram are the result of pivots—they began as very different products from what they eventually evolved into, according to CB Insights.[253] Slack actually began as a company called Tiny Speck that developed a game called Glitch, which was launched in 2011. Stewart Butterfield, founder of Slack, who had already founded and sold Flickr, decided that Glitch wasn't viable.

Instead, he decided to build up the messaging platform that Tiny Speck built in the course of developing Glitch. Slack launched in 2014 and now has more than eight million daily active users, carrying a valuation of more than $7 billion. As of June 20, 2019, Slack is now a publicly traded company.[254]

Step 11: Attract Investors

You've got a product with sales, and now you're ready to pitch investors. Now it's time to raise capital, which is much easier said than done. It's hard because you have to convince risk-adverse investors that you and your product deserve their hard-earned money.

Investors aren't interested in your hard-luck story—all they care about is the opportunity to partner with an entrepreneur who can generate consistent sales and large profits. So that is what your fundraising efforts must focus on—why investing in your product will create big profits for investors. You do this by researching your market, identifying the key metrics that show why your product is a good investment, and creating a compelling narrative around your product.[255]

Let's explore this in a bit more depth:

1. Research your market: While you want to be hyper focused on your customer and your product, your market's got to be large enough to merit investment. Venture capitalists want to find the next Facebook, not a niche company that will never scale. Get behind the boldest idea possible that will penetrate the largest market possible because these are the types of ideas and businesses investors want to fund.

2. Identify key metrics: Investors want strong metrics suitable to your product/service niche. They can and will reduce your business to a spreadsheet with a bottom-line profit calculation because the numbers have to work. Good metrics will help make your case, facilitating investment with bad metrics won't attract investors. It's that simple.

3. Create a compelling narrative: The story around your product must be simple—complexity kills investment. That's because

investors wade through hundreds, if not thousands of pitches a year, and they have no time or interest to figure out whether your service is the next Uber or not. You've got to do it for them. Creating a compelling story leads naturally to a conclusion that your company will end up being worth billions goes a long way toward convincing investors.

Because so many start-ups fail, attracting investors and raising capital is critical to success. Teresa Esser, author of *The Venture Cafe: Secrets, Strategies and Stories from America's High-Tech Entrepreneurs*, believes that a key to success in attracting investors is connecting with organizations that support, educate, and mentor entrepreneurs. Do a Google search in your area for start-up accelerators and incubators, Esser suggested on *The Rocco Forino Show*. Contact your city, local colleges, and the U.S. Small Business Administration to see what free resources are available. Getting started and growing bigger with this type of support can make a big difference because there are usually investors and bankers watching to see who has business models that are viable and scalable, according to Esser's comments on *The Rocco Forino Show* podcast.

"Through one of these accelerators or incubators maybe you get a small loan to buy a truck and start a food truck business," Esser said on *The Rocco Forino Show*. "Bankers and investors will notice if you did a good job with that food truck business. If you did, then it will be easier to get more funding to buy a second truck or to expand into catering. Anyone can start on the entrepreneurial track because there is a lot of support out there—I know because I provide some of it." Esser recommends visiting www.venturecafe.com and seeing if there is a Thursday gathering in your community where you can meet other entrepreneurs and connect with investors to discuss ideas and projects.

If your community isn't supportive of entrepreneurs with resources such as incubators, accelerators, investor networks, venture capitalists, and free resources for start-ups, you may need to move to a community where these resources exist. "You need to connect at the start with someone who knows how to start a business, has a history of making money and has a plan because that person can help guide you," Esser says. "If you don't have access to people who can help guide you, you might have to pick up and go somewhere else and relaunch. Many people go off to college or move somewhere else where the start-up atmosphere is more inspiring. Then you can learn what you need to learn and come back and start that business." However, that is the problem that struggling OZs need to figure out and prevent. If a local entrepreneur moves and becomes successful in a city like Austin, Texas, or Miami Florida, why would they move back to a city or town that was not supportive of their business or start-up when they needed it most, what is the incentive?

Step 12: Get to Know Family Offices and Wealth Managers

Now that you have gone through all the steps of what it takes to build a successful business, the next step is to get your business in front of investors that want to invest in entrepreneurs and start-ups located in OZs. Family offices, which are private wealth management firms that serve groups of ultra-high-net-worth investors. These investors outsource all their financial and investment management activities to Family offices, which then invest their money for them. There are also thousands of individual private equity investors with capital to invest. Both Family offices and private equity investors have significant amounts of capital to invest, which means that you don't have to get a lot of small investors to invest in your venture. Family offices make their own decisions which means it can be easier to raise capital from them than through VC firms, which have more involved decision-making processes.

Networking with the right family offices and high–net-worth investors can streamline your capital raising efforts. Many family offices and high–net-worth investors specialize in investing in specific niches, so if you can find these types of investors who invest in your niche, you have a higher potential for success. In fact, family offices share deal flow with other related family offices, so if you bring a good deal to them, there is a chance that they will introduce you to others in the sector. However, before you approach specific family offices and high-net-worth investors, conduct some due diligence. Before you approach a family office about an investment, understand what that particular family office invests in and whether your business is a good fit. Working with family offices is all about building a relationship, so don't pitch a deal immediately when you're introduced. When you do build a relationship and are ready to pitch a deal, make sure you have established a clear path to profitability and exit. Investors need to understand how and when they can make a profit and cash out their investment.

DealConnect Hub is an investment platform that matches investors and QOFs with entrepreneurs just like yourself. Our private investor network offers a heavily discounted plan for entrepreneurs under 30 years old, because we want to support young investors and those from distressed communities. Now is a great time to get your start-up moving since many investors and QOFs are under strict time constraints to deploy their capital to invest in entrepreneurs located in OZs.

Step 13: Increase Your Start-Up's Visibility

You're reading this book because you believe in the potential of QOFs and OZs. That means you need to connect with QOFs to raise capital for your startup or business. Before you take that step, you need to put a more professional face on your business by occupying an office, manufacturing, or coworking space in the most desirable OZ in your area. This is because in order for the QOF to be compliant it has to invest in startups or businesses that are located in or will relocate to an OZ community as described in chapter 4. If you want to first start with a coworking space, search through coworking companies with locations across the country such as Spring Place, Impact Hub, WeWork, Industrious, and Knotel. Check out coworking search engines and apps such as Coworker, WorkHardAnywhere, Workfrom, and LiquidSpace.

Then, you need to position yourself to make connections with the right investors. To ensure that OZs, QOFs, and investors are aware of you, you've got to list your business's location on DealConnect Hub. QOFs and investors only receive tax incentives when they invest in businesses or real estate that is located in an OZ. Geo-locating your business on the DealConnect Hub map will ensure investors and QOFs that your business is properly located in an OZ and that you are seeking to raise capital from investors.

While OZs and QOFs offer a great deal of potential, right now there is no efficient method for OZs, QOFs, and OZs businesses to connect with each other. In other words, there are many investors seeking businesses with growth potential, but it's very difficult to find them. Going to conferences isn't an efficient use of your time because investors in your niche or your geographical area may not be at the same conferences. Those conferences are designed to collect fees and are not an efficient means for connecting people, making the process frustrating and as a result a lot of investment capital is held in limbo on the sidelines. DealConnect Hub specializes in matching your business with investors in the same niche and geography. Our platform matches businesses in specific sectors with investors seeking to invest in those sectors. DealConnect Hub will offer a variety of niche marketing opportunities, including *Shark*

Tank-like investment pitch conferences to get you and your business in front of the right investors.

Advantages of listing your business on the DealConnect Hub include:

1. Being the first to be discovered by QOFs and investors seeking to invest in entrepreneurs, start-ups, developers, and existing businesses.

2. Matching entrepreneurs directly to investors who match their exact investment filters. So no more wasting time reaching out to the wrong investors who don't specialize in your business sector or geography.

3. Raising more capital from private equity investors and family office institutions than on any other network.

4. Gaining access to live investor events, conferences, and pitch events.

5. Building your business's brand by appearing on The Rocco Forino Show or DealConnect Hub podcasts.

6. Discovering and connecting with like-minded businesses who want to build a business ecosystem in your OZ community.

7. Use data visualization and map viewing to find the best OZs that are pro-business, have little to no taxes, and have the best quality of life for you and your employees.

Starting a business in an OZ is a great way to position your start-up for success. The best OZ communities are maximizing support for their OZ businesses as well as making a strong case to QOFs and investors. Following the steps in this chapter will provide you and your business with a leg up on other start-ups that aren't as well prepared to succeed or are even aware of the hard work and preparation that is necessary to succeed in attracting capital.

If you want your business to create the largest possible impact and improve your community, consider how positioning it as an impact investment opportunity can attract impact investment capital. Chapter 8 outlines the advantages of impact investing, the types of businesses that are succeeding at impact investing, and what investors are looking for in impact investing. Creating a business that can change your community for the better will not only help your community, but create additional opportunities for your start-up to raise capital.

Chapter 8

IMPACT INVESTING

Now that you've learned the ins and outs of raising capital, it's time to consider how to best use the capital that you're raising to fully incorporate positive social impact into your OZ investments, which was the purpose and intent of the 2017 TCJA. Social impact investing is an investing approach that reflects personal social values, designed to create a positive social and/or environmental difference. "Impact investing is defined as investing in something that reflects your social values," said Morgan Simon, author of *Real Impact: The New Economics of Social Change*, on an episode of *The Rocco Forino Show* podcast. Investors who implement impact investing might bank with a community development bank that reinvests in the community rather than a large national bank like Wells Fargo that has a history of defrauding millions of customers by opening fake accounts and selling them products they didn't understand or need.[256]

When investors seek to both make a profit and improve the world around them, they are investing for impact. Impact investors channel capital into companies that offer solutions to major social and environmental challenges, including poverty, pollution, hunger, and global warming. Essentially, the end goal of impact investing is to achieve the principles for responsible investing that were established in 2006.[257] These include no poverty, zero hunger, good health and well-being, gender equality, industry, innovation and infrastructure, reduced inequalities, sustainable cities and communities, climate action, life below water, life on land, peace, justice and strong institutions, partnerships, quality education, affordable and clean energy, clean water and sanitation, responsible consumption and production, and decent work and economic growth.[258]

Simon divides impact investing into two categories: transformative and palliative. "Impact investing can be done in a way that is transformative, which really addresses the underlying structural problems and fixes them for the long term or the typical palliative approach which is much less effective and only involves mitigating the impact of something but not making structural change," she said on the podcast. "For example, palliative impact investing might simply decelerate climate change rather than actually stopping it or make poor people slightly less miserable rather than helping them climb out of poverty. What we really want to do as investors is to be as transformative as possible to address the root causes of problems and make systemic change."

An example of palliative impact would be reforming the payday loan industry to create more affordable loans for low-income Americans, Simon noted. While lower interest rate loans would certainly help, they wouldn't do anything to address the fundamental structural problem behind payday lending—the fact that low-income Americans can't pay their utility bills at the end of the month. It isn't that they budget poorly or can't get better loans, it is that they don't have sufficient income to pay for the necessities of life. Payday loans are a short-term solution that exacerbates and compounds the problem rather than attempting to solve it, leaving borrowers in worse circumstances.

"So the real question is how do we create enterprises that actually offer wage scales so that everyone can get their financial needs met and not need a loan at any interest rate towards the end of the month because they are running out of money," Simon said. "Are we making it easier to be poor or are we actually stopping poverty? The opportunity we have with impact investing is to create systemic, lasting change while also fulfilling financial goals." Impact investing is growing in popularity. More than 1,340 organizations worldwide manage $502 billion of impact investment assets.[259] Most of that capital—in excess of 60 percent—is managed by asset managers, while foundations manage 21 percent, banks and diversified financial institutions manage 4 percent, and family offices manage 2 percent.[260]

Impact investing and OZs are a natural fit. OZs were designed to create positive social impact in America's poorest communities. That's why OZ stakeholders must consider the ultimate objective of specific OZ investments. Operating from an impact investing perspective, an investor's goal should be to add more to an OZ community than it extracts. "If we're impact investors, then whoever we are calling the beneficiary should, in fact, be the primary beneficiary," said Simon on *The Rocco Forino Show* podcast. "That involves looking at what the rate of return the community is receiving versus the investor rate of return. That doesn't mean investors should accept sub-market returns; rather, it means that everyone in the transaction is being treated fairly." One way to achieve this goal is to ensure that a company receiving impact investing funds makes a profit and is productive before the impact investors receive returns. Simon notes that this type of blended structure ensures that both the investor and the company being invested in are equally invested in the company's ultimate success. This stands in contrast to traditional highly leveraged private equity investments, such as the now-defunct Toys "R" Us, where it was loaded up with so much debt that all the value was extracted out of it, leaving a massive void in communities across the country. This void ranged from empty commercial real estate spaces that communities rely on for property taxes to employees who received pink slips with a laughable $60 per employee in severance pay.[261] These are the types of jobs that keep workers poor, provide no upward mobility for people, and cause workers to build up debt instead of assets. These jobs extract value from communities, leaving millions of Americans mired in poverty they can't escape.[262]

When considering an investment in OZs with the intention to make a positive impact, both the investors and the beneficiaries should benefit. If you are planning a real estate investment, for example, will that investment help the community achieve more affordable housing or will it push long-time residents out of their neighborhoods as the community gentrifies? Consider how you can profitably add an affordable housing component to a more traditional multi-family development rather than focusing exclusively on high-end units. If you are planning to invest in an OZ business, invest sufficient funds so that the business can pay its employees a living wage. Employees who are employed at a living wage are more loyal and more likely to add value back into an organization than those who are poorly paid. In addition, well-paid employees spend more, which multiplies the value of those well-paying jobs within a community.

Before proceeding with an investment, you should create or adopt an assessment tool so you can evaluate your investments to determine if you've achieved your impact objectives.

One danger of impact investing is that it can be used as window dressing for investment managers who want the benefit of investing for impact without actually investing for impact. The London

School of Economics described this practice—known as "impact washing"—as "rampant."[263]

Speaking on the podcast, Simon agreed, saying, "I'm skeptical of people on the 40th floor of a Wall Street investment bank saying that they are going to move into impact investing. They think they'll figure out how to change the world without accountability to make sure they are actually making investments that people want, so it seems like it is more about impact washing than actual impact. This is why my book is called *Real Impact*. It's the idea that yes, there is real impact to be had, but we have to actually make sure that it's real." That means investors need to engage with the communities they invest in and collaborate with community members to determine what investments will do the most to improve conditions there. "Clean" coal is a great example of impact washing, Simon noted, because "there is no way to make coal clean. The whole point is that fossil fuel is not clean, but by putting that label on is a way to show that you're doing something, that you are painting it green but it isn't really green."

"In the same way, you're seeing more traditional financial institutions coming into impact investing who really don't have the history or the on the ground connections to know if that impact is real or not. You can wind up calling something an impact portfolio, but when you look under the hood, it's just a reorganization of the Fortune 500," she said. The bottom line, Simon said, is that it's important to evaluate any proposed OZ impact investment carefully before investing—to be a conscious consumer of impact investing. "If you are offered an impact investment or an impact portfolio, take the time to really go through and question the fund manager or advisor. Find out what companies and investments were included and why as well as asking if the manager is engaged in shareholder activism to try to improve practices. Social change is always a work in progress. It's not that you're going to have the most beautiful portfolio on day one, but that you're really showing progress and commitment."

Types of Impact Investing

Anyone can achieve impact in investing, regardless of their occupation, age, or role. For example, anyone with a connection to a pension fund or endowment can propose a shareholder resolution, which recommends a specific course of action to a publicly traded company. While shareholder resolutions are non-binding, they place financial pressure on company boards. "In the U.S., shareholder proposal filings have historically played an important role in advancing corporate governance and in highlighting key risks related to environmental and social issue," noted an article published in the Harvard Law School Forum on Corporate Governance and Financial Regulation.[264] "Shareholder proposals have also served as a driving force for greater corporate awareness of environmental and social risk, such as climate change risk management, diversity and inclusion in the workplace and sustainability reporting." The number of environmental and social shareholder resolutions filed in 2017 exceeded the number of governance proposals for the first time. Resolutions falling under this category sought to influence corporate behavior in climate change, environmental impact, political contributions, human rights, and human capital management.[265]

While it may seem idealistic to think that shareholder resolutions can force corporate change, there's ample evidence to support their utility. In the late 1960s, a group of Vietnam War protestors called the Medical Group for Human Rights, purchased shares in Dow Chemical, the company that manufactured napalm, a chemical that maimed and burned Vietnamese civilians. Their resolution led to the eventual cessation of napalm production by Dow, after a federal court upheld the right of shareholders to introduce resolutions.[266] Shareholder pressure led to the eventual dismantling of apartheid in South Africa after shareholders at hundreds of companies pressured board to quit doing business with the racist government regime there.[267]

As a student at Swarthmore College, a liberal arts college in Swarthmore, Pennsylvania, Simon was an activist who joined the college's committee on investor responsibility. That committee filed the first shareholder resolution since the apartheid era asking Lockheed Martin Corporation to add sexual orientation to their non-discrimination policy. "After presenting at their annual meeting, the company ultimately decided to change that policy," Simon noted on my podcast that this was the beginning of a wave of companies making changes in this area that led to national legislation. "For me, it was an opportunity to see as an individual you could have the leverage to influence change in discriminatory corporate policies when people could come together to make a difference," she continued. "It very much inspired me, and inspired thousands of students across the country to come together in the Responsible Endowment Coalition, which at its height included more than 100 campuses across the country that managed hundreds of billions of dollars in endowment money."

Simon related that it wasn't as hard as you might think to persuade vice presidents at these colleges to support this type of corporate resolution, because social and financial consequences are closely aligned in this area. After all, the LGBTQ population makes up about 10 percent of the U.S. population, which is an important constituency in terms of hiring employees and purchasing products and services. "As a financial steward, as a fiduciary for the school, he was very much behind the idea that we should make sure that companies are doing the best by their shareholders," Simon said. "As a mission-based institution, the college also believed deeply in the safety, security and rights of people regardless of their sexual orientation."

That's one example of impact investing. Another example is basing your purchasing decisions on your values. For example, I always buy my coffee from Starbucks because of their commitment to the environment, fair trade for coffee farmers, and their employees. Starbucks serves coffee in paper rather than foam cups, which is better for the environment. Since 2000, Starbucks has not only purchased coffee on fair trade terms but also funded more than $14 million in loans to fair trade coffee cooperatives in an effort to help coffee farmers manage risk and create better businesses.[268] Finally, the fact that Starbucks pays their employees decent wages, provides health benefits and also offers educational benefits so that they can get college degrees. I've handed these values down to my daughters, who now understand that they can influence corporate behavior and stay aligned with their values through their purchasing decisions.

Another example of impact investing is directly investing in start-ups and businesses designed for social and/or environment impact. Venture capitalists and private equity investors committed to investing on a large-scale engage in this practice. A number of large financial institutions have recently launched impact investing VC funds, including Bain Capital's $390 million double impact fund.[269] Bain reports that more private equity funds are incorporating impact requirements, including environmental, social, and governance goals, known as ESG, into their strategies.[270]

Social impact accelerators such as VillageCapital invest in start-ups through an accelerator, which supports start-ups through mentorship and training. VillageCapital has an incredibly high survival rate for businesses that made it through its innovative training program—90 percent are still in business.[271] The Hult Prize offers $1 million in seed funding for the student team that wins a global competition around a scalable impact business solution. The 2013 winner of the Hult Prize, Aspire Food Group, scales the farming of insects as a food source in the United States and Africa. A U.S.-based program raises food-grade crickets on a commercial scale, which are made into protein bars and delivered directly to consumers.[272] "I went to medical school to help thousands. I left to help millions," said Mohammed Ashour, the company's founder.[273]

Jobs Trap People in Poverty

Many Americans believe that jobs are the solution to poverty. However, this is far from true. Modern capitalism ensnares the working poor in jobs that leave them locked into generational poverty. Low wages, lack of benefits, and lack of opportunity for advancement all sentence the poor to decades stuck in an endless cycle of desperately trying—but failing—to make ends meet. Gary Fields, a professor at Cornell University and author of *Working Hard, Working Poor* (Oxford University Press, 2011), believes that the world has a global employment problem because the jobs that are created are exactly the types of jobs that keep people poor.[274] Research from the International Labor Organization supports this claim. The World Employment and Social Outlook: Trends 2019 reports that "poor quality employment is the major issue for global labor markets, with millions of people forced to accept inadequate working conditions."[275]

While the economy and corporate profits have grown tremendously during the past 40 years, wages have not, especially for workers who lack a college education.[276] In the 46 years since 1973, productivity has grown by 77 percent, while hourly pay has risen by 12 percent.[277] Linking the federal minimum wage to those productivity gains would translate to a federal minimum wage of more than $20 an hour, rather than the current rate of $7.25 an hour.[278] In the United

States, the working poor are better off than the non-working poor, mainly because employment is a gateway to other benefits, such as the earned income credit. However, the earned income credit doesn't give back enough to lift low-wage workers in industries like fast food or occupations like home healthcare worker or adjunct professors out of poverty.

In fact, 3.1 million workers—or 3 percent of all full-time workers—earn wages below the poverty rate.[279] In 2019, cities such as McAllen, Laredo, and Brownsville, Texas, all have poverty rates of their full-time workforces in excess of 10 percent.[280] CBS News reports that approximately 65 million Americans worked in low-paid service jobs last year, jobs that are extremely difficult to upgrade in the future. A research paper entitled "Can Low Wage Workers Get Better Jobs?" concluded that these workers are three times more likely to completely stop working than to move up to a better job in any given year. Based on a research review of 175,000 people in low-quality jobs—jobs that feature low pay, unpredictable schedules, and few or no benefits—the authors concluded that high school graduates have much less of a chance to move into higher payer jobs than college graduates. The few high school graduates that move into higher paying jobs gain traction through occupations such as truck driving, clerks, automotive technicians, and repair workers.

"Most poor people are working at least one, if not two or three jobs and they are still poor," Simon said. "As impact investors, we need to really think about how to invest in companies that create quality jobs that offer living wages, insurance, retirement plans and the chance to advance. These are all different aspects of not just helping people, but also of creating a better workforce that is more loyal, who don't have to be constantly replaced and who are already trained." Lack of benefits is a major issue for low-wage jobs. When workers or their family members get sick, they either have to stay on the job, stay home without pay, or risk getting fired. OZ investors should not only focus on well-paying jobs in the companies they invest in, but also ensure that benefits, such as sick pay, retirement account match, and vacation pay, are included. Employees especially value sick days so that they can recover from their own illnesses or be available to help their relatives with their illnesses.

Stacked Decks

A major challenge for entrepreneurs interested in starting an impact-focused business is raising capital. Of course, raising capital is a challenge for everyone, but it's an especially large challenge for disadvantaged entrepreneurs and entrepreneurs from distressed communities, as I've mentioned earlier in the book. Simon noted on my podcast that less than 2 percent of VC is channeled to black or Latino start-up founders.

"That means there's a massive lack of funding for certain populations and there's a presumption that even to get a company to the point of qualifying for VC funding you're supposed to first have a friends and family round, where you raise money from your friends and family," Simon related. "That's really quite laughable, because for some of us, our friends and families don't have this kind of money. One of my mentees was Latina, grew up in downtown LA, both of her parents were hard working and scrapping to get by. I took her to see an entrepreneur who very casually said, 'I raised $500,000 from family and friends.' I know that if she walked up and down her block, talking to people who loved her to death, she might raise $50. The idea that your friends and family should be able to give you enough money to start a company is preposterous. It makes entrepreneurship more of a privilege than a birthright. That's why we need to be thinking more about how do we get people to that first capital raising opportunity, to the place where a venture capitalist would consider them."

The dog-walking start-up Wag is a perfect example about how Wall Street and Silicon Valley value start-ups that actually produce little or no value. Wag's value proposition—such as it is—rests on uberizing dog-walking. In 2018, Wag announced a $300 million investment from SoftBank's Vision Fund, the world's largest technology investor.[281] However, less than two years later, Wag went through multiple rounds of layoffs and management changes. Former employees allege that the company fails to guarantee the safety of the pets that contractors take care of and offers poor customer service.[282] Under the care of Wag dog walkers, dogs have died, been abused, or been lost.[283] Despite the millions of dollars invested, Wag has yet to demonstrate it has a sustainable business model. Instead of investing in companies that lack a clear path to profitability, investors should analyze prospective investments based on their fundamentals, and invest in companies that offer the chance to impact communities while also making a profit. At an Opal Conference in June, Harold Hughes, board chair of endowment at St. John's College in Annapolis, Maryland, noted that he met an entrepreneur in North Carolina with a viable business model who was having trouble raising $750,000 in capital, then read a story about how Wag raised $300 million for a dog-walking business, which really makes no sense. Investors need to stop wasting money on companies that continue to lose money and make an elite few people wealthy at the cost of many hardworking employees and community stakeholders. Impact investing focuses on businesses that demonstrate a sustainable path to profitability as well as the potential to make a positive impact on a community.

Bringing Impact Investing to Opportunity Zones

Many of the distressed communities that form the vast majority of OZs are home to some of America's most successful entrepreneurs, executives, athletes, entertainers, and investors. Like many of us, when they started businesses or moved up in their careers, they moved on from their hometowns and never looked back. OZs provide the chance for the thousands of successful entrepreneurs, investors, athletes, entertainers, and executives to make an impact on the communities where they were raised. By investing in QOFs designed to maximize the social impact of investments, successful individuals and families can give back while making a profit.

At an Opal Group conference about OZ investing, Prashant Doshi, a venture capitalist and founder of Shreem, LLC noted that the tax incentives offer the ideal situation for investors looking to give back, especially to the communities that they and their families came from. "Recently, I went back to Hoboken, New Jersey, where I grew up," he said. "Visiting there after 33 years, it looks nothing like it did when I was growing up. My Dad came to America from India and started from scratch first in Chicago and later in New Jersey with the idea to make money and do good. He left India because of all the corruption there. So based on his message, there has been a division in the purpose of my existence. However, with opportunity zones there is the chance to do both. If you adopt this philosophy to change your mental model, investment can be both profitable and do a dramatic amount of good in opportunity zone communities."

Harold Hughes, board chair of endowment at St. John's College in Annapolis, MD, noted that the tax breaks, especially the elimination of taxation after a holding period of ten years, is a major benefit for businesses, which means that they can afford to participate in projects that might otherwise not make economic sense. "We do know that if you have a long-term return of 6 percent, the elimination of taxation can make a big difference," he added.

Eric Stephenson, director of Align Impact an independent impact investment firm, said that the major questions with OZ investing is how capital will impact the communities where it is invested. "The potential for better outcomes occurs when community endowments, impact investors and others are at the table with opportunity zone communities, helping high-net-worth families figure out how they can make an impact," he said.

Impact investing is designed to help distressed communities in exactly the ways envisioned by Congress when the 2017 TCJA legislation was passed. Many entrepreneurs are joining the trend, starting businesses designed to address, and remediate social and environmental ills. There are many ways that OZs, QOFs, and OZ businesses can collaborate to maximize the positive impact of investments in distressed communities by creating well-paying jobs and affordable housing. Foundations are becoming a major player in OZ and social impact investing, while also supporting accountability and reporting standards. Such standards are designed to measure the impact of OZ investing.

OZs and impact investing are natural partners because the purpose of OZs is to improve distressed communities across America. The Initiative for a Competitive City, a non-profit dedicated to improving economic prosperity in America's inner cities, published a report focusing on the potential for OZs to make meaningful change in distressed communities entitled, *What It Will Take for Opportunity Zones to Create Real Opportunity in America's Economically Distressed Areas*.[284] The report identifies four keys to positioning OZs to succeed in their mission of battling economic distress and making social change: focusing on places in need, concentrating on non-real estate business investment, aligning investments with community priorities, and creating transparency and accountability.

The Initiative sees a potential best-case scenario for OZ investments, in which "investors would invest in places with genuine needs—not necessarily the most distressed areas, but not areas that would develop without the aid of the tax incentive. They would invest mainly in non-real estate businesses and would do so in ways that make economic sense for the communities in which they invested, catalyzing further development as part of a well-grounded economic development strategy."

A report by the Federal Reserve Bank of Chicago about OZs notes: "Opportunity zone investment strategies can promote inclusive growth, if carefully targeted to invest in marginalized areas, increase the availability of living wage jobs in historically disinvested areas and/or increase access to capital for low-income and minority residents. Reinvesting within disinvested communities is one key element of inclusive growth. However, investments must be consistent with local goals and needs."[285] PolicyLink, a non-profit focused on creating an equitable economy, recommends that investors, developers, local officials, philanthropy, and communities prioritize equitable growth, development without displacement, and creating healthy communities.[286]

Kamil Homsi noted that investors in OZs should be willing to trade off some return for the potential to really make a difference in communities that lack access to capital. He believes it is unrealistic to expect OZ investing to yield high returns because the purpose of the legislation that created it is to help disadvantaged communities. OZs are a great way for investors to give back to communities that need help, he believes. "Opportunity zone investing is a place where you compromise and invest partly for love and partly for money," Homsi said. For investors with diversified portfolios, an investment in a QOF for social impact represents a small portion of their overall assets. Serious impact investors are willing to trade higher returns for high impact when investing in OZs because this type of investment would represent a portion of a well-diversified portfolio. Some investment will have higher returns with lower impact, and others will have higher impact with slightly lower returns.

As more investors want to create impact with their capital, there are increasing opportunities for investors to invest private capital in low-income communities. Take Enterprise Community Investment, which strives to create affordable housing and connect the disadvantaged to opportunity through private investment. This company, based in Columbia, Maryland, has invested $43.6 billion, helping create 585,000 homes.[287] Since 1982, the organization has used asset management, a community loan fund, conventional equity, development, grants, housing credit investments, new markets tax credits, and other strategies to make a significant difference in the lives of millions.

Square Roots leverages innovative advanced hydroponic technology and an indoor growing platform to provide fresh food without the carbon footprint of big agriculture.[288] By focusing on sustainable cultivation practices, Square Roots uses less water and less land, revitalizes neighborhoods, and creates well-paying jobs. Indoor farming creates a reliable supply chain regardless of the weather, allowing the company to deliver farm to table fresh produce within 24 hours of packing. Square Roots is the face of sustainable, non-farm based agriculture.

Foundations are a natural partner for OZ stakeholders. Innovative foundations are stepping up and funding OZ initiatives designed to improve distressed communities, provide returns to investors, and track investment impact. The Rockefeller Foundation and the Kresge Foundation for example, committed $25 million in grants and unfounded guarantees to QOFs with the most compelling proposals for fulfilling those three objectives. Unfounded guarantees are a type of impact investment under which these foundations would assume losses in the event of a failed fund investment.[289]

The Beeck Center for Social Impact and Innovation at Georgetown University was tasked with reviewing the 150 submissions and will report out data designed to help investments and fund managers evaluate QOFs as a vehicle for impact investing. Rockefeller and Kresge decided to move forward with 21 of the funds that made proposals. These grants will be used to strengthen fund structure, offerings, and impact standards. Community foundations are uniquely situated to facilitate collaboration between OZ stakeholders as they understand community needs, are deeply connected to local officials and business leaders and have access to capital. Potential roles that foundations can fulfill in facilitating impactful OZ activity include sponsoring local start-up incubators and accelerators, bringing together stakeholders, helping set local agendas, creating awareness of the potential impact of OZ investing, and involving local residents.[290]

In a report "How Philanthropies Leverage OZs," Knight Foundation notes that "…it is clear that philanthropies have a critical role in helping cities realize the full economic and social impact of Opportunity Zones. Foundations often possess the community legitimacy necessary to convene disparate urban stakeholders around hard challenges and intriguing possibilities. They have the discretionary capital necessary to make investments in community development enterprises and other local institutions so that these organizations can leverage Opportunity Zones. They have the patient, risk-tolerant capital necessary to invest in QOFs, aligned funds, or individual transactions. They have the respect for evidence-driven decision making that is conducive to catalyze, capture, codify, and communicate new norms and models as they emerge."[291]

QOFs have a major role to play in impact investing. That's because investing in OZ is, by definition, impact investing. The question that QOFs and their investors must ask themselves is how committed they are to making an impact through their OZ investments. Is the social change that these communities desperately need the priority? Or is making a profit, getting out, and moving onto the next investment the top priority? A partnership between the Federal Reserve Bank of New York, The U.S. Impact Investing Alliance, and the Beeck Center at Georgetown University is focusing on sustainable approaches that QOFs can employ to ensure that they achieve the outcome that OZ legislation intended, which is creating positive economic and social outcomes. To that end, these organizations recommend an approach that stresses guiding principles that facilitate effective and equitable investment and implementation, reporting frameworks that promote impact investments at scale and measuring outcomes beneficial to all stakeholders.

Structuring and Evaluating Social Impact Investments

A bedrock principal of impact investing is to add more value than you extract from a community. You want a win-win for both your investors and the community you are investing in, which is entirely possible if you go about it the right way. The Working World, which builds cooperative businesses in low income countries,[222] structures deals by first helping grow wealth for the companies who receive an investment and then lowering risks so that the fund is protected for future projects within the larger community, according to Simon in *Real Impact*. Companies receiving investments are closely supported through small initial investments, the creation of a detailed business plan and timeline and ongoing monitoring of the business plan and investment repayment. Simon further notes in *Real Impact* that The Working World criteria for investment dictates that repayments must come from a productive output of the investments. In other words, if the investment is ineffective at helping the cooperative gain profitability, no repayment is due. This moves the risk to the investor, rather than just the receiver of the investment, creating a strong incentive for investor due diligence and support. The Working World also lives by the stipulation that the cooperative it invests in must receive a greater return than the investor. As Simon notes in *Real Impact*, "Like any tool, capital is useless unless human hands pick it up and build something with it." Cooperatives receiving investments must put significant effort into executing their business plan. Because cooperative members receive a substantial benefit from The Working World financing, they are usually more motivated to work hard so that the cooperative's business succeeds." Simon further noted: "Intimately tying investor and worker success, while ultimately prioritizing the asset accumulation of workers, serves to both motivate the workers and ensure their fair treatment while still ensuring that investors benefit from enhanced profitability." However, in cases where cooperative members fail to put in the necessary "sweat equity," The Working World can repossess equipment that it funded to get some of its capital back to invest in other businesses.

The Working World financed an employee purchase of Republic Windows and Doors in Chicago, which reopened as New Era Windows in May of 2013.[293] In 2008, the same workers occupied the Republic Windows and Doors factory after being told their plant would close with no notice. Later, when the workers were again subject to a mass layoff in 2013 by a different owner, the workers collaborated with The Working World to form a new company and cooperative completely owned by the workers.[294] "We decided to make a co-op because we were tired of our life being in someone else's hands," said window maker Melvin "Ricky" Macklin.[295] "To save money, workers shifted equipment from the old factory building to a cheaper new location by themselves in 80 tractor trailer loads," according to *The Nation*. "This coop is one of 25 that The Working World has financed here in the United States during the past several years without any losses," according to Simon.

Impact investing possesses the potential to transform OZ barren, poverty-stricken communities to thriving neighbornou where Americans of all ethnicities and backgrounds can prosper. This type of investing fulfills the intention of OZ legislation as laid out by Congress in the 2017 TCJA. Investors who truly invest for impact can ensure that OZs live up to their potential and break the toxic impact of inequality in America.

Developing a Social Impact Framework

Because OZ legislation didn't include accountability or reporting frameworks, the onus is on QOFs and their investors to create transparency and accountability around their OZ investments. The U.S. Impact Investing Alliance, the Beeck Center for Social Impact + Innovation at Georgetown University, and the Federal Reserve Bank of New York convened a series of round tables to discuss how to ensure that OZ investment results in economic development that will benefit communities, facilitating well-paying jobs, and affordable housing.

The Beeck Center and the U.S. Impact Investing Alliance followed those discussions with the creation of a model framework that stakeholders can use to evaluate the investments undertaken by QOF managers.[296] This framework offers guiding principles designed to steer investments and implementation, a reporting framework with common core criteria, and flexible additions as well as customizable outcome measurements. Guiding principles center around criteria designed to realize the potential of OZs to combat income inequality. To create robust principles, QOF managers need to engage with the community and integrate their needs into the objectives of the fund. QOF investments should attempt to generate equitable community benefits and create responsible exists. Managers who stay transparent and hold themselves accountable will employ processes that are fair and clear. QOFs should also commit to monitor, track, and measure progress against impact objectives and share those results with other stakeholders.

These best practices framework begins with a statement of a QOF's investment and community engagement intention. The QOF should state its geographic focus, intended investment focus, target investment size, and impact objective as well as basic fund demographics. The QOF should be transparent as to how large it is, how much there is in the fund in eligible deferred gain assets, the types of investors in the QOF, where those investors live and what the QOF's structure is. Your QOF should define its community engagement parameters by providing public notices of any development, discussing how it will assess community needs and plans to engage with the local community. There should also be a disclosure of any collaboration with local non-governmental agencies, such as community foundations and how the QOF is furthering regional economic development strategies. Core community impact should be defined by the jobs, entrepreneurship, affordable housing, and infrastructure improvements. Drilling down into the jobs aspect of community impact, the framework recommends evaluating jobs by the number of employees, net new jobs created, net number of employees from low and moderate income communities and employment of targeted disadvantaged groups. Jobs should also be measured by the number of job created that pay more than $25.00 per hour and offer benefits. These jobs should also put employees on the path to wealth building rather than leaving them mired in poverty. When analyzing business starts, consideration should be given to the types of industries, the percentage of women, or minority-owned enterprises and percentage of first-time business owners. Affordable housing should be measured by the net new number of affordable units, number of net additional individuals housed, percentage of affordable units, and number of affordable units renovated.

The best outcomes lead to lasting community impact the form of responsible exits where all stakeholders b wealth creation. As I've stressed, impact investing works b investors leave more in a community that they take ou. strategies should be considered at the beginning of a spe investment, not at the end. When creating an exit strategy, QOF managers should employ approaches such as shareholder first right of refusal, employee stock ownership plans, and management continuity, the Beeck Center and the U.S. Impact Investing Alliance framework adds. Reassuring OZ stakeholders and community members of your commitments to the community by issuing a broad commitment to preserving community wealth is suggested. Finally, the framework strongly suggests the adoption of transparent outcomes reporting, stating, "QOF managers should commit to working forthrightly and transparently with independent evaluators and researchers on reporting."[297] As I mentioned in the qualified opportunity fund chapter, analysis and reporting on outcomes can add to a collective understanding of the local economic impact of your QOF's investments. A reporting framework should include impact goals, intended impact, community engagement, and post-exit reporting.

In an article published in *Barron's Magazine*, Fran Seegull, executive director of the Alliance, notes that the premise behind OZ legislation "will only meet its objective of achieving positive economic and social outcomes for these communities if we understand where funds are flowing and how capital is helping drive positive social and economic change."[298] Four U.S. Senators, Cory Booker, Tim Scott, Maggie Hassan, and Todd Young, introduced bipartisan legislation in the Senate in May to restore and strengthen reporting requirements that were stripped out of OZ legislation in 2017. The bill would direct the U.S. Treasury Department to collect a variety of data from QOFs to assess the impact on underserved communities and would be reported to Congress annually.[299]

Building a Social Impact Start-Up

OZs are natural homes for entrepreneurs seeking to drive social change through start-ups. The World Economic Forum offers strategies for start-up founders interested in social entrepreneurship that can easily be applied to OZ start-up founders.[300] They advise starting off by figuring out what societal problems you want to solve and how to solve them. Once you develop a simple solution, get feedback. Work hard, record and accept feedback, remain confident, and move through setbacks. Collaborate with others and empower them to execute your vision. Finally, scale up your solution to create a catalyst for social change. You can also follow many of the steps I outlined in Chapter 7 about capital raising.

There are more inspiring examples of social entrepreneurs than you might think. While starting any type of business is grueling work with no guarantee of success, creating a business that you really believe in makes the grind more worthwhile. Consider Cody Friesen, an associate professor at Arizona State University, who invented innovative solar panels that use air and humidity to create clean drinking water.[301] Winner of the Lemelson-MIT Prize, Friesen is a serial entrepreneur focused on renewable energy technology.[302] His earlier inventions include the world's first and only rechargeable metal-air battery, which is now sold through NantEnergy after Friesen exited.[303] Metal air batteries are high energy density batteries that can store energy from renewable energy, offering the potential to create batteries for cars and other types of mechanized equipment. His second entrepreneurial venture, Zero Mass Water, was established to deliver clean drinking water to residents of 33 countries in six continents through his new invention.[304] The solar panels that provide the cleaning drinking water are known as SOURCE Hydropanels. They are employed across the world in schools in Mexico, Syrian refugee camps in Lebanon, and Jordan and in fire stations in Puerto Rico after Hurricane Maria, according to MIT. In an effort to encourage social impact entrepreneurship, Friesen founded the Arizona State University Innovation Open. This student start-up competition awards $250,000 annual in prize money. As part of his efforts to create sustainable water supplies across the globe, he donated the prize money from receiving the Lemelson-MIT prize to Conservation International, which will provide SOURCE Hydropanels to a Bahia Honduras community in Columbia.[305]

Zack Rosenberg, founder of SBP, was named one of the World Economic Forum's 2018 Social Entrepreneurs of the Year for building a company that reduces the gap between disaster and recovery.[306] His business facilitates quick recovery from disasters by rebuilding damaged homes in disaster areas at 40 percent of the cost of market rate contractors and in a little more than two months. Rosenberg offers his rebuilding model to other organizations through an open-source model and provides training to non-governmental organizations across the globe to encourage wide adoption.

Conscious Company named 31 social entrepreneurs to watch in 2018. Emily Kirsch, founder and CEO of Powerhouse, a coworking space and venture fund that backs clean-energy entrepreneurs. Powerhouse, founded in 2013, has worked with 58 clean-energy start-ups and organizations that have created hundreds of jobs, generated hundreds of millions of dollars of revenue and raised capital in the millions for start-ups across the country. Located in Oakland, California, Powerhouse is designed to connect start-ups, corporations and investors to create a sustainable American energy system.[307] Impact-oriented coworking spaces and investor networks are a great way to connect with entrepreneurs already sold on impact investing. Impact HUB, with locations around the world, including Oakland, San Francisco, and Los Angeles, CA; London, UK; Johannesburg, South Africa; Singapore; and Oaxaca, Mexico, is a coworking space and event venue for start-ups who want to create positive impact.

Impact HUB is designed to educate and support start-up founders with innovative programs, access to thought leaders and connections with other start-up founders with the goal of creating a better world. Through frequent events, large coworking spaces, free trade beverages, and snacks, Impact HUB facilitates connections between start-up founders in the hope of creating a better world. Another impact-oriented network is the Business Alliance for Local Living Economies, which represents a consortium of communities, entrepreneurs, businesses, and investors who seek to create local communities that work for everyone.[308] The Social Enterprise Alliance seeks to facilitate social entrepreneurs, who start businesses designed to foster positive social change.[309] This organization holds a yearly summit, offers a mentorship program and offers chapters in 17 cities, including Tampa, FL, Chicago, IL, San Francisco, CA, and New York City. The organization also offers webinars on topics such as Crowdfunding for Social Entrepreneurs, Digital Marketing, Social Media for Social Impact, and Social Finance. Arcus, formerly Regalii, which began as a platform through which immigrants could inexpensively send remittances to relatives in Latin America, originally raised $146,000 through 34 investors on the WeFunder crowdfunding platform.[310] The company was originally founded at Y Combinator. In the past five years, the company has pivoted several times, now focusing on domestic bill pay operations using virtual cards and tokenization in partnerships with major banks.

Accessing capital is one of the biggest challenges you'll face in terms of getting an impact start-up off the ground. One of the best ways to meet investors interested in investing in your start-up is to join DealConnect Hub, which offers membership discounts for emerging entrepreneurs under thirty years of age who have an OZ or social impact start-up.

Invest in the Future

OZs are already bringing hope to cities like Fresno, CA; Cleveland, OH; and Washington, DC, where community leaders are proactively aligning community goals with attractive projects in designated OZs. Fresno streamlined its zoning code to eliminate barriers to investment in downtown and major transit corridors within OZs.[311] Cleveland hopes to build off areas of growth to spark growth in adjacent, strategic commercial corridors in distressed neighborhoods.[312] Washington DC is promoting investment in a large number of tracts zoned for institutional use by contributing public land and financing in specific areas to ensure job opportunities for local residents and businesses.[313] These and many other use cases that I've mentioned in this book demonstrate how OZs can truly represent an inflection point in combating inequality in America. As the Urban Institute notes, OZs possess the potential to become "the nation's largest economic development program."[314]

This potential can be fulfilled when OZs, QOFs, OZ businesses, community foundations, business leaders, entrepreneurs, communities, and other stakeholders collaborate to address economic inequality with investments that provide opportunity for all. Through ongoing investment, communities can ultimately transform from those on government-benefit life support to those that offer everyone wealth-building opportunities. When the viscous cycle of inequality is broken from within, communities can truly prosper. Driven by impact investing, OZs can truly benefit from the tax incentives included in the 2017 TCJA, transforming distressed communities into areas where residents can gain dignity and upward mobility.

CONCLUSION

Like many opportunity zone communities, the economy of Erie, Pennsylvania, has been locked in a downward spiral. It's a familiar story—good jobs moving south, leaving behind low-paying service jobs and a community desperate for better times. While a downtown revitalization plan successfully plays up the city's location on the Lake Erie Bayfront, decaying industrial buildings circle the city, echoing the reality that the city's economic prosperity evaporated decades ago. The city has lost more than 30 percent of its population since the 1960s, while its percentage of residents living below the federal poverty rate is nearly twice the national average.[315] Attempts to spark revitalization with a pedestrian-friendly downtown mall and an airport-based transportation hub failed. Now, with the community's economic future at stake, Erie is making great strides to capitalize on its OZs as way forward to building a more prosperous economic future.

Before launching the Flagship OZ, the city's economic development agency, Erie's economic development leaders carefully studied other Midwestern cities that have reinvented themselves. Then, they created the Erie Innovation District, designed to stem brain drain, revitalize downtown, and replace low-wage jobs with sustainable employment. The district launched the Secure Erie Accelerator, a program that brings ten start-ups to Erie each summer for a ten-week boot camp.[316] Primarily focused on the industrial internet of things and the security space, the Secure Erie Accelerator leverages the community's industrial past and Mercyhurst University's expertise in intelligence and cyber security. Major employers and community foundations then created the Erie Downtown Development Corporation and an equity fund to support redevelopment projects. These efforts build a robust base that the city sought to build upon as soon as the ink was dry on the OZ provisions of the 2017 TCJA. OZ legislation offered the potential to accelerate Erie's economic reinvention by bringing in tax-advantaged outside capital. While outside QOFs have been slow to emerge, the city isn't leaving anything to chance. The OZ website is attractive, designed to appeal to investors: "Erie, Pennsylvania has the market momentum, institutional capacity and diverse portfolio that opportunity zone investors are looking for." Describing itself as a "one-stop shop for investors and developers entering the Erie market for the first time," officials encourage investors to contact them to "help you identify deal flow, identify local QOFs, connect with developers and investment grade business opportunities."

Erie's base in industrial manufacturing, advantages in healthcare and education, reasonable cost of living, and proximity to recreation should help boost its case for OZ capital. The Lake Erie College of Osteopathic Medicine, with more than 4,000 students spread across several campuses, is the country's largest medical school.[317] Erie also sits on Lake Erie and offers the only sand beaches in Pennsylvania on Presque Isle State Park. Pittsburgh, Cleveland, Buffalo, and Canada are within a two-hour drive. These advantages, along with a below-average cost of living, should help Erie's boost its case for OZ capital.

Local companies and economic development agencies are investing in the city, including $150 million of OZ projects in the city core.[318] However, despite all that the community has staked on OZs and the head start it has in terms of its approach to the process, Erie, like virtually all other Tier-2 and Tier-3 cities, is struggling to build momentum in its quest to raise capital from outside investors and QOFs. There are a number of reasons for this situation. Many investors fear that investing in Tier-2 and Tier-3 OZ communities could result in below market rate returns. Before they invest, they want to see more outside investors and capital flowing into OZs. It's a catch-22—without significant outside investment, investors won't move first. However, without some investors taking a chance and starting to invest, there will never be enough capital to make a difference in cities such as Erie. Erie's economic development officials report that even impact investors are reluctant to invest. Apparently, these investors state that the projects they've seen aren't compelling enough and don't promise enough in potential returns, which makes me wonder if they are actually impact investors or if they are engaging in impact washing. Erie's economic development leaders believe their projects meet impact criteria. The lack of deal flow feeds this fear of moving first. Because investors have no visibility into what other investors are doing, they aren't willing to take a chance on being the first—or only—investor in a Tier-2 or Tier-3 OZ. Widespread deal flow would help unlock the log-jam of investor capital, creating genuine first-mover advantage. First-mover advantage means scooping up the best deals early and getting favorable prices and terms on business and real estate deals. Once deal flow is unlocked, a bandwagon effect is created, with more investors investigating deals and closing them. There's one last issue that may cause problems for OZs in certain states—the issue of whether their state conforms to federal Internal Revenue Code rules on OZs. When an OZ is located in a state that doesn't conform to these rules, investors in those OZs may owe state capital gains taxes on their OZ profits either at the personal level, corporate level, or both. Fortunately, most states conform to the Internal Revenue code rules on OZs. There's also the possibility that non-conforming states will decide to conform. Whether this happens or not is up to the state legislatures of individual non-conforming states.

The issue of whether Tier-2 and Tier-3 OZ communities offer the potential for higher returns seems pretty clear-cut to me. I believe that there's ample potential for higher returns precisely because so many projects in distressed communities are available at pennies on the dollar. Think New York City in the 1980s—more on that later. Because OZ investment deals are available at such attractive rates, the potential for absolute returns for communities can be quite high. Imagine the compounding effect when subsequent investors pile on and create new clusters of investment. As these investments build on each other, DealConnect Hub will light up, guiding even more investors to visualize and track investments in specific OZs.

The lack of external investment in OZs such as Erie, PA and Baltimore, MD, demonstrates that communities such as these still have more work to do. Economic development leaders in Tier-2 and Tier-3 cities must convince investors that their investment deals offer either a high return or high impact or a combination of both. That means economic development agencies should be working double time to assure investors that they are taking the lead in building investor momentum and interest by publicizing their efforts and acting as a hub for local deals. Investors want to know that the OZ communities are active and have skin in the game, which is an important sign of commitment. I've detailed the steps that OZ leaders can take to encourage investment in Chapter 5. The strongest recommendation I would make is to start an accelerator or incubator program, if there isn't one in place already. A commitment to incubators and accelerators creates an innovation ecosystem that builds on itself. Involving local business leaders, an OZ's economic development team, university professors, and start-up experts provides the support that start-ups need to succeed. Once an incubator or accelerator program is established, companies that graduate from the program usually stay local, growing and creating jobs while contributing back to the OZ's emerging start-up culture.

Establishing an innovation ecosystem—along with the other steps I detail in Chapter 5—will go a long way toward convincing reluctant investors to invest in OZs as an alternative to all the other options available. As I've mentioned repeatedly, raising capital is a highly competitive business. Every day family offices, high-net-worth investors, and wealth managers are deluged with new investment opportunities. These opportunities span the investment universe, from private equity to VC to traditional stocks and bonds, gold and commodities and so on. OZs are one tiny sliver of a large investment universe. However, they are a compelling alternative for the right investors, those who prefer value plays with large upside. Imagine the potential returns for investing in a beaten-down community at pennies on the dollar as the economic turnaround gains momentum and that community reinvents itself. You're talking Miami in 2008 or New York City in 1985.

Consider the profits that investors in New York City real estate and businesses reaped who took a chance on a broken-down and nearly bankrupt city in the 1970s and 1980s. New York City hit rock bottom in 1975 when its debts exceeded its assets by hundreds of millions of dollars.[319] Behind the debt crisis were extensive local welfare benefits, the recession of the mid-1970s, middle-class flight to the suburbs, rising crime and industrial decline. The city narrowly avoided default, despite the federal government's refusal of aid.[320] During the 1970s, real estate prices in New York City declined by an average of 12.4 percent.[321] Several boom and bust periods followed, but overall real estate prices increased by 250 percent between 1974 and 2006.[322] In the ten years since the financial crisis, New York City housing prices have increased by 30 percent.[323]

These are just averages, but imagine replicating the feat of buying real estate in New York City at a low, holding and then selling without paying any taxes on your capital gains—this is the potential that many OZ communities possess. With many OZ investments, there's the chance to profit on an early-stage start-up as well as the real estate that the start-up occupies. Because as a company gets larger and gains value, it's likely that any property that it owns will get more valuable too, increasing the overall value of your investment. In addition, any stand-alone real estate investments are also likely to appreciate as a community's economy gains ground and property values rise.

When the next recession ultimately strikes, investors will be faced with a choice of investing their capital gains in traditional safety sectors, such as gold and Treasury bonds, bills or notes, or in the new asset class of OZs. It's unlikely that Treasuries will appreciate much more than they already have, given that interest rates have already been cut three times in 2019. Gold isn't an investment that yields ongoing income—it's generally a store holder of wealth used to preserve gains and act as a hedge against inflation. If Shiller is correct about future returns, relative performance will be low over the next thirty years—on average 4 percent a year. Compared with those potential returns, investing in businesses and real estate in Tier-2 and Tier-3 cities can yield phenomenal returns, just like investments in New York City in 1985. Dalio's views outlined in Chapter 2 support this case, because OZ investing will put capital in the hands of the bottom 60 percent of communities by investing in companies that will produce well-paying jobs that will enable people to afford decent housing and the potential to build wealth. The bottom-up approach of investing in OZ businesses and real estate at bargain basement prices will do even better if a catalyst appears that will further increase value. This investing approach builds value not only for the investors and QOFs who do the investing, but also for the communities, residents, and other OZ stakeholders involved.

Every investor should consider what might happen to tax rates should the economy fall into recession and the portion of society that ranks as have-nots continues to grow in size. As investment returns plummet in a recession, local and state tax rates typically go up to make up for the loss of tax revenues that local governments experience. In addition, municipalities reassess real estate periodically, which usually leads to real estate tax increases. Frequently, these reassessments place higher values on real estate at a time when real estate prices are falling, placing a major tax burden on tax payers at a time when their incomes are getting squeezed. A recession coupled with the already enormous wealth gap can lead to a rise in protests such as the Occupy Wall Street movement that occurred in 2011–2012, following the financial crisis. Protests that can influence the make-up of Congress and state legislatures during a recession might lead to significantly higher tax rates for wealthy individuals and corporations. If you're an investor, entrepreneur or high-net-worth individual who has capital gains to invest, now is the time to invest in OZs to avoid these potential scenarios. That's because the alternative solution is the government wastefully deploying your tax dollars for you, just as it did in spending $1.7 billion on building the Obamacare website.[324] Then there's the issue of the Pentagon losing track of $1 trillion through accounting errors.[325] Although on the surface, taxing the wealthy sounds like a great idea to solve America's wealth inequality, the problem is the government is clearly wasteful with your taxes and is even worse at deploying money to the people that the taxes were intended to help. It is more efficient for wealthy individuals to deploy their capital into OZs to create wealth and prosperity for American's in the bottom 60 percent than to waste it through taxation where everyone loses. At some point, those that have benefitted from American capitalism need to offer a helping hand to the millions who are still struggling. I encourage all investors to seriously consider investing in OZs for positive social impact. If OZs take off, many will benefit, including communities, investors, developers, entrepreneurs, and start-ups. Once there's positive evidence that impact investing in OZs works, developers, entrepreneurs and start-ups will be inspired to use what they've learned about raising capital to make impact investments that build wealth for everyone.

Invest in Real Businesses, Not in Unprofitable Tech Unicorns

If there's an investment type that's the antithesis of OZs, that would be many of the speculative money-losing ventures that have failed to make a profit during the past decade. Theranos, the blood testing start-up founded by Elizabeth Holmes, is a perfect example. After raising $700 on the promise of diagnosing diseases with a simple finger prick, Theranos was exposed as a fraud.[326] Venture capitalists sunk millions into Theranos, revealing a flawed capital raising model where typically the only potential winners are the initial investors and the company's owners.[327] However in this example, it backfired and investors lost money in Theranos. At the height of its valuation, Theranos was valued at $9 billion, but as the scandal around the company grew, that valuation along with the company's credibility was erased. This negatively impacted early investors, including Tim Draper of the VC firm Draper Fisher Jurvetson, Trump administration Education Secretary Betsy DeVos, Walmart founding family the Waltons, Rupert Murdoch, Cox Enterprises, and Mexican tycoon Carlos Slim.[328] The Silicon Valley capital raising model places an immense amount of pressure on valuations and growth, while start-up founders scramble to cut corners and falsify results to justify those valuations.

Startups that lack the potential to ever make a profit are sucking up more capital to the detriment of businesses that actually have a legitimate chance to succeed and employ Americans at a living wage. "At the same time as money is essentially free for those who have money and credit worthiness, it is essentially unavailable to those who don't have money and creditworthiness, which contributes to the rising wealth, opportunity and political gaps," Dalio wrote in a LinkedIn article entitled The World Has Gone Mad and the System is Broken. He continued, "...the 'trickle-down' process of having money at the top trickle down to workers and others by improving their earnings and creditworthiness is not working, the system of making capitalism work well for most people is broken."[329] The last time so few IPOs were profitable was in 1999, at the end of the Dotcom bubble.[330] Apparently, the lessons from that $5 trillion bust weren't taken to heart.[331] Venture capitalists, start-up founders, and American culture at large exhibits a fascination with money-losing unicorns, which Matt Stoller, author of *Goliath: The 100 Year War Between Monopoly Power and Democracy* (Simon and Schuster, 2019), characterizes counterfeit capitalism."[332] Counterfeit capitalism describes the practice of investing large amounts of capital in money-losing operations with the intent of dominating a particular category. That dominance is achieved through predatory pricing, which drives competitors out of entire categories of businesses by underpricing goods and services. This pricing strategy can only be maintained when a business is sustained by massive amounts of outside capital, supplied by venture capitalists and private equity. This method of financing start-ups is predicated on the belief that the start-up grows to the point where it controls an entire market, pricing can be raised at will. Then, the company will be immensely profitable, because there is no competition and consumers have no choice about where to obtain the services that the company provides.

Eventually, private equity and venture capital investors seek to monetize their investments through exiting from these investments, which is where the initial public offering, or IPO market, comes in. When private investors can offload money-losing companies to the public through an IPO, they have the opportunity to cash out on lucrative terms and transfer any as much of the remaining risk to other investors and employees holding stock options.

"Sustaining money-losing businesses on private or public capital undermines the very premise of capitalism," Stoller said. "Capitalism works because companies that thrive take a bunch of inputs and create a product that is more valuable than the sum of its parts. That creates additional value and in such a model companies have to compete by making better goods and services," Stoller wrote.[333] However, if there is no competition, then the need to create value doesn't exist so financiers can run businesses—and eventually entire economies—based on access to capital. That means the player with the access to the most capital wins by crowding out the competition and engaging in predatory pricing. This mind-set also encourages start-up founders to focus on smoke and mirrors rather than building legitimate profitable businesses, because that's where the big money is. The example of WeWork reveals how damaging this business model is. Adam Neumann, the founder of WeWork, was handsomely awarded with a $1.7 billion exit package to leave the company he grew into a global brand. That global brand ultimately lost $219,000 per hour for a total loss of $1.9 billion in 2018.[334] Does that sound like the type of company that will offer sustainable benefit to America, its workers, and its customers?

After nine years with WeWork, Neumann's net worth is now worth almost half of Howard Schultz's net worth of $4.0 billion,[335] who took nearly forty-eight years to build Starbucks, from a single store located in Seattle into an international brand employing 180,000 people.[336] Starbucks is not only a highly successfully company that has handsomely rewarded its shareholders, it is also known for treating its employees and suppliers fairly. Starbucks has successfully weathered recessions and financial crises. In contrast, WeWork may disappear during the next recession, when its customers abandon their short-term desk leases and return to working from home or from the many Starbucks locations rent free.

Stoller's ideas about counterfeit capitalism align with other attempts to define capitalism and align it with values—or a lack of values. Oprah's embrace of *"The Secret,"* a book published in 2006, popularized positive thinking and a certain amount of mysticism around capitalism, according to an article published in *The New Yorker*. Mystique and hero-worship about tech and tech entrepreneurs continued to grow throughout the past decade, as the super-wealthy founders, including Bill Gates, Mark Zuckerberg, and Steve Jobs spoke about their roles as callings that would transform society. They created the impression their companies were here to transform society and the economy into something better. This viewpoint embraced a softer, kinder version of capitalism. In 2008, Bill Gates began to speak about creative capitalism at the World Economic Forum in Davos in 2008.[337] As inequality has risen and social division has increased, more companies, and celebrities are talking about ways to reinvent capitalism. Obviously, that's a major focus of impact investing—to reinvent capitalism as a way to banish poverty, global warming, and other challenges. The Conference Board, a roundtable of executives from America's top companies, recently asserted a need for "sustaining capitalism," which seeks improved education and infrastructure as well as fiscal discipline. In an article published in *The Chicago Tribune*, the Committee for Economic Development of The Conference Board wrote, "'Sustaining capitalism' also calls for greater vigilance against crony capitalism—a corruption that both business and government leaders must reject if they want their pro-capitalism preaching to be believed. CEOs can build on this road map, identify our capitalistic system as in need of ongoing maintenance and improvement, and assert that what is good for America is ultimately good for the economy and business."[338] Then there's Marc Benioff, CEO of Salesforce, who placed what he calls "compassionate capitalism" at the center of his bestselling book, *Trailblazer: The Power of Business as the Greatest Platform for Change* (Currency, 2019). There's more and more widespread support for capitalism as a force for good, instead as a vehicle for making as much money as possible, regardless of the impact on the planet, people, and other living beings.

Clearly, Starbucks is the type of business that exemplifies the best side of capitalism, while Theranos and many others represent it' dark side. OZs were designed to build on the best side of capitalism, the potential for it to be a force of good, and positively impact the lives of millions who have been excluded from its benefits to date. Bad examples of capitalism distract investors and start-up founders from the real endeavor of investing in and building companies and products that improve people's lives, make profits, and contribute to society. Imagine the good that all the capital that has been poured into money losing ventures such as Theranos could do in businesses that were actually making a profit, paying employees a living wage and making a positive contribution to society. Imagine if even a tenth of the capital that was wasted on all the money-losing companies that have come to the markets in the last 25 years was invested in communities like Erie, PA and Birmingham, AL through OZs. The communities, investors, residents, and beneficiaries of this capital would be engaged in the productive and profitable endeavor of building wealth, together. If capital was actually invested in communities across the country instead of being concentrated among the privileged few, consumers would be actually able to afford an appropriate price for services such as coworking and ride sharing. Leveraging OZs as an instrument to more fairly distribute the rewards of capitalism and create a more level playing field is what this book is all about. OZs deserve a chance to do what they were built to do—rebuild communities to give their residents an equal shot at building wealth for their families.

Opportunity Zones as a Value Investing Play

For family offices and private equity investors who wisely avoid chasing unprofitable tech unicorns, Tier-2 and Tier-3 cities such as Waterbury, CT, and Greenville, SC, stand out as potential home runs via a value investing play. Instead of moving into gold and U.S. Treasury bonds, bills, and notes when the inevitable recession occurs, moving capital from the stock market to OZs is a strong value investment opportunity. "The whole idea of investing is to lay out money now to get more money back later," said Warren Buffett. "If you buy a farm or business or an apartment building, you expect it to appreciate and generate income. However, you could buy all the gold in the world, but it's not going to produce anything. People like gold because they hope that someone will buy it from them for a higher price in the future."[339] Buffett offered this example about the value of tangible assets in comparison to gold to Berkshire Hathaway shareholders: "If you take all of the gold in the world, which is 165 metric tons, and put it all together that would result in a cube 67 feet long. At present prices that gold is selling for $7 trillion. Compare that to the value of the entire stock market in the United States, which is worth about $20 trillion. Would you rather have a third of all of the businesses in the United States as an investment or would you rather look at that cube? As another example if you take all of the farmland in the United States, that's about a billion acres of farmland that's a million and a half square miles, about half of the land in the United States. You add in seven Exxon Mobiles and leave yourself $1 trillion for walking around incidentals. That adds up to the value of that cube of gold. Would you rather have that 67-foot cube or would rather have all the farmland in the United States, plus seven Exxon Mobiles, plus $1 trillion to stick in your pocket? I think that's an easy decision. But people like their gold. When they get afraid of money, terrified of money, they run to gold and hope that someone will pay more for it next year because it isn't going to produce anything. That cube is just going to sit there and stare at you. If you own it you can fondle it you can sit on top of it do whatever makes you feel good, but it's not going to deliver anything to you."[340]

In contrast to gold, OZ investing is designed to produce income and price appreciation. OZ investing is open to all investors and individuals with capital gains to reinvest, including lawyers, doctors, architects, athletes, and entertainers.

In *Margin of Safety: Risk-Averse Value Investing for the Thoughtful Investor* (Harper Collins, 1991) billionaire hedge fund manager Seth Klarman writes, "Because investing is as much an art as a science, investors need a margin of safety. A margin of safety is achieved when securities or equities are purchased at prices sufficiently below underlying value to allow for human error, bad luck or extreme volatility in a complex, unpredictable and rapidly changing world."[341] The optimal method for achieving a margin of safety is to invest in undervalued assets. OZs are essentially distressed undervalued assets. Therefore, viewing real estate and business investments through the lens of distressed—or value—investing brings an entirely different perspective to this ignored corner of OZ investing. Because the capital that has already flowed into OZs was mainly invested in real estate in Tier-1 cities, business investments, and developments in Tier-2 and Tier-3 cities have largely been ignored. As I finish writing this book, it is estimated that starting in 2017 only $2 billion has been raised to deploy to OZs. In fact, just two companies, WeWork[342] and Uber,[343] have raised a combined $46 billion more than all of the OZs in America. To make the point even more somber, Uber lost $5.2 billion in the second quarter of 2019 alone.[344] Ultimately investors will start to come to their senses and realize that they have risked their capital on a few grandiose corporate dreams that have no clear path to profitability over investing with diversification in OZs that possess significant margins of safety and potential for substantial profits.

Viewing investment in distressed OZs in cities such as St. Louis, MO, and Columbia, SC, provides a similar entry point that investing in New York City did in 1985. Tier-2 and Tier-3 cities are where value investors—or those who decide to adopt a value investing philosophy—can gain an edge. That advantage comes in the form of investing in undervalued assets that offer the potential for outsized returns. Value investing focuses strictly on absolute performance and ignores relative performance. Value investors avoid the forecasting game altogether because they focus on the fundamental analysis of a potential deal, a strategy that aims to "buy at a bargain and wait." This is the perfect investment strategy for OZ investing, because investors have to hold their investments for at least five and ten years respectively to take advantage of all the tax incentives. It also takes time for OZ businesses to mature and yield significant profits. That means that once an attractive deal is discovered, time is on the side of the investor.

Klarman emphasizes this point in his book: "The securities owned by value investors are not buoyed by such high expectations. To the contrary, they are usually unheralded or just ignored. In depressed financial markets, it is said, some securities are so out of favor that you cannot give them away."[345] That's currently the case with Tier-2 and Tier-3 OZs. There's significant potential for price appreciation as OZ investing gains momentum. Even if you are the first investor in an OZ, if you've correctly evaluated the fundamentals of the deals you're investing in as well as the potential of the OZ to gain traction with other investors, you're more likely to fair much better than the many OZ investors who play it safe with luxury real estate investments in Tier-1 cities.

Benjamin Graham and Warren Buffett, two other famous proponents of value investing, are also firm believers in a fundamental approach to evaluating investment opportunities. "Price is what you pay. Value is what you get," Buffett famously said. All too often, investors blow their money on what seems like a great growth investment opportunity, only to later find out that the initial price was inflated and that there's really not much value there. WeWork and its investors are a perfect example of a growth investment "opportunity" gone wrong. Investing isn't a popularity contest and it's not about picking the one perfect opportunity. It's also not about focusing on the day-to-day price of an asset. As Buffett told CNBC, "It is the business that I look at. When you are just looking at price of something you're not investing. If you buy something bitcoin or cryptocurrency, you're really not looking at an asset that will produce anything. But if you buy an apartment building or a business, you need to look at how the business is going perform."[346]

Value investing focuses on fundamental analysis, not speculation, price, or popularity. Instead, as Graham puts it, "The stock investor is neither right nor wrong because others agreed or disagreed with him; he is right because his facts and analysis are right."[347] Fear of being first is understandable. However, investors who fail to take advantage of investing in OZs may miss out on one of the most profitable and impactful investment opportunities in generations.

That's why it makes sense for investors interested in OZs to persevere in finding the deals that align with their niche and geographical preferences. Consider how a smaller investment at the right time in a city such as Round Rock, TX, or Cleveland, OH, can make a major difference to the local economy, encouraging other investors to follow suit and invest. In Erie, Pennsylvania, local business leaders, foundations, and the community has already committed significant capital and resources to set the table for success. So far their accelerator has worked with 20 security and tech start-ups. One of those companies may be the next Fortinet, a leading cybersecurity company with $2.15 billion in revenue, specializing in firewalls, endpoint security, and intrusion prevention.[348] There are a multitude of solid investment deals in Tier-2 and Tier-3 cities from Maine to California. Through DealConnect Hub, you have the chance to view multiples lucrative deals; do some due diligence and determine which opportunities are the best fit for your particular investment niche and style.

Bringing America Together

In the absence of change, communities will continue to stagnate, inequality will continue to grow and unprofitable companies will continue to reap the benefits of capital investment while profitable alternatives are overlooked. In this scenario, sooner, rather than later, the next recession will come. Eventually, it will force investors to make a choice. They can either start the process all over again by investing in money-losing start-ups, by perpetuating the system that has created so much division and so many problems. Or, they can make a different choice—invest in OZ related deals with the potential to bring wealth and prosperity to all stakeholders across the United States. It's time to offer a helping hand to those who haven't had the chance to participate in the equity side of American capitalism by investing in OZs. With capital behind them, start-up founders and developers will have the chance to grow their businesses, offer stable and well-paying employment in their communities and build some capital of their own.

Even more significant change can occur when start-ups have an impact investing focus. Consider SolarCity, Tesla Motors, and Revolution Foods, all financed by DBL Partners, an impact venture capital fund. The intersection of OZs and impact investing is timely, as 86 percent of millennials believe that business success should be measured by social impact rather than merely profits. A generation of millennial start-up founders are reaping the benefit of cashing in on success. These investors—and many others—stand to make a real difference by applying their capital gains to QOFs with impact investing objectives. With those funds in hand, OZ businesses can set about tackling the difficult problems we face, including poverty, the inability of millions to afford retirement, rising infant mortality, crumbling infrastructure, and skyrocketing college costs.

The inability to build wealth through investment is what keeps many individuals, families, and communities from succeeding. OZs offer the chance to change that dynamic, so that more people than ever before have the chance to realize the American dream and prosper from American capitalism. OZs offer a way to mend the divisions that have created so much anger, hatred, and inequality. When investors, community leaders, entrepreneurs, and community residents work together on growing businesses through OZ investments, commonalities can be re-established. It's my hope that after reading this book, wealthy investors will realize that struggling residents of inner-city OZs aren't so very different from they were when they were starting out. In the same way, I hope that the residents of those OZs will realize that the investors who seek to rebuild their communities are offering something positive and valuable that will improve their lives. By working together for a common purpose, both the investors and the communities can create a common bond to rebuild cities and counties across the country for a more prosperous and sustainable future.

Through collaboration, at least some of the walls of division can come down, replaced by cooperation. Then, as investment continues to move the needle in these communities, creating jobs, affordable housing, and a sustainable economy, the divide will melt even further. Capitalism will actually rebuild these communities by ensuring that everyone in the process has access to building wealth. Instead of making the rich richer and the poor poorer, the new asset class of OZ investing can be used so that everyone can participate in wealth building. That's what will ultimately stamp out inequality.

Each OZ stakeholder has the chance to contribute to positive change in a unique way:

- Communities can identify promising impact start-ups and key developments

- Business leaders can sponsor incubators and accelerators focused on impact investing

- Entrepreneurs can take aim at the most pressing problems their communities face and create scalable solutions

- Investors can commit to deploying their capital gains with QOFs focused on impact investments

- QOFs can invest time and energy to identify impact entrepreneurs

With all those stakeholders collaborating—maximizing their efforts for OZ success—OZs can finally tap into a significant amount of the $6 trillion in capital gains sitting on the sidelines. That capital, properly invested in promising OZ businesses and developments, can grow start-ups in all industry sectors. Enough to provide communities like Erie with the chance to climb out of 30 years of economic devastation. With even a small cohort of growing companies, those OZs will build on that success, attracting even more capital. That will create a virtuous cycle, as more capital enters the community, creating more businesses, more jobs and more affordable housing along with improved access to education and healthcare. That's *all* it takes to make a difference—to transform a struggling community into a thriving community.

The goal of this book is to provide education and offer investors perspective on the challenges communities and entrepreneurs face due to their lack of access to capital, mentors, and connections. To remedy this challenge, I provide information and resources to communities, developers, QOFs, and start-ups on the best ways to reach out to investors to begin to close the gap that has separated the haves and the have nots for so long. By providing a glimpse of the challenges that I faced over 20 years ago, my goal is to prevent residents of distressed communities from having to experience similar yet unnecessary challenges. By uniting investors with, start-ups, developers, and QOFs, I hope to provide a basis from which they can bridge their differences. America's divisions can't be healed easily or quickly. But through a process of learning about each other and working collaboratively to solve the problems that our society faces, I hope that we can at least begin the process of rediscovering the spirit that has created the most powerful and productive country in the world. We can unite to rebuild our country, by dedicating energy and hard work toward that effort, contributing what each of us as the ability to offer. For investors, that's their capital. For communities, it's their investment in and knowledge of their communities. For start-up founders, it's their ideas and energy. For individuals, it's ensuring that their elected officials and community leaders position their communities to benefit from OZ investment. Consider how the nation's 8,762 OZs could benefit from the hard work of entrepreneurs, backed by investment capital.

Rebuilding both economic and social division is a major theme of this book. It won't be possible to rebuild America unless the gap that separates the haves from the have-nots is repaired at the same Mending the connection between classes can be accomplish through investments in entrepreneurs and businesses as a means to exert transformative impact on the economy and on the country. Rebuilding must happen on a number of levels—beginning at the core, where the broken meritocracy must be democratized to allow all Americans to participate in wealth building. Then, the capital markets, including investors must refocus on funding profitable companies—companies that create products and services that make the world a better place. America and Americans needs the OZ program to succeed—to do its job and rebuild this great country into one where all have an equal chance to build wealth and prosperity.

Educating a very diverse group of OZ stakeholders is only the beginning of the work that needs to be done to enable OZs to reach their full potential. It's now up to you—investors, community leaders, entrepreneurs, community residents, and other stakeholders—to use what you've learned and connect. Get out of your comfort zone and actively work to ensure that your community's OZs reach their full potential. Join the DealConnect Hub network and leverage this tool so that all stakeholders can join together and benefit from the vast investment opportunities across this country. As Gary Vaynerchuk puts is: "You can't just read about push ups. You gotta do them."[349] It's time for everyone to do their part to rebuild America.

CKNOWLEDGEMENTS

I would like to express my most sincere gratitude and appreciation for all those individuals who helped me create this book.

My brother-in-law, Michael Romaniello who first introduced me to the opportunity zone investment initiative. He is the cyber security head and accountant at Lenkowski Lonergan & Co. in Middlebury, Connecticut. Thank you for all your help and contributing your insights and examples as well as working with us to build the top 400 OZ ranking.

Richard Wilson for encouraging me to become a thought leader and pointing me in the direction to write this book. It was at your conferences and events that I connected with the leaders who made tremendous contributions to this book.

My friend, Kamil Homsi Co-Founder and CEO of the GRC Investments Group a single-family office in Dubai/UAE. Thank you for introducing me to numerous members of the family office and wealth management community. I also appreciate the wealth of knowledge you shared on opportunity zone investing on my podcasts and at the many investor networks you attend. The entire opportunity zone community shall flourish from your tireless advocacy regarding the benefits of investing in opportunity zones for positive social impact.

Teresa Esser who is a wealth of knowledge on both entrepreneurship and investing. She is the Managing Partner of

Silicon Pastures an Angel investing network based in Milw WI. She wrote the book *The Venture Café*, one of the comprehensive books on startup culture and what it takes to become a successful entrepreneur. Her contributions to building successful investors ecosystems via the Venture Café model has been replicated across numerous cities. Your model, which you generously shared on my podcast, is one that the opportunity zone communities should embrace to jumpstart investment and entrepreneurship in their communities.

Morgan Simon for your fearless leadership building bridges between finance and social justice. She wrote the book *Real Impact, The New Economics of Social Change.* She is the founding partner of the Candide Group, a social impact investment firm that seeks to foster social benefit alongside financial return. Morgan created a great model and framework for investors to use when evaluating opportunity zone deals for positive social impact, which she kindly shared on my podcast. Your many experiences across the fields of social impact and social justice have provided me with a deeper level of understanding of the work and energy it takes to become a social impact investor.

Ray Dalio for sharing your principles as well as your concerns around the growing wealth gap in America. Thank you for making your economic theories and book *A Template For Understanding Big Debt Crises* available to the public. This book is such an important guide to understanding what principles and actions policy makers, central banks, governments and investors can deploy to navigate future financial crises. Your position on the wealth gap and theory on the limited monetary policy tools during the next financial crisis supports the case for why investing in opportunity zones will be such an important economic tool. Dalio founded Bridgewater Associates and has grown it into the largest hedge fund in the world. Dalio himself has been named to Time magazine's list of the 100 most influential people in the world.

Gary Vaynerchuk for inspiring a new generation of entrepreneurs to adopt an immigrant work ethic and to focus on building startups and solutions that make them happy about waking up in the morning. Your ever-growing positive contributions to shaping the thought process around building a realistic, yet healthy and focused mindset in the pursuit of entrepreneurship is what this country needs. Thank you for all your contributions on the topics of entrepreneurship, grit mentality and success. Your contributions on these topics are much needed and very well appreciated.

My Friend and business attorney, Dave Pite who is always there when needed and without question. I appreciate all your help, generosity and added humor to everything you undertake. I look forward to working with you in the decades to come.

CONTACT INFORMATION

Email: rocco@rocforcap.com

Investment site: https://www.roccoforinocapital.com

DealConnect Hub Site: https://www.dealconnecthub.com

Instagram: https://www.instagram.com/roccoforino

Facebook: https://www.facebook.com/roccoforinocapital

Twitter: https://twitter.com/RocForCap

YouTube: Rocco Forino Capital

Apple Podcasts: https://podcasts.apple.com/us/podcast/the-rocco-forino-show/id1467422006

Soundcloud: https://soundcloud.com/roccoforinocapital

TuneIN: https://tunein.com/podcasts/Business--Economics-Podcasts/The-Rocco-Forino-Show-p1227955/

Stitcher: https://www.stitcher.com/podcast/rocco-forino/the-rocco-forino-show

iHeart Radio: https://www.iheart.com/podcast/269-the-rocco-forino-show-46372238/

Definition Terms

1031 Exchange

This type of sale is named for IRS code 1031, which allows investors to defer paying capital gains on investment properties when they are sold, so long as another "like-kind" property is purchased with the profits gained by the sale. This type of transaction is also known as a "Starker Exchange." (See Starker Exchange.)

70% Test

Real state and qualified opportunity zone businesses are allowed to regard documented working capital as qualified opportunity zone property for up to thirty-one months. A qualified opportunity fund (QOF) must generally hold at least 90 percent of its assets in qualified opportunity zone property and 70 percent of the tangible property "owned or leased" by a business must be qualified opportunity zone property for a business to be considered a qualified opportunity zone business.

90% Test

All qualified opportunity funds (QOFs) must hold at least 90 percent of its assets in qualified opportunity zone properties. These holdings may include qualified opportunity zone stock, qualified opportunity zone partnership interests, or direct investments in businesses which conduct the majority of their operations within a qualified opportunity zone. In order to validate this 90 percent margin, the fund must measure it average percentage of investment semi-annually, at the end of its first six months of operation and again at the end of the year.

Accelerator (Incubator)

Accelerators invest in early-stage start-ups in exchange for business equity, providing coworking space, advice, mentoring, networking, and support so that the start-up can succeed.

Assets

In the context of opportunity zone regulations, qualified assets are defined as:

• Any qualified opportunity zone business property

• A qualified opportunity zone stock, or

• A qualified opportunity zone partnership interest

The program encourages long-term development by making the sale of QOF assets tax-free after a 10-year holding period.[350]

Authority

The ability to establish trust and credibility by attracting or drawing your target audience to you.

Avatar

Represents your ideal target investor or client. When you define your target avatar, you create a detailed persona of your target investor or client. Then you use that avatar to create marketing materials specifically targeted to that person or business.

Basis

Basis has many meanings in finance, but most frequently refers to the difference between the price and expenses in a transaction when calculating taxes. Such usage relates to "cost basis" or "tax basis," and is used when capital gains (or losses) are calculated for income tax filings. A security's basis is the purchase price after commissions or other expenses. It is also known as cost basis or tax basis. This figure is used to calculate capital gains or losses when a security is eventually sold. For example, assume you purchase 1,000 shares of a stock for $8 per share. Your cost basis is equal to the total purchase price, or $8,000.

Blind Pooled Investments

A blind pool is a direct participation program or limited partnership that lacks a stated investment goal for the use of the funds that are raised from investors. In a blind pool, money is raised from investors, usually based on the name recognition of a particular individual or firm. There are usually few restrictions or safeguards in place for investor security. Blind pools are also known as "blank check underwriting" or a "blank check offering."

Capital Gains Deferral

Capital gains tax benefits flowing from opportunity zone investments depend on how long an investment is held. For investments disposed of on or before December 31, 2026, deferred capital gains reinvested in an opportunity zone must be recognized at that point.[351] For qualified opportunity zone businesses or property held for ten years or longer, the sale of such assets is tax free.[352]

Cash Flow

How much money your business or start-up has at the end of the week, month, or financial period after all bills, expenses, and taxes are paid.

Community Foundations

A grant making public charity that is devoted to improving a specific community and the lives of the people who live there.

Cooperative

A business, farm, or other organization operated and controlled by individuals who work for and/or use the products or services produced.

Deal Sponsor

Is generally responsible for bringing capital to a deal as well as supporting the goals and objectives of an individual or company through their various expertise.

Direct Business Investment

An investment of capital in a business enterprise in exchange for an equity stake in this enterprise. Some direct businesses are willing to sell an equity stake in their business in exchange for capital whereas others may want to sell the entire business.

Due Diligence

Due diligence is an investigation or audit of a potential investment or product to confirm all facts, that might include the review of financial records. Due diligence refers to the research done before entering into an agreement or a financial transaction with another party.

Due Diligence Questionnaire

Also known as a DDQ or due diligence checklist that is used to extract information that will improve your chances of getting a deal done if you can respond to the questionnaire promptly and accurately.

Eligible Capital Gain

When investing capital gains in a qualified opportunity fund (QOF), investors can defer paying taxes on any gains until 2026 or eliminate a capital for investments held for ten years or longer. If those investments meet the five- or seven-year holding period requirement, investors receive the exemption. If investors hold the investment for a 10-year period they pay no capital gains on the appreciation from the new capital gain generated by the QOF investment. Eligible capital includes gains received from investments in stocks, bonds, mutual funds, exchange traded funds, real estate, art, cryptocurrency, and other types of investment and real estate.[353] Capital gains eligible for deferral include[354]:

1. Capital gains that are considered a capital gain under federal income tax purposes

2. Capital gains that would be recognized in the absence of the deferral

3. Capital gains that do not involve exchanges with related parties

Empathy

Your ability to understand what your potential customers or employees are going through by seeing challenges through their eyes.

Employee Stock Ownership Program

Also known as ESOPs. A program of ownership investment in which a company's workforce either buys or receives shares in the company that employs them. Companies that offer ESOPs either provide shares in the company to employees as part of their compensation, as incentive compensation, or as part of a program by a company exclusively run by employees.

Environmentally Friendly

Building a business or maintaining a lifestyle that is sustainable and reduces, minimizes or eliminates harm to the ecosystem or environment.

Equity Stake

A percentage of shares in a start-up company held by stock owners. These owners can include the founder, employees, investors, friends, and family members who have all contributed to the start-up's success.

Family Office

A private investment firm set up to serve ultra-high-net-worth individuals and families. These firms offer a customized management solution that takes care of the entirety of these individual's financial and investment needs so that they can actively participate in the management of their money and assets. Many founders of companies that have recently gone public or who sell their businesses set up family offices to manage their new-found wealth.

Form 8996

A corporation or partnership uses Form 8996 to certify that it is organized to invest in qualified opportunity zone properties. Additionally, corporations or partnerships file Form 8996 annually to report that the qualified opportunity zone meets the investment standard of section 1400Z-2 or to figure the penalty if it fails to meet the investment standard.

Grit

Persistence and mental toughness in the face of obstacles without ever giving up in pursuing of the end goal.

High Net Worth

Individuals or families with a net worth of between $1 and $5 million.

Hurdle Rate

The minimum rate of return that a fund manager should generate before he or she can charge a performance fee.

Impact Investing

A type of investing designed to generate financial returns as well as positive and measurable environmental and social impact.

Impact Washing

Using impact investing as window-dressing to get attention and attract capital without the intention of making a meaningful impact with those investments.

Inclusion

For the purposes of opportunity zones, inclusion events occur when investors experience events that trigger capital gains. When these events occur, deferred gains are triggered, meaning they become taxable for the investor. In general, inclusion events are triggered when an investor either cashes out a portion of their investment in a qualified opportunity fund (QOF) by receiving a distribution great than their basis or reduces a direct investment in a qualified opportunity fund.

Income-and-Assets Test

This is simply another term used for the compliance testing required by opportunity zone businesses and qualified opportunity fund (QOF) to verify that the businesses or investments they report as tax deferred, in fact, follow the letter of the law.[355]

Ineligible Businesses

In order to encourage positive development of the opportunity zone areas, certain business types have been deemed ineligible for the opportunity zone program. These businesses include: private or commercial golf courses, country clubs, massage parlors, hot tub facilities, suntan facilities, racetracks or other establishments used for gambling, and any store which claims its principal business to be the sale of alcoholic beverages for consumption off premises.

Investment Structure

Qualified opportunity funds (QOFs) must be organized as either a corporation or a partnership. A number of different types of entities are acceptable, including a partnership, LLC, LLP, C-corp, S-corp, or other pass-through entity.

IRS Compliance Reporting

In the context of opportunity zone investing, IRS compliance reporting is the series of reports the investor must file with the IRS to ensure the properties follow all the dictates of the opportunity zone regulations. This includes passing the 90 percent test and the 70 percent test, as well as proving that any business properties fall within the preview of acceptable business practices. The opportunity zone or opportunity zone property must also be located within a designated opportunity zone. (See *90% Test, 70% Test, Qualified Opportunity Zone Business, and Ineligible Properties.*)

Job

A paid position of regular employment and a flawed economic metric that only tracks income distribution, ignoring long-term and often inter-generational poverty aka asset distribution (see definition of wealth).

Like-Kind Properties

In order for an investor to be eligible for a 1031 or Starker Exchange, the investor must place the gains her or she makes from the sale of her first property toward the investment of a like-kind property. Like-kind property rules dictate that both the original and replacement properties must be of "the same nature or character, even if they differ in grade or quality." In other words, you can't exchange farming equipment for an apartment building, because they're not the same asset. In terms of real estate, you can exchange almost any type of property, as long as it's not personal property.

Key Performance Indicator

A key performance indicator is a measurable value that demonstrates how effectively a company is achieving key business objectives. Organizations use key performance indicators at multiple levels to evaluate their success at reaching targets.

Maintenance

Opportunity zone businesses and qualified opportunity funds (QOFs) must self-certify their eligibility for opportunity zone deferment benefits through the completion of Form 8996, investors must engage in a process of data and tax maintenance, reporting to the IRS twice a year with the results of their 90 percent test or 70 percent test.

Net Present Value

A type of analysis that discounts the value of all future cash flows that a business is expected to generate back to the present.

Niche

A highly specific market segment or highly specific geographic segment.

Opportunity Zone

Opportunity zones are economically distressed census tracts, or areas contiguous with these census tracts, which qualify for the opportunity zone program under guidelines set forth by 2017's Tax Cuts and Jobs Act. Communities qualify for the opportunity zone program in one of three ways; they report:

● a median poverty rate of at least 20 percent

● a median family income of no more than 80 percent of the median family income for non-metropolitan areas or

● a median family income of no more than 80 percent of the greater statewide median income or the overall metropolitan median family income for tracts within metropolitan areas

Taxpayers who invest in qualified opportunity zones are eligible for exclusive capital gains tax incentives.

Poverty Reduction

The ability to rethink how we measure job creation and use social impact investment dollars to redefine and engage a broader set of measurable metrics to ensure the desired result of reducing poverty is actually achieved.

Qualified Opportunity Fund

A qualified opportunity fund (QOF) is a corporation or U.S. partnership that has dedicated itself to investing at least 90 percent of its holdings in one or more opportunity zones. These funds are governed by IRS section 1400Z-2, and must self-certify with the IRS.

Qualified Opportunity Zone Business

Qualified opportunity zone businesses must possess tangible property owned or leased by this business that is qualified opportunity zone business property acquired by a qualified opportunity fund (QOF) after December 31, 2017. The use of this property must occur within a qualified opportunity zone during the substantial period of the opportunity zones investment. The qualified opportunity zone business must earn at least 50 percent of its gross income from the active conduct of business within a qualified opportunity zone. In addition, a substantial portion of the intangible property of such an entity must also be used in the active conduct of business in the zone. Finally, less than 5 percent of the average of the aggregate unadjusted bases of the property of the business can be attributable to non-qualified financial property. Businesses excluded from the opportunity zone program include golf courses, country clubs, massage parlors, hot tub facilities, suntan facilities, racetracks, gambling operations, or liquor stores

Qualified Opportunity Zone Property

Qualified opportunity zone properties may include:

• Partnership interests in business which operate within a qualified opportunity zone,

• Stock ownership in business which conduct most or all of their operations within a qualified opportunity zone, or

• Properties such as real estate located within a qualified opportunity zone.

QOFs acquiring property that is already in use in a qualified opportunity zone will only qualify for the opportunity zone designation if that property receives substantial improvement. Substantial improvement is defined as improvements equal to the fund's initial investment in the property. Investment must be made within a thirty-month period after acquiring the property.

Recycling Capital

The opportunity zones program provides a mechanism that allows investors to recycle capital upon sale of a designated opportunity zone investment. Qualified opportunity funds (QOFs) have a one-year grace period to sell assets and reinvest the proceeds into another opportunity zone investment, and thus avoid the penalties of fees that can be associated with falling out of opportunity zone compliance.

Rollover

The opportunity zone program allows investors to roll over a capital gain into a qualified opportunity fund (QOF) through a simple three-step process:

1. Determine which gains qualify for deferral. These include capital gains that would otherwise be recognized by January 1, 2027, without the deferral that are treated as capital gains for federal tax purposes. Gains that arise from a sale or exchange from a related party do not qualify for opportunity zone deferral.

2. Invest eligible capital gains into a qualified opportunity fund (QOF) within 180 days of the realization of those capital gains.

3. Report that rollover to a qualified opportunity fund (QOF) to the IRS via form 8996.

Section 1202

Also known as the Small Business Stock Gains Exclusion, permits capital gains from the sale of specific types of small businesses stock to be exempt from federal capital gains tax. The stock must be issued by a U.S. C-corp. and cannot be any of the following types of businesses: hotel, restaurant, financial institution, farm, mining company or a business related to architecture, law, or engineering.

Section 1231 Gain

Real of depreciable business property held for more than a year. Investors with a Section 1231 gain can invest gross gains from the sale of Section 1231 property in a qualified opportunity fund (QOF) within 180 days of the gain or within 180 days of the due date of the tax return of the entity from which they received the gain.

Shareholder Resolution

Is a non-binding recommendation to the board of directors of a public corporation regulated by the U.S. Securities and Exchange Commission. Proposed by shareholders, resolutions are presented and voted upon at the corporation's annual meeting and through the annual proxy vote. In order for an individual stockholder to file a shareholder resolution, they must be a beneficiary or an owner of at least $2,000 of common stock and they must have owned the stock for at least one year.

Social Entrepreneur

A business founder who starts a company with the intention to effect social change.

Social Impact Report

A report that describes the positive or negative social impact of investment.

Social Justice

Achieving true social justice involves taking the lead from the affected community and community members to achieve collective priorities identified by those communities.

Starker Exchange

A Starker Exchange is essentially a 1031 exchange; this particular variant was named after person who brought the first lawsuit to explore the details of this purchase. At its core, it describes a like-kind exchange which is deferred. Like-kind property is defined by the IRS as properties that possess the "same character" regardless of whether or not the property is improved.

Startup

A new company that is in the beginning stages of its operation.

State Tax Conformity

All states have their own tax rules. However, there are many areas of overlap with federal tax rules. Every time there is a major tax code update, such as when the 2017 federal Tax Cuts and Jobs Act, states must decide how to incorporate changes into their own tax code. State tax conformity describes the extent to which individual states align their tax codes with that of the federal Internal Revenue Code. Some states comply for the purpose of personal income taxes and corporate income taxes, while others comply for one or the other or neither. Other states automatically conform—known as automatic rolling conformity—while others exclude certain aspects of the tax code from conformity. State conformity to opportunity zone provisions is in flux, so states that may not conform now, may change and conform in the future. In some cases, even if an investor's home state conforms to the opportunity zone personal income tax treatment, the state in which they invest may not. That could disqualify the investor from receiving an income tax credit for the taxes paid in a state due to non-conformity on opportunity zones. Whether a state has a personal or corporate capital gains tax also bears on opportunity zone taxation; states that have neither personal nor corporate capital gains tax offer a favorable opportunity zone investing environment because there are no concerns about conformity. Before investing in a qualified opportunity fund (QOF), consult a tax advisor to determine whether state and local tax codes conform to Internal Revenue Code for the purposes of opportunity zone investing and how that might impact an opportunity zone investment.

Step-Up in Basis

A step-up in basis reflects the changed value of an asset. In the case of investing in qualified opportunity funds it can mean tax exclusion or tax exemption. When you invest your capital gains in a qualified opportunity fund, your initial taxes owed will be excluded by 10 percent if you hold that investment for five years. Hold that investment for an additional two years—for a total of seven years—and you receive an additional 5 percent tax exclusion. By holding the opportunity zone investments for a total of seven years, (10 percent for five years and +5 percent for the additional two years) 15 percent of the original gain will be excluded from taxation.

Tier-1 Cities

Tier 1 is a way to describe a premier city, a major city, a city rich in resources and possibilities. While there are no official lists of all Tier-1 cities, several come to mind in the U.S.: New York, Los Angeles, Chicago, Houston, and Atlanta. Some of the things these cities have in common are the very qualities of Tier-1 cities. These characteristics include:

- Airports with ample nonstop national and international access

- An abundance of hotel inventory, including top hotel brands

- Lively dining, entertainment, and cultural options for visitors

- Major metropolitan hub

- Strong destination travel infrastructure in place (rail, public transportation, taxis)

- Reputation for world-class services and amenities

It is important to remember that tiers are descriptions, not designations. As such, they are subject to perception.

Tier-2 Cities

Defining a Tier-2 city is a bit harder to do. As in Tier 1, this distinction is a subjective description of amenities, economics, and opportunities. Typically, Tier-2 cities are mid-sized thriving cities with a number of economic drivers. Tier-2 cities include Charlotte, NC; Dallas, TX; Portland, OR; Cincinnati, OH; or Denver, CO.

Other characteristics of Tier-2 cities include:

● More affordable business markets and opportunities

● Attracts a regional drive market

● Still provides attractive dining, cultural, and entertainment options

● Convention facilities with less than 500,000 gross square feet

● Adequate hotel accommodations with many major chains

● Airports may be International, though some are regional, typically fewer nonstop flights to major hubs

● Largest convention venue generally a single hotel or conference center

● Productive local industries and business climate

Tier-3 Cities

Tier-3 designations follow the same pattern as the other two tiers, adjusted for size and scale. These cities may be older, former Tier-2 cities that may have lost some of their industries, or they may be younger, smaller cities who are just coming into their own. While they may register as third tier, it is important not to think of these cities as third class. Tier-3 cities include Waterbury, CT; Charleston, SC; Concord, NC; Saint George, UT; or Erie, PA.

Some defining features include:

- Regional airport with less nonstop or direct airlift

- Largest convention venue generally a single hotel or conference center

- Convention facilities less than 500,000 gross square feet

- Attracts a regional drive market

- May have distinctive leisure travel appeal

Ultra-High Net Worth (UHNWI)

Ultra-high net-worth individuals (UHNWI) are defined as people with investable assets of at least $30 million, usually excluding personal assets and property such as a primary residence, collectibles, and consumer durables.

Vesting

To receive or earn the right to a present or future asset, payment or benefit. Prior to vesting, an individual does not have the right to use or benefit from that asset, payment, or benefit. There is, in many cases, no guarantee that the payment, asset, or benefit will reach the stage where the individual will receive the payment, asset, or benefit. In the case of stock options, for example, options vest at a specific market price. The stock of the company offering the options may not reach that price, in which case the options are worthless.

Wealth

A great quantity or store of money, valuable possessions, property, or other riches usually acquired beyond the possession of a job and typically thorough a combination of hard work, starting a business, receiving an inheritance, pursing an education, and making investments.

NOTES

[1] "The One Percent Have Gotten $21 Trillion Richer Since 1989. The Bottom 50% Have Gotten Poorer," *New York Magazine*, June 16, 2019, http://nymag.com/intelligencer/2019/06/the-fed-just-released-a-damning-indictment-of-capitalism.html. Accessed Oct. 26, 2019.

[2] "Facts: Wealth Inequality in the United States," Inequality.org, 2018, https://inequality.org/facts/wealth-inequality. Accessed Oct. 26, 2019.

[3] Hilary Leav, "How Many Family Offices Are There in the United States?" Family Office Exchange, Aug. 9, 2019, https://www.familyoffice.com/insights/how-many-family-offices-are-there-united-states. Accessed Oct. 26, 2019.

[4] Will Keaton, "Ultra-High Net-Worth Individual (UHNWI)," Investopedia.com, Sept. 11, 2019, https://www.investopedia.com/terms/u/ultra-high-net-worth-individuals-uhnwi.asp. Accessed Oct. 11, 2019.

[5] Alicia McElhaney, "Is Anyone Actually Investing in Opportunity Zone Funds?" Institutional Investor, May 23, 2019, https://www.institutionalinvestor.com/article/b1fjptxryzv07y/Is-Anyone-Actually-Investing-in-Opportunity-Zone-Funds. Accessed Oct. 29, 2019.

[6] Blake Christian, "What You Need to Know About the Federal Opportunity Zone Program," AccountingToday.com, Feb. 28, 2019, https://www.accountingtoday.com/opinion/what-you-need-to-know-about-the-federal-qualified-opportunity-zone-program. Accessed Sept. 24, 2019.

[7] "The Tax Benefits of Investing in Opportunity Zones," Economic Innovation Group, Jan. 2018, https://eig.org/wp-content/uploads/2018/01/Tax-Benefits-of-Investing-in-Opportunity-Zones.pdf. Accessed Oct. 9, 2019.

[8] "8 Best Money Market Accounts for October 2018," Bankrate.com, Oct. 8, 2019, https://www.bankrate.com/banking/money-market/rates/#money-market-rates-banks. Accessed Oct. 25, 2019.

[9] Marcus Galindo, "Opportunity Zone Program Falls Short of Fundraising Goal Amid Investor Skepticism," Primor.com, July 11, 2019, https://www.primior.com/opportunity-zone-program-falls-short-of-fundraising-goal-amid-investor-skepticism. Accessed Oct. 8, 2019.

[10] Marcus Galindo, "Opportunity Zone Program Falls Short of Fundraising Goal Amid Investor Skepticism," Primor.com, July 11, 2019, https://www.primior.com/opportunity-zone-program-falls-short-of-fundraising-goal-amid-investor-skepticism. Accessed Oct. 8, 2019.

[11] Marcus Galindo, "Opportunity Zone Program Falls Short of Fundraising Goal Amid Investor Skepticism," Primor.com, July 11, 2019, https://www.primior.com/opportunity-zone-program-falls-short-of-fundraising-goal-amid-investor-skepticism. Accessed Oct. 8, 2019.

[12] Marcus Galindo, "Opportunity Zone Program Falls Short of Fundraising Goal Amid Investor Skepticism," Primor.com, July

11, 2019, https://www.primior.com/opportunity-zone-program-falls-short-of-fundraising-goal-amid-investor-skepticism. Accessed Oct. 8, 2019.

[13] "Shutdown Delays IRS Regulation's for Qualified Opportunity Zones," Thompson Hine, Jan. 28, 2019, http://thompsonhine.com/publications/shutdown-delays-irs-regulations-for-opportunity-zones. Accessed Oct. 2, 2019.

[14] Marcus Galindo, "Opportunity Zone Program Falls Short of Fundraising Goal Amid Investor Skepticism," Primor.com, July 11, 2019, https://www.primior.com/opportunity-zone-program-falls-short-of-fundraising-goal-amid-investor-skepticism. Accessed Oct. 8, 2019.

[15] Alicia McElhaney, "Is Anyone Actually Investing in Opportunity Zone Funds?" Institutional Investor, May 23, 2019, https://www.institutionalinvestor.com/article/b1fjptxryzv07y/Is-Anyone-Actually-Investing-in-Opportunity-Zone-Funds. Accessed Oct. 29, 2019.

[16] Marcus Galindo, "Opportunity Zone Program Falls Short of Fundraising Goal Amid Investor Skepticism," Primor.com, July 11, 2019, https://www.primior.com/opportunity-zone-program-falls-short-of-fundraising-goal-amid-investor-skepticism. Accessed Oct. 8, 2019.

[17] "Facts: Wealth Inequality in the United States," Inequality.org, 2018, https://inequality.org/facts/wealth-inequality. Accessed Oct. 26, 2019.

[18] Michael Groathaus, "Some of the U.S.'s Biggest Companies Are Founded By Immigrants," *Fast Company*, July 26, 2018, https://www.fastcompany.com/90202816/some-of-the-u-s-s-biggest-companies-are-founded-by-immigrants. Accessed Sept. 21, 2019.

[19] Quoted in J.L. Elkhorne, "Edison: The Fabulous Drone," *73*, vol. XLVI no. 3, July 1967, p. 52. Available at http://www.arimi.it/wp-content/73/03_March_1967.pdf. Accessed Sept. 21, 2019.

[20] "Rocco Forino on the Value of Investing in Entrepreneurs," Rocco Forino Capital, Apr. 15, 2018, https://roccoforinocapital.com/rocco-forino-on-the-value-of-investing-in-entrapreneurs. Accessed Sept. 21, 2019.

[21] "Rocco Forino on the Value of Investing in Entrepreneurs," Rocco Forino Capital, Apr. 15, 2018, https://roccoforinocapital.com/rocco-forino-on-the-value-of-investing-in-entrapreneurs. Accessed Sept. 21, 2019.

[22] "Rocco Forino on the Value of Investing in Entrepreneurs," Rocco Forino Capital, Apr. 15, 2018, https://roccoforinocapital.com/rocco-forino-on-the-value-of-investing-in-entrapreneurs. Accessed Sept. 21, 2019.

[23] John Cook, "Jeff Bezos Had to Take 60 Meetings to Raise $1 Million for Amazon, Giving Up 20% to Early Investors," *GeekWire*, Dec. 1, 2013, https://www.geekwire.com/2013/jeff-bezos-60-meetings-raise-1m-amazoncom-giving-20-early-investors/amp. Accessed Aug. 10, 2019.

[24] Matt Rosoff, "Jeff Bezos Told What May Be the Best Startup Investment Story Ever," *Business Insider*, Oct. 20, 2016, https://amp.businessinsider.com/jeff-bezos-on-early-amazon-investors-2016-10. Accessed Sept. 21, 2019.

[25] Matt Rosoff, "Jeff Bezos Told What May Be the Best Startup Investment Story Ever," *Business Insider*, Oct. 20, 2016, https://amp.businessinsider.com/jeff-bezos-on-early-amazon-investors-2016-10. Accessed Sept. 21, 2019.

[26] "Marc Benioff couldn't get any VCs to give him money when launching Salesforce—now it's worth $124 billion," CNBC.com, Nov. 8, 2019, https://www.cnbc.com/2019/11/08/marc-benioff-no-vcs-would-give-him-money-to-launch-salesforce.html. Accessed Dec. 3, 2019.

[27] "Marc Benioff couldn't get any VCs to give him money when launching Salesforce—now it's worth $124 billion," CNBC.com, Nov. 8, 2019, https://www.cnbc.com/2019/11/08/marc-benioff-no-vcs-would-give-him-money-to-launch-salesforce.html. Accessed Dec. 3, 2019.

[28] Marc Benioff couldn't get any VCs to give him money when launching Salesforce—now it's worth $124 billion," CNBC.com, Nov. 8, 2019, https://www.cnbc.com/2019/11/08/marc-benioff-no-vcs-would-give-him-money-to-launch-salesforce.html. Accessed Dec. 3, 2019.

[29] Polina Marinova, "DraftKings' First Investor: 'You'll See DraftKings as a Public Company," Fortune.com, April 4, 2018, https://fortune.com/2018/04/04/jeff-fagnan-draftkings-public/. Accessed Dec. 4, 2019.

[30] Andrea Browne Taylor, "Slide Show: 8 *Shark Tank* Fails That Turned Into Big Successes," *Kiplinger*, Feb. 22, 2019, https://www.kiplinger.com/slideshow/business/T049-S001-8-shark-tank-fails-that-turned-into-big-successes/index.html. Accessed Sept. 17, 2019.

[31] Andrea Browne Taylor, "Slide Show: 8 *Shark Tank* Fails That Turned Into Big Successes," *Kiplinger*, Feb. 22, 2019, https://www.kiplinger.com/slideshow/business/T049-S001-8-shark-tank-fails-that-turned-into-big-successes/index.html. Accessed Sept. 17, 2019.

[32] Connie Chen, "The 8 Most Successful Businesses That Got Their Start on '*Shark Tank*,'" *Business Insider*, June 14, 2019, https://www.businessinsider.com/biggest-shark-tank-success-stories-2018-3. Accessed Sept. 17, 2019.

[33] "Sunnyvale, California," DataUSA, https://datausa.io/profile/geo/sunnyvale-ca. Accessed Sept. 21, 2019.

[34] City of Waterbury, "Economic Development", https://www.waterburyct.org/economicdevelopment. Accessed July 20, 2019.

[35] City of Waterbury, "Economic Development", https://www.waterburyct.org/economicdevelopment. Accessed July 20, 2019.

[36] Post University, "Post Moving 400 Associates to Downtown Waterbury," Apr. 2018, https://post.edu/blog/2018/04/post-moving-400-associates-to-downtown-waterbury. Accessed July 20, 2019.

[37] "Waterbury, Connecticut," DataUSA, https://datausa.io/profile/geo/waterbury-ct. Accessed July 20, 2019.

[38] IRS, "Opportunity Zones Frequently Asked Questions", https://www.irs.gov/newsroom/opportunity-zones-frequently-asked-questions. Accessed July 19, 2019.

[39] Ray Dalio, *Principles for Navigating Big Debt Crises*, available at https://www.principles.com/big-debt-crises. Accessed Sept. 17, 2019.

[40] Ray Dalio, *Principles for Navigating Big Debt Crises*, available at https://www.principles.com/big-debt-crises. Accessed Sept. 17, 2019.

[41] Board of Governors of the Federal Reserve System, "Report on the Economic Well-Being of U.S. Households in 2018," May 2019, https://www.federalreserve.gov/publications/2019-economic-well-being-of-us-households-in-2018-dealing-with-unexpected-expenses.htm. Accessed Sept. 17, 2019.

[42] Ray Dalio, *Principles for Navigating Big Debt Crises*, available at https://www.principles.com/big-debt-crises. Accessed Sept. 17, 2019.

[43] Ray Dalio, *Principles for Navigating Big Debt Crises*, available at https://www.principles.com/big-debt-crises. Accessed Sept. 17, 2019.

[44] Ray Dalio, *Principles for Navigating Big Debt Crises*, available at https://www.principles.com/big-debt-crises. Accessed Sept. 17, 2019.

[45] Ray Dialo, "Our Biggest Economic, Social and Political Issue—The Two Economies: The Top 40% and the Bottom 60%," *Bridgewater Daily Observations*, Oct. 23, 2017, https://economicprinciples.org/downloads/bwam102317.pdf. Accessed Sept. 17, 2019.

[46] "Is the United States on the Brink of a Revolution?" TheConversation.com, Sept. 25, 2019, https://theconversation.com/is-the-united-states-on-the-brink-of-a-revolution-123244. Accessed Oct. 7, 2019.

[47] Cameron Huddleston, "Unemployment is Low, Wages are Up — But Cost of Living in America Keeps Rising," GOBankingRates.com, Dec. 27, 2018, https://www.gobankingrates.com/making-money/economy/rising-cost-of-living-in-america. Accessed Oct. 20, 2019.

[48] Laura Davison, "Here's How U.S. Businesses Actually Used Their Tax Cuts," *Bloomberg*, Jan. 16, 2019, https://www.bloomberg.com/news/articles/2019-01-16/here-s-how-u-s-businesses-actually-used-their-tax-cuts. Accessed Oct. 9, 2019.

[49] Kathryn Kranhold, "Big businesses promised wage hikes from Trump's tax cuts. What actually happened?" NBC News, Feb. 12, 2019, https://www.nbcnews.com/politics/congress/big-businesses-promised-wage-hikes-trump-s-tax-cuts-what-n970081. Accessed Oct. 19, 2019.

[50] Emanuel Kopp, Daniel Leigh and Susan Tambunlertchai, "US Business Investment: Rising Market Power Mutes Tax Cut Impact," IMF Blog, Aug. 18, 2019, https://blogs.imf.org/2019/08/08/us-business-investment-rising-market-power-mutes-tax-cut-impact. Accessed Oct. 31, 2019.

[51] Ray Dialo, "Our Biggest Economic, Social and Political Issue—The Two Economies: The Top 40% and the Bottom 60%," *Bridgewater Daily Observations*, Oct. 23, 2017, https://economicprinciples.org/downloads/bwam102317.pdf. Accessed Sept. 17, 2019.

[52] Ray Dialo, "Our Biggest Economic, Social and Political Issue—The Two Economies: The Top 40% and the Bottom 60%," *Bridgewater Daily Observations*, Oct. 23, 2017, https://economicprinciples.org/downloads/bwam102317.pdf. Accessed Sept. 17, 2019.

[53] Colleen Campbell, "The Forgotten Faces of Student Loan Default," The Center for American Progress, Oct. 16, 2018, https://www.americanprogress.org/issues/education-postsecondary/news/2018/10/16/459394/forgotten-faces-student-loan-default. Accessed Oct. 22, 2019.

[54] Thomas Frank, "Is Meritocracy to Blame for Our Yawning Class Divide?" *The New York Times*, Sept. 10, 2019, https://www.nytimes.com/2019/09/10/books/review/the-meritocracy-trap-daniel-markovits.html. Accessed Oct. 16, 2019

[55] Michael Hobbs, "The 'Glass Floor' is Keeping America's Richest Idiots At The Top," *Huffington Post*, Oct. 10, 2019, https://www.huffpost.com/entry/the-glass-floor-is-keeping-americas-richest-idiots-at-the-top. Accessed Oct. 30, 2019.

[56] Richard V. Reeves and Katherine Guyot, "Fewer Americans Are Making More than Their Parents Did—Especially If They Grew Up in the Middle Class," The Brookings Institute, July 25, 2018, https://www.brookings.edu/blog/up-front/2018/07/25/fewer-americans-are-making-more-than-their-parents-did-especially-if-they-grew-up-in-the-middle-class. Accessed Oct. 9, 2019.

[57] "Fewer Americans are making more than their parents did — especially if they grew up in the middle class," The Brookings Institute, July 26, 2018, https://www.brookings.edu/blog/up-front/2018/07/25/fewer-americans-are-making-more-than-their-parents-did-especially-if-they-grew-up-in-the-middle-class/. Accessed Dec. 3, 2019.

[58] Ray Dialo, "Our Biggest Economic, Social and Political Issue—The Two Economies: The Top 40% and the Bottom 60%," *Bridgewater Daily Observations*, Oct. 23, 2017, https://economicprinciples.org/downloads/bwam102317.pdf. Accessed Sept. 17, 2019.

[59] Ray Dialo, "Our Biggest Economic, Social and Political Issue—The Two Economies: The Top 40% and the Bottom 60%," *Bridgewater Daily Observations*, Oct. 23, 2017, https://economicprinciples.org/downloads/bwam102317.pdf. Accessed Sept. 17, 2019.

[60] Ray Dialo, "Our Biggest Economic, Social and Political Issue—The Two Economies: The Top 40% and the Bottom 60%," *Bridgewater Daily Observations*, Oct. 23, 2017, https://economicprinciples.org/downloads/bwam102317.pdf. Accessed Sept. 17, 2019.

[61] Ray Dalio, *Principles for Navigating Big Debt Crises*, available at https://www.principles.com/big-debt-crises. Accessed June 17, 2019.

[62] Ray Dalio, *Principles for Navigating Big Debt Crises*, available at https://www.principles.com/big-debt-crises. Accessed June 17, 2019.

[63] William J. O'Neill, *How to Make Money in Stocks: A Winning System in Good Times or Bad*, 4th ed. (New York: McGraw-Hill Education, 2009), p. 229.

[64] William J. O'Neill, *How to Make Money in Stocks: A Winning System in Good Times or Bad*, 4th ed. (New York: McGraw-Hill Education, 2009), p. 229.

[65] William J. O'Neill, *How to Make Money in Stocks: A Winning System in Good Times or Bad*, 4th ed. (New York: McGraw-Hill Education, 2009), p. 229.

[66] Kimberly Amadeo, "2008 Financial Crisis: The Causes and Costs of the Worst Crisis Since the Great Depression," *The Balance*, May 11, 2019, https://www.thebalance.com/2008-financial-crisis-3305679. Accessed June 20, 2019.

[67] U.S. Department of LaborBureau of Labor Statistics, "Labor Force Statistics from the Current Population Survey", https://data.bls.gov/timeseries/LNS14000000. Accessed June 20, 2019.

[68] Federal Reserve Bank of St. Louis Economic Research, "Corporate Profits After Tax", https://fred.stlouisfed.org/series/CP. Accessed June 20, 2019.

[69] Ray Dalio, *Principles for Navigating Big Debt Crises*, available at https://www.principles.com/big-debt-crises. Accessed June 20, 2019.

[70] Ray Dalio, *Principles for Navigating Big Debt Crises*, available at https://www.principles.com/big-debt-crises. Accessed June 20, 2019.

[71] Matt Krantz, "Stock Market Crash Near? Nobel Laureate Sees 'Bubbles Everywhere,'" Investor's Business Daily, Oct. 25, 2019, https://www.investors.com/etfs-and-funds/sectors/stock-market-crash-robert-shiller-i-see-bubbles-everywhere. Accessed Oct. 4, 2019.

[72] Matt Krantz, "Stock Market Crash Near? Nobel Laureate Sees 'Bubbles Everywhere,'" Investor's Business Daily, Oct. 25, 2019, https://www.investors.com/etfs-and-funds/sectors/stock-market-crash-robert-shiller-i-see-bubbles-everywhere. Accessed Oct. 4, 2019.

[73] Ray Dalio, *Principles for Navigating Big Debt Crises*, available at https://www.principles.com/big-debt-crises. Accessed June 20, 2019.

[74] Ray Dalio, *Principles for Navigating Big Debt Crises*, available at https://www.principles.com/big-debt-crises. Accessed June 20, 2019.

[75] Richard Feloni, "Ray Dialo Shares Top Lessons from His Career at Bridgewater," *Business Insider*, July 2, 2019, https://www.businessinsider.com/ray-dalio-shares-top-lessons-from-career-at-bridgewater-2019-7. Accessed Sept. 21, 2019.

[76] Christopher A. Coes and Tracy Hadden Loh, "National Opportunity Zones Ranking Report," Locus Smart Growth America, Dec. 2018, https://smartgrowthamerica.org/app/uploads/2018/12/LOCUS_opportunity-zones-FINAL.pdf. Accessed Sept. 17, 2019.

[77] "Opportunity Zones: Tapping into a $6 Trillion Market," Economic Innovation Group, Mar. 21, 2018, https://eig.org/news/opportunity-zones-tapping-6-trillion-market. Accessed Sept. 17, 2019.

[78] Steve Bertoni, "An Unlikely Group of Billionaires and Politicians Has Created the Most Unbelievable Tax Break Ever," *Forbes*, July 18, 2018, https://www.forbes.com/sites/forbesdigitalcovers/2018/07/17/an-unlikely-group-of-billionaires-and-politicians-has-created-the-most-unbelievable-tax-break-ever. Accessed July 9, 2019.

[79] Jared Bernstein and Kevin A. Hassett, "Unlocking Private Capital to Facilitate Economic Growth in Distressed Areas," Economic Innovation Group, Apr. 2015, https://eig.org/wp-content/uploads/2015/04/Unlocking-Private-Capital-to-Facilitate-Growth.pdf. Accessed Sept. 21, 2019.

[80] Anthony Noto, "Amazon's HQ2 Proves 'Opportunity Zone' Tax Breaks Are Flawed, Senator Says," New York Business Journal, Feb. 16, 2019, https://www.bizjournals.com/newyork/news/2019/02/06/amazons-hq2-proves-opportunity-zone-tax-breaks-are.html. Accessed Sept. 17, 2019

[81] "Opportunity Zones: Tapping into a $6 Trillion Market," Economic Innovation Group, Mar. 21, 2018, https://eig.org/news/opportunity-zones-tapping-6-trillion-market. Accessed Sept. 17, 2019.

[82] Steve Bertoni, "An Unlikely Group of Billionaires and Politicians Has Created the Most Unbelievable Tax Break Ever," *Forbes*, July 18, 2018, https://www.forbes.com/sites/forbesdigitalcovers/2018/07/17/an-unlikely-group-of-billionaires-and-politicians-has-created-the-most-unbelievable-tax-break-ever/#69b20b781485. Accessed July 9, 2019.

[83] "HQ2 and Opportunity Zones: The Big Picture," Economic Innovation Group, Nov. 16, 2018, https://eig.org/news/hq2-and-opportunity-zones-the-big-picture. Accessed July 9, 2019.

[84] "Opportunity Zones: A New Economic Development Tool for Low-Income Communities," Economic Innovation Group, Feb. 2018, https://eig.org/wp-content/uploads/2018/02/Guidance-for-Governors-FINAL.pdf. Accessed June 18, 2019.

[85] IRS, "Instructions for Form 2553", https://www.irs.gov/pub/irs-pdf/i2553.pdf. Accessed June 26, 2019.

[86] IRS, "Opportunity Zones Frequently Asked Questions", https://www.irs.gov/newsroom/opportunity-zones-frequently-asked-questions. Accessed July 19, 2019.

[87] "What is an LLC?" Nolo.com, https://www.nolo.com/legal-encyclopedia/llc-basics-30163.html. Accessed Dec. 3, 2019

[88] Roberta Codemo, "Difference Between an LLC and an LLP," LegalZoom, https://www.legalzoom.com/articles/difference-between-llc-and-llp. Accessed June 26, 2019.

[89] "PitchBook-NVCA Venture Monitor," PitchBook, July 10, 2019, https://pitchbook.com/news/reports/2q-2019-pitchbook-nvca-venture-monitor. Accessed Sept. 21, 2019.

[90] "What is a Benefit Corporation?" CooleyGo.com, https://www.cooleygo.com/what-is-a-benefit-corporation/. Accessed Dec. 28, 2019.

[91] "What is a Benefit Corporation?" CooleyGo.com, https://www.cooleygo.com/what-is-a-benefit-corporation/. Accessed Dec. 28, 2019.

[92] "Why is Benefit Corp Right for Me?" BenefitCorp.net, https://benefitcorp.net/businesses/why-become-benefit-corp. Accessed Dec. 28, 2019.

[93] "Why is a Benefit Corp Right for Me?" BenefitCorp.net, https://benefitcorp.net/businesses/why-become-benefit-corp. Accessed Dec. 28, 2019.

[94] "5 Reasons to Become a Benefit Corporation," Entrepreneur.com, May 24, 2017, https://www.entrepreneur.com/article/294213. Accessed Dec. 28, 2019.

[95] "It Pays to Become a B Corporation," Harvard Business Review, Dec. 6, 2019, https://hbr.org/2016/12/it-pays-to-become-a-b-corporation. Accessed Dec. 28, 2019.

[96] "Benefit Corporations: What Are the Advantages, Disadvantages, and Impact on Not for Profit Organizations?" CohnReznick, Oct. 31, 2014, https://www.cohnreznick.com/insights/benefit-corporations-what-are-advantages-disadvantages-and-impact-not-profit-organizations. Accessed Dec. 28, 2019.

[97] "Benefit Corporations: What Are the Advantages, Disadvantages, and Impact on Not for Profit Organizations?" CohnReznick, Oct. 31, 2014, https://www.cohnreznick.com/insights/benefit-corporations-what-

are-advantages-disadvantages-and-impact-not-profit-organizations. Accessed Dec. 28, 2019.

[98] "Benefit Corporations: What Are the Advantages, Disadvantages, and Impact on Not for Profit Organizations?" CohnReznick, Oct. 31, 2014, https://www.cohnreznick.com/insights/benefit-corporations-what-are-advantages-disadvantages-and-impact-not-profit-organizations. Accessed Dec. 28, 2019.

[99] "State by State Status of Legislation," BenefitCorp.net, 2019, https://benefitcorp.net/policymakers/state-by-state-status?state=wisconsin

[100] "About B Corps," BCorporation.Net, https://bcorporation.net/about-b-corps. Accessed Dec. 28, 2019.

[101] "B Corp. Directory," BCorporation.net, http://bcorporation.net/directory?sort_by=search_api_aggregation_1&sort_order=ASC. Accessed Dec. 28, 2019.

[102] "Certified B Corporation," BCorporation.net, https://bcorporation.net. Accessed Dec. 28, 2019.

[103] "State conformity to federal provisions: exploring the variances," Deloitte, July 10, 2017, https://www2.deloitte.com/content/dam/Deloitte/us/Documents/Tax/us-tax-state-conformity-to-federal-provisions-exploring-the-variances.pdf, Accessed Nov. 6, 2019

[104] "Federal opportunity zones offer state tax opportunities, complexities," PriceWaterhouseCoopers, Jan. 8, 2019, https://www.pwc.com/us/en/state-local-tax/newsletters/salt-insights/assets/pwc-federal-opportunity-zones-offer-state-tax-opportunities.pdf, Accessed Nov. 7, 2019

105 "California Punts on Qualified Opportunity Zone Conformity," EisnerAmper, Sept. 19, 2019, https://www.eisneramper.com/qualified-opportunity-zone-conformity-re-blog-0919/, Accessed Nov. 7, 2019

106 "State conformity to federal provisions: exploring the variances," Deloitte, July 10, 2017, https://www2.deloitte.com/content/dam/Deloitte/us/Documents/Tax/us-tax-state-conformity-to-federal-provisions-exploring-the-variances.pdf

107 "Not All States Are On Board with the Tax Benefits of Qualified Opportunity Zones," Aprio, 2019, https://www.aprio.com/not-all-states-are-on-board-with-the-tax-benefits-of-qualified-opportunity-zone-investments/?cn-reloaded=1&cn-reloaded=1

108 Native American Financial Services Association, "Opportunity Zones in Indian Country," Mar. 8, 2019, https://nativefinance.org/news/opportunity-zones-in-indian-country. Accessed July 8, 2019.

109 IRS, "Special Rules for Capital Gains Invested in Opportunity Zones", https://www.irs.gov/pub/irs-drop/rr-18-29.pdf. Accessed July 8, 2019.

110 "Investing in Qualified Opportunity Funds," Internal Revenue Service, Dec. 19, 2019, https://www.irs.gov/pub/irs-drop/td-9889.pdf

111 Jay Steinman et al, "Seeking to Capitalize on the Opportunity Zone Program? Move Quickly to Take Full Advantage," *Miami Herald*, Jan. 18, 2019. Available at https://www.duanemorris.com/articles/seeking_to_capitalize_on_opportunity_zone_program_move_quickly_take_full_advantage_0119.html. Accessed July 8, 2019.

[112] Tony Nitti,"IRS Publishes Final Opportunity Zone Regulations: Putting it All Together," Forbes.com, Dec. 23, 2019,https://www.forbes.com/sites/anthonynitti/2019/12/23/irs-publishes-final-opportunity-zone-regulations-putting-it-all-together/#1febe8562551. Accessed Dec. 29, 2019.

[113] Lisa Zarlenga, John Cobb, Caitlin Tharp, "Final Opportunity Zone Regulations Provide Some Much-Needed Clarit," Steptoe, Dec. 27, 2019, https://www.steptoe.com/en/news-publications/final-opportunity-zone-regulations-provide-some-much-needed-clarity.html. Accessed Dec. 29, 2019.

[114] "Investing in Qualified Opportunity Funds," Internal Revenue Service, Dec. 19, 2019, https://www.irs.gov/pub/irs-drop/td-9889.pdf

[115] "Treasury releases final opportunity zone regulations," CohnReznick, Dec. 20, 2019, https://www.cohnreznick.com/insights/treasury-releases-final-opportunity-zones-regulations. Accessed Dec. 31, 2019.

[116] "Investing in Qualified Opportunity Funds," Internal Revenue Service, Dec. 19, 2019, https://www.irs.gov/pub/irs-drop/td-9889.pdf. Accessed Jan. 1, 2020.

[117] Lisa Zarlenga, John Cobb, Caitlin Tharp, "Final Opportunity Zone Regulations Provide Some Much-Needed Clarit," Steptoe, Dec. 27, 2019, https://www.steptoe.com/en/news-publications/final-opportunity-zone-regulations-provide-some-much-needed-clarity.html. Accessed Dec. 29, 2019.

[118] Rich Blumenreich, Tom West, Joe Scalio and Orlando O'Connor, "Impressions of final regulations for opportunity zones," KPMG, Dec. 20, 2019, https://home.kpmg/us/en/home/insights/2019/12/tnf-kpmg-

report-initial-impressions-final-regulations-opportunity-zones.html. Accessed Jan, 1, 2020.

[119] Lisa Zarlenga, John Cobb, Caitlin Tharp, "Final Opportunity Zone Regulations Provide Some Much-Needed Clarit," Steptoe, Dec. 27, 2019, https://www.steptoe.com/en/news-publications/final-opportunity-zone-regulations-provide-some-much-needed-clarity.html. Accessed Dec. 31, 2019.

[120] "Investing in Qualified Opportunity Funds," Internal Revenue Service, Dec. 19, 2019, https://www.irs.gov/pub/irs-drop/td-9889.pdf. Accessed Jan. 1, 2020.

[121] Investing in Qualified Opportunity Funds," Internal Revenue Service, Dec. 19, 2019, https://www.irs.gov/pub/irs-drop/td-9889.pdf. Accessed Jan. 1, 2020.

[122] "Investing in Qualified Opportunity Funds," Internal Revenue Service, Dec. 19, 2019, https://www.irs.gov/pub/irs-drop/td-9889.pdf. Accessed Jan. 1, 2020.

[123] "Lisa Zarlenga, John Cobb, Caitlin Tharp, "Final Opportunity Zone Regulations Provide Some Much-Needed Clarit," Steptoe, Dec. 27, 2019, https://www.steptoe.com/en/news-publications/final-opportunity-zone-regulations-provide-some-much-needed-clarity.html. Accessed Dec. 29, 2019.

[124] Lisa Zarlenga, John Cobb, Caitlin Tharp, "Final Opportunity Zone Regulations Provide Some Much-Needed Clarit," Steptoe, Dec. 27, 2019, https://www.steptoe.com/en/news-publications/final-opportunity-zone-regulations-provide-some-much-needed-clarity.html. Accessed Dec. 29, 2019.

[125] Tony Nitti,"IRS Publishes Final Opportunity Zone Regulations: Putting it All Together," Forbes.com, Dec. 23, 2019,https://www.forbes.com/sites/anthonynitti/2019/12/23/irs-

publishes-final-opportunity-zone-regulations-putting-it-all-together/#1febe8562551. Accessed Dec. 29, 2019.

[126] Tony Nitti,"IRS Publishes Final Opportunity Zone Regulations: Putting it All Together," Forbes.com, Dec. 23, 2019,https://www.forbes.com/sites/anthonynitti/2019/12/23/irs-publishes-final-opportunity-zone-regulations-putting-it-all-together/#1febe8562551. Accessed Dec. 29, 2019.

[127] "Treasury releases final opportunity zone regulations," CohnReznick, Dec. 20, 2019, https://www.cohnreznick.com/insights/treasury-releases-final-opportunity-zones-regulations

[128] Lisa Zarlenga, John Cobb, Caitlin Tharp, "Final Opportunity Zone Regulations Provide Some Much-Needed Clarit," Steptoe, Dec. 27, 2019, https://www.steptoe.com/en/news-publications/final-opportunity-zone-regulations-provide-some-much-needed-clarity.html. Accessed Dec. 29, 2019.

[129] Lisa Zarlenga, John Cobb, Caitlin Tharp, "Final Opportunity Zone Regulations Provide Some Much-Needed Clarit," Steptoe, Dec. 27, 2019, https://www.steptoe.com/en/news-publications/final-opportunity-zone-regulations-provide-some-much-needed-clarity.html. Accessed Dec. 29, 2019.

[130] "Investing in Qualified Opportunity Funds," Internal Revenue Service, Dec. 19, 2019, https://www.irs.gov/pub/irs-drop/td-9889.pdf. Accessed Dec. 31, 2019.

[131] Lisa Zarlenga, John Cobb, Caitlin Tharp, "Final Opportunity Zone Regulations Provide Some Much-Needed Clarit," Steptoe, Dec. 27, 2019, https://www.steptoe.com/en/news-publications/final-opportunity-zone-regulations-provide-some-much-needed-clarity.html. Accessed Dec. 31, 2019.

132 "Investing in Qualified Opportunity Funds," Internal Revenue Service, Dec. 19, 2019, https://www.irs.gov/pub/irs-drop/td-9889.pdf. Accessed Dec. 31, 2019.

133 Tony Nitti,"IRS Publishes Final Opportunity Zone Regulations: Putting it All Together," Forbes.com, Dec. 23, 2019,https://www.forbes.com/sites/anthonynitti/2019/12/23/irs-publishes-final-opportunity-zone-regulations-putting-it-all-together/#1febe8562551. Accessed Dec. 29, 2019.

134 "Investing in Qualified Opportunity Funds," Internal Revenue Service, Dec. 19, 2019, https://www.irs.gov/pub/irs-drop/td-9889.pdf. Accessed Dec. 31, 2019.

135 Tony Nitti,"IRS Publishes Final Opportunity Zone Regulations: Putting it All Together," Forbes.com, Dec. 23, 2019,https://www.forbes.com/sites/anthonynitti/2019/12/23/irs-publishes-final-opportunity-zone-regulations-putting-it-all-together/#1febe8562551. Accessed Dec. 31, 2019.

136 "Treasury releases final opportunity zone regulations," CohnReznick, Dec. 20, 2019, https://www.cohnreznick.com/insights/treasury-releases-final-opportunity-zones-regulations

137 Rich Blumenreich, Tom West, Joe Scalio and Orlando O'Connor, "Impressions of final regulations for opportunity zones," KPMG, Dec. 20, 2019, https://home.kpmg/us/en/home/insights/2019/12/tnf-kpmg-report-initial-impressions-final-regulations-opportunity-zones.html

138 Rich Blumenreich, Tom West, Joe Scalio and Orlando O'Connor, "Impressions of final regulations for opportunity zones," KPMG, Dec. 20, 2019, https://home.kpmg/us/en/home/insights/2019/12/tnf-kpmg-

report-initial-impressions-final-regulations-opportunity-zones.html

[139] Thomas J. Hillegonds and Katie K. Roskam, "QOZ Final Rules Part 1: More Flexibility to Invest Capital Gains," Varnum, Dec. 30, 2019, https://www.varnumlaw.com/newsroom-publications-qoz-final-rules-investment-window-changes-and-types-of-capital-gains-that-may-be-invested. Accessed Jan. 1, 2020.

[140] Thomas J. Hillegonds and Katie K. Roskam, "QOZ Final Rules Part 1: More Flexibility to Invest Capital Gains," Varnum, Dec. 30, 2019, https://www.varnumlaw.com/newsroom-publications-qoz-final-rules-investment-window-changes-and-types-of-capital-gains-that-may-be-invested. Accessed Jan. 1, 2020.

[141] Jimmy Atkinson, "The First Venture Capital Opportunity Zone Fund: Podcast with Brian Phillips," OpportunityDB, Oct. 9, 2019, https://opportunitydb.com/2019/10/brian-phillips-056. Accessed Oct. 18, 2019.

[142] Will Kenton, "Section 1202," Investopedia.com, May 13, 2019, https://www.investopedia.com/terms/s/section-1202.asp. Accessed Oct. 26, 2019.

[143] Will Kenton, "Section 1202," Investopedia.com, May 13, 2019, https://www.investopedia.com/terms/s/section-1202.asp. Accessed Oct. 26, 2019.

[144] Benjamin Smith, "How to Do a 1031 Exchange: Rules & Definitions for Investors," *Real Wealth Network*, Sept. 2019, https://www.realwealthnetwork.com/learn/how-to-do-a-1031-exchange-rules-definitions. Accessed Sept. 21, 2019.

[145] IRS, "Like-Kind Exchanges: Real Estate Tax Tips", https://www.irs.gov/businesses/small-businesses-self-

employed/like-kind-exchanges-real-estate-tax-tips. Accessed July 8, 2019.

146 "Opportunity Fund or 1031 Exchange: Which Offers Better Tax Advantages for Real Estate Investors?" *Fundrise*, https://fundrise.com/education/blog-posts/opportunity-fund-1031-exchange-tax-advantages-for-real-estate-investors. Accessed July 8, 2019.

147 "Investing in Qualified Opportunity Funds," Internal Revenue Service, Dec. 19, 2019, https://www.irs.gov/pub/irs-drop/td-9889.pdf. Accessed Dec. 31, 2019.

148 IRS, "Opportunity Zones Frequently Asked Questions", https://www.irs.gov/newsroom/opportunity-zones-frequently-asked-questions. Accessed July 19, 2019.

149 Wendi L. Kotzen, Linda B. Schakel, Molly R. Bryson and Christopher A. Jones, "Overview of Qualified Opportunity Zone Program," Ballard Spahr LLP, May 1, 2019, https://www.ballardspahr.com/alertspublications/legalalerts/2019-05-01-update-on-qualified-opportunity-zones. Accessed July 8, 2019.

150 IRS, "IRS Issues Guidance Relating to Deferral of Gains for Investment in A Qualified Opportunity Fund," Apr. 17, 2019, https://www.irs.gov/newsroom/irs-issues-guidance-relating-to-deferral-of-gains-for-investments-in-a-qualified-opportunity-fund. Accessed Sept. 21, 2019.

151 IRS, "Opportunity Zones Frequently Asked Questions,", https://www.irs.gov/newsroom/opportunity-zones-frequently-asked-questions. Accessed July 19, 2019.

[152] IRS, "Opportunity Zones Frequently Asked Questions,", https://www.irs.gov/newsroom/opportunity-zones-frequently-asked-questions. Accessed July 19, 2019.

[153] "Opportunity Zones: Tapping into a $6 Trillion Market," Economic Innovation Group, Mar. 21, 2018, https://eig.org/news/opportunity-zones-tapping-6-trillion-market. Accessed Sept. 17, 2019.

[154] Teresa Esser, *The Venture Café: Secrets, Strategies and Stories from America's High-Tech Entrepreneurs* (New York: Warner Books, 2002).

[155] Sarah Perez, "U.S. Adults Now Spend Nearly 6 Hours Per Day Watching Video," TechCrunch.com, July 31, 2018, https://techcrunch.com/2018/07/31/u-s-adults-now-spend-nearly-6-hours-per-day-watching-video. Accessed Sept. 21, 2019.

[156] Quoted in "Churchill and the Commons Chamber," Parliament of the United Kingdom, https://www.parliament.uk/about/living-heritage/building/palace/architecture/palacestructure/churchill. Accessed Sept. 21, 2019.

[157] Elizabeth Stinson, "How Much Impact do Starchitects Have on a City's Economy?" *Architectural Digest*, Mar. 29, 2018, https://www.architecturaldigest.com/story/how-much-impact-do-starchitects-have-on-citys-economy. Accessed Sept. 21, 2019.

[158] Timothy Lattener, "Atlanta Planning Commissioner is on a Mission to Stop Ugly Building Construction," *Architectural Digest*, Jan. 11, 2019, https://www.architecturaldigest.com/story/atlanta-planning-commissioner-stop-ugly-building-construction. Accessed Sept. 21, 2019.

[159] Elizabeth Stinson, "How Much Impact do Starchitects Have on a City's Economy?" *Architectural Digest*, Mar. 29, 2018,

https://www.architecturaldigest.com/story/how-much-impact-do-starchitects-have-on-citys-economy. Accessed Sept. 21, 2019.

160 Lyra Kilston, "Good Design is For Everyone: The Evolution of Low-Income Housing in L.A.," KCET, Mar. 16, 2015, https://www.kcet.org/shows/artbound/good-design-is-for-everyone-the-evolution-of-low-income-housing-in-la. Accessed Sept. 21, 2019.

161 Michael Friedrich, "How to Create Safer Public Housing Projects," CityLab, Nov. 30, 2018, https://www.citylab.com/design/2018/11/affordable-public-housing-design-crime-safety-research/577009. Accessed Sept. 21, 2019.

162 Sumedha Sood, "How Miami Got Its Art Scene," BBC Travel, Nov. 30, 2010, http://www.bbc.com/travel/story/20101129-travelwise-how-miami-got-its-art-scene. Accessed Sept. 21, 2019.

163 "Romero Britto," Artnet.com, http://www.artnet.com/artists/romero-britto/. Accessed Dec. 3, 2019.

164 "Mr. E," Artnet.com, http://www.artnet.com/artists/mister-e/. Accessed Dec. 3, 2019.

165 "Lefty Out There," VerticalGallery.com, https://verticalgallery.com/collections/lefty-out-there. Accessed Dec. 3, 2019.

166 "52 Places to Go in 2017," *The New York Times* Travel, Jan. 4, 2017 https://www.nytimes.com/interactive/2017/travel/places-to-visit.html. Accessed Sept. 21, 2019.

167 Stereo Williams, "How Atlanta Became the New Cultural Capital of America," *The Daily Beast*, Apr. 11, 2017,

https://www.thedailybeast.com/how-atlanta-became-the-new-cultural-capital-of-america. Accessed Sept. 21, 2019.

[168] "A Game Plan for Eating Well in Atlanta," *The New York Times*, Jan. 30, 2019, https://www.nytimes.com/2019/01/29/dining/atlanta-restaurants-super-bowl.html. Accessed Sept. 21, 2019.

[169] Atlanta Startup Battle, https://atlantastartupbattle.com. Accessed Aug. 3, 2019.

[170] U.S. Small Business Administration Office of Advocacy, "2019 Small Business Profile", https://cdn.advocacy.sba.gov/wp-content/uploads/2019/04/23142719/2019-Small-Business-Profiles-US.pdf. Accessed Sept. 21, 2019.

[171] J.J. McCorvey, "Atlanta's Black Tech Founders are Changing Entrepreneurship in America. Can They Avoid Silicon Valley's Mistakes?" *Fast Company*, Aug. 5, 2019, https://www.fastcompany.com/90378268/atlantas-black-tech-founders-are-changing-entrepreneurship-in-america-can-they-avoid-silicon-valleys-mistakes. Accessed Sept. 21, 2019.

[172] Ashley Lyle, "Founders of Black-Owned Private Member Club The Gathering Spot Talks Purchasing A3C and LA Opening," *Forbes*, Mar. 15, 2019, https://www.forbes.com/sites/ashleylyle/2019/03/15/founders-of-black-owned-private-member-club-the-gathering-spot-talks-purchasing-a3c-and-la-opening/#4af50109750f. Accessed Aug. 3, 2019..

[173] Ashley Lyle, "Founders of Black-Owned Private Member Club The Gathering Spot Talks Purchasing A3C and LA Opening," *Forbes*, Mar. 15, 2019, https://www.forbes.com/sites/ashleylyle/2019/03/15/founders-of-black-owned-private-member-club-the-gathering-spot-talks-

purchasing-a3c-and-la-opening/#4af50109750f. Accessed Aug. 3, 2019.

[174] Carlyn Pounders, "New Venture to Propel Black Tech Ecosystem Launches in Atlanta," *UrbanGeekz,* Feb. 7, 2019, https://urbangeekz.com/2019/02/new-venture-to-propel-black-tech-ecosystem-launches-in-atlanta. Accessed Sept. 21, 2019.

[175] J.J. McCorvey, "Atlanta's Black Tech Founders are Changing Entrepreneurship in America. Can They Avoid Silicon Valley's Mistakes?" *Fast Company*, Aug. 5, 2019, https://www.fastcompany.com/90378268/atlantas-black-tech-founders-are-changing-entrepreneurship-in-america-can-they-avoid-silicon-valleys-mistakes. Accessed Sept. 21, 2019.

[176] Hana Schank, "Blight is Eating American Cities. Here's How Mobile, Alabama, Stopped It," *Fast Company*, June 10, 2019, https://www.fastcompany.com/90298534/blight-is-eating-american-cities-heres-how-mobile-stopped-it. Accessed Sept. 21, 2019.

[177] City of Memphis, "Welcome to the Blight Authority of Memphis", http://www.blightauthoritymemphis.com. Accessed Sept. 21, 2019.

[178] J.B. Wogan, "It Takes a Village: The Idea Behind Memphis' Anti-Blight Strategy," Governing the States and Localities, May 17, 2016, https://www.governing.com/topics/urban/gov-memphis-blight-elimination-charter.html. Accessed Sept. 21, 2019.

[179] City of Colorado Springs, "Rapid Response Team", https://coloradosprings.gov/economic-development/page/rapid-response-team?mlid=9241. Accessed Sept. 21, 2019.

[180] Mindy Fetterman, "Why Downtown Parking Garages May be Headed for Extinction," Pew Charitable Trust, Dec. 12, 2017,

https://www.pewtrusts.org/en/research-and-analysis/blogs/stateline/2017/12/12/why-downtown-parking-garages-may-be-headed-for-extinction. Accessed Sept. 21, 2019.

[181] Angie Schmitt, "American Cities are Drowning in Car Storage," *StreetsblogUSA*, July 12, 2018, https://usa.streetsblog.org/2018/07/12/american-cities-are-drowning-in-car-storage. Accessed Sept. 21, 2019.

[182] "New Free Software Helps Create Walkable Cities of the Future," Forbes.com, Nov. 13, 2019, https://www.forbes.com/sites/juliabrenner/2019/11/13/new-free-software-helps-architects—city-planners-create-walkable-cities-of-the-future/#2d735bc098b8. Accessed Dec. 3, 2019.

[183] Alayna Fuller, "Advantage Valley Pitch Book Showcasing Regional Opportunity Zones Unveiled," *The Herald-Dispatch*, Huntington, WV, June 23, 2019, https://www.herald-dispatch.com/news/advantage-valley-pitch-book-showcasing-regional-opportunity-zones-unveiled/article_c16af3ad-ed37-57fa-8cc3-b1e6f00499f4.html. Accessed Sept. 21, 2019.

[184] Jay Miller, "Cuyahoga County Collaboration to Promote Opportunity Zone Investments," *Craig's Cleveland Business*, Mar. 21, 2019, https://www.crainscleveland.com/government/cuyahoga-county-collaboration-promote-opportunity-zone-investments. Accessed Sept. 21, 2019.

[185] Rich Barbieri, "Economists' Fears of a 2020 Recession in the US Surge," CNN Business, June 6, 2019, https://www.cnn.com/2019/06/03/economy/us-recession-risk-nabe/index.html. Accessed Sept. 21, 2019.

[186] "US Business Cycle Expansion and Contractions," *National Bureau of Economic Research*, *https://www.nber.org/cycles/cyclesmain.html*. Accessed Dec. 3, 2019.

[187] Sarah Philips, "A Brief History of Facebook," *The Guardian*, July 25, 2007, https://www.theguardian.com/technology/2007/jul/25/media.new media. Accessed July 26, 2019.

[188] Lydia DePillis and Ivory Sherman, "Amazon's Extraordinary 25-Year Evolution," CNN Business, https://www.cnn.com/interactive/2018/10/business/amazon-history-timeline/index.html. Accessed July 26, 2017.

[189] "Scott Plans Bill to Extend Opportunity Zone Investment Deadline," *Bloomberg* Tax, June 13, 2019, https://news.bloombergtax.com/daily-tax-report/scott-to-unveil-opportunity-zone-deadline-delay-bill-before-recess. Accessed Sept. 21, 2019.

[190] Richard C. Wilson, *Capital Raising: The Proven 5-Step System for Raising Capital from Private Investors*, available at https://capitalraising.com/wp-content/uploads/2017/02/Capital raising-Book-by-Richard-C-Wilson-1.pdf. Accessed Sept. 21, 2019.

[191] Gary Vaynerchuk, "How to Sell," GaryVaynerchuk.com, Apr. 2019, https://www.garyvaynerchuk.com/how-to-sell. Accessed Sept. 21, 2019.

[192] Gary Vaynerchuk, "The GaryVee Content Strategy: How to Grow and Distribute Your Brand's Social Media Content," GaryVaynerchuk.com, Mar. 2019, https://www.garyvaynerchuk.com/the-garyvee-content-strategy-how-to-grow-and-distribute-your-brands-social-media-content. Accessed Sept. 21, 2019.

[193] Maurice Kugler et al, "Entrepreneurship in Low-Income Areas," U.S. Small Business Administration Office of Advocacy, Sept. 2017, https://www.sba.gov/sites/default/files/437-

Entrepreneurship-in-Low-income-Areas.pdf. Accessed July 7, 2019.

[194] Lewis Howes, "Gary Vaynerchuk on Insecurity, Fame and Killing It in Business," *Entrepreneur*, Feb. 4, 2018, https://www.entrepreneur.com/article/308426. Accessed July 7, 2019.

[195] Catherine Clifford, "Self-made millionaire Gary Vaynerchuk: This is the real secret to success," CNBC.com, March 13, 2017, https://www.cnbc.com/2017/03/13/self-made-millionaire-gary-vaynerchuk-shares-real-secret-to-success.html. Accessed Dec. 4, 2019.

[196] Lewis Howes, "Gary Vaynerchuk on Insecurity, Fame and Killing It in Business," *Entrepreneur*, Feb. 4, 2018, https://www.entrepreneur.com/article/308426. Accessed July 7, 2019.

[197] Cheryl Conner, "Overcoming the Greatest Challenge in Business: Your Own Insecurity," *Forbes*, May 4, 2013, https://www.forbes.com/sites/cherylsnappconner/2013/05/04/overcoming-the-biggest-challenge-in-business-your-own-insecurity/#23b918a43aa4. Accessed Sept. 21, 2019.

[198] "Gary Vaynerchuk: It's Better to Be Fast than Perfect," *Inc.* Video, https://www.inc.com/gary-vaynerchuk/askgaryvee-episode-144-be-fast-not-perfect.html. Accessed Sept. 21, 2019.

[199] Jeff Haydon, "Matt Damon Says 1 Simple Decision Transformed His Career (and Will Make All the Difference in Your Life), *Inc.*, https://www.inc.com/jeff-haden/matt-damon-says-1-simple-decision-transformed-his-career-will-make-all-difference-in-your-life.html. Accessed Oct. 5, 2019.

[200] Jeff Haydon, "Matt Damon Says 1 Simple Decision Transformed His Career (and Will Make All the Difference in Your Life), *Inc.*, https://www.inc.com/jeff-haden/matt-damon-says-1-simple-decision-transformed-his-career-will-make-all-difference-in-your-life.html. Accessed Oct. 5, 2019.

[201] Jeff Haydon, "Matt Damon Says 1 Simple Decision Transformed His Career (and Will Make All the Difference in Your Life), *Inc.*, https://www.inc.com/jeff-haden/matt-damon-says-1-simple-decision-transformed-his-career-will-make-all-difference-in-your-life.html. Accessed Oct. 5, 2019.

[202] Lesley Messer, "'Good Will Hunting' Turns 20: 9 Stories About the Making of the Film," ABC News, Dec. 5, 2017, https://abcnews.go.com/Entertainment/stories-making-good-hunting/story?id=51592706. Accessed Oct. 4, 2019.

[203] Henry Adoso, "Biography: DreDre," LiveAbout.com, Mar. 22, 2019, https://www.liveabout.com/biography-of-dr-dre-2857158. Accessed Sept. 21, 2019.

[204] Rick Juzwiak, "Dee Barnes is the Truth on *The Defiant Ones*, HBO's DreDre Documentary," *Jezebel*, July 12, 2017, https://themuse.jezebel.com/dee-barnes-is-the-truth-on-the-defiant-ones-hbos-dr-d-1796811852. Accessed Sept. 21, 2019.

[205] Asawin Suebsang, "The F.B.I. Agent Who Hunted N.W.A.," *The Daily Beast*, Apr. 14, 2017, https://www.thedailybeast.com/the-fbi-agent-who-hunted-nwa. Accessed Sept. 21, 2019.

[206] Jen Yamato, "'Straight Outta Compton' Fact-Check: How True is the Explosive N.W.A. Biopic?" *The Daily Beast*, July 12, 2017, https://www.thedailybeast.com/straight-outta-compton-fact-check-how-true-is-the-explosive-nwa-biopic. Accessed Sept. 20, 2019.

207 "DreDre," Biography.com, June 21, 2019, https://www.biography.com/musician/dr-dre. Accessed Sept. 21, 2019.

208 David Browne, "'The Defiant Ones': DreDre and Jimmy Lovine's Wild Adventure," *Rolling Stone*, July 7, 2017, https://www.rollingstone.com/tv/tv-features/the-defiant-ones-dr-dre-and-jimmy-iovines-wild-adventure-195006. Accessed Sept. 21, 2019.

209 "Dre is the CEO of Aftermath Entertainment," Capital Xtra, https://www.capitalxtra.com/artists/dr-dre/lists/facts/ceo-aftermath-entertainment. Accessed Sept. 21, 2019.

210 "Interscope Artists", https://www.interscope.com/artists. Accessed Sept. 21, 2019.

211 Steven Tweedle, "How Jimmy Lovine Ran Into DreDre on the Beach and Persuaded Him to Start Beats Over a Sneaker Line," *Business Insider*, Oct. 15, 2014, https://www.businessinsider.com/the-story-of-how-beats-by-dr-dre-was-started-2014-10. Accessed Sept. 21, 2019.

212 Zack O'Malley Greenberg, "DreDre's Net Worth: $800 Million in 2019," *Forbes*, June 18, 2019, https://www.forbes.com/sites/zackomalleygreenburg/2019/06/18/dr-dre-net-worth-800-million-in-2019/#667b3c9f7a26. Accessed Sept. 21, 2019.

213 Aaron Morrison, "A Look Back at DreDre's $70 Million USC Donation in 2013," *Black Enterprise*, Mar. 25, 2015, https://www.blackenterprise.com/dr-dres-70-million-usc-donation-seeks-innovators. Accessed Sept. 20, 2019.

214 Salvador Rodriguez, "A Brief History of Beats, Apple's $3 Billion Acquisition," *The Los Angeles Times*, May 29, 2014,

https://www.latimes.com/business/technology/la-fi-tn-apple-beats-brief-history-20140528-story.html. Accessed Sept. 20, 2019.

[215] "About," Economic Growth Business Indicator, http://egbi.org/about. Accessed Sept. 21, 2019.

[216] Gary Vaynerchuk, "The Straightest Road to Success," GaryVaynerchuk.com, Feb. 3, 2015, https://www.garyvaynerchuk.com/the-straightest-road-to-success. Accessed Sept. 21, 2019.

[217] Juian Haynes II, "Want to Get More Done and Be More Successful? Adopt an Immigrant Mentality," *Inc.*, Dec. 13, 2017, https://www.inc.com/julian-hayes-ii/want-to-get-more-done-be-more-successful-adopt-an-immigrant-mentality.html. Accessed Sept. 21, 2019.

[218] Hollie Wong, ""Immigrants 'Have it Better than Ever,' with 'Ungodly' Opportunities, Says CEO Gary Vaynerchuk," CNBC MakeIt, July 13, 2017, https://www.cnbc.com/2017/07/13/immigrants-have-better-opportunities-than-ever-ceo-gary-vaynerchuk.html. Accessed Sept. 21, 2019.

[219] "70 Highly Motivational Dwayne 'The Rock' Johnson Quotes," Addicted2Success.com, Dec. 27, 2018, https://addicted2success.com/quotes/57-highly-motivational-dwayne-the-rock-johnson-quotes. Accessed Nov. 5, 2019.

[220] Hollie Wong, "Immigrants 'Have it Better than Ever,' with 'Ungodly' Opportunities, Says CEO Gary Vaynerchuk," CNBC MakeIt, July 13, 2017, https://www.cnbc.com/2017/07/13/immigrants-have-better-opportunities-than-ever-ceo-gary-vaynerchuk.html. Accessed Sept. 21, 2019.

[221] Nicole Rodriguez, "Immigrants Preferred By Employers Over Native Workers, Report Says," *Newsweek*, Nov. 27, 2017, https://www.newsweek.com/immigration-facilitates-workplace-discrimination-against-americans-report-says-723681. Accessed Sept. 21, 2019.

[222] Mark L. Rockefeller, "America's Grittiest Entrepreneur: How an Army Sergeant Created an $100 Million Lifestyle Brand," *Forbes*, July 18, 2017, https://www.forbes.com/sites/marklrockefeller/2017/07/18/americas-grittiest-entrepreneur-how-an-army-sergeant-created-a-100-million-lifestyle-brand/#6f2c85986d82. Accessed Aug. 31, 2019.

[223] Mark L. Rockefeller, "America's Grittiest Entrepreneur: How an Army Sergeant Created an $100 Million Lifestyle Brand," *Forbes*, July 18, 2017, https://www.forbes.com/sites/marklrockefeller/2017/07/18/americas-grittiest-entrepreneur-how-an-army-sergeant-created-a-100-million-lifestyle-brand/#6f2c85986d82. Accessed Aug. 31, 2019.

[224] Eliza Berman, "The True Story Behind the Movie 'Joy,'" *Time*, Dec. 27, 2015, https://time.com/4161779/joy-movie-accuracy-fact-check. Accessed Aug. 31, 2019.

[225] Eliza Berman, "The True Story Behind the Movie 'Joy,'" *Time*, Dec. 27, 2015, https://time.com/4161779/joy-movie-accuracy-fact-check. Accessed Aug. 31, 2019.

[226] Eliza Berman, "The True Story Behind the Movie 'Joy,'" *Time*, Dec. 27, 2015, https://time.com/4161779/joy-movie-accuracy-fact-check. Accessed Aug. 31, 2019.

[227] Justin Kan, "What's the Right Mindset for a Startup Company," Quora, June 12, 2019, https://www.quora.com/Whats-the-right-mindset-for-a-start-up-company/answer/Justin-Kan. Accessed Aug. 31, 2019.

228 Young Entrepreneur Council, "How Mindfulness Can Drastically Improve Your Business," *Inc.*, Apr. 18, 2019, https://www.inc.com/malak-saleh/nphub-nurse-training-clinical-education-krish-chopra-30-under-30-2019.html. Accessed Sept. 21, 2019.

229 Elon Musk, "Work Like Hell Quote," AZQuotes.com, https://www.azquotes.com/quote/705674. Accessed Nov. 6, 2019.

230 Yale Middleton, "62 Unforgettable Arnold Schwarzenegger Quotes," Addicted2Success.com., Feb. 15, 2016, https://addicted2success.com/quotes/62-unforgettable-arnold-schwarzenegger-quotes. Accessed Nov. 6, 2019.

231 "Actor Will Smith's Work Ethic," Character-Education.info, http://www.character-education.info/resources/Will_Smith's_Character.htm. Accessed Oct. 8, 2019.

232 Denzel Washington, "Without Commitment, You'll Never Start, But More Importantly, Without Consistency, You'll Never Finish," speech given at the NAACP Image Awards 2017, Speakola.com, https://speakola.com/arts/denzel-washington-naacp-image-awards-2017. Accessed Oct. 22, 2019.

233 Asad Meah, "46 Inspirational Gary Vaynerchuk Quotes on Success," AwakentheGreatnessWithin.com, https://www.awakenthegreatnesswithin.com/46-inspirational-gary-vaynerchuk-quotes-on-success. Accessed Oct. 6, 2019.

234 Julia Takoreva, "What is a Minimum Viable Product, and Why Do Companies Need One?" *Forbes*, Feb. 27, 2018, https://www.forbes.com/sites/quora/2018/02/27/what-is-a-minimum-viable-product-and-why-do-companies-need-them/#23d4690382ca. Accessed Sept. 21, 2019.

[235] RTS Labs, "What Every Startup Should Know About Building a Minimum Viable Product," Medium, Apr. 8, 2017, https://medium.com/@rtslabs/what-every-startup-should-know-about-building-a-minimal-viable-product-357299b6eb36. Accessed Sept. 21, 2019.

[236] Justin Kan, "How Should Entrepreneurs Go About Finding a Good Product/Market Fit?" Quora, June 12, 2019, https://www.quora.com/How-should-entrepreneurs-go-about-finding-a-good-product-market-fit/answer/Justin-Kan. Accessed Aug. 20, 2019.

[237] Riz Pasha, "35 Kevin Harrington Quotes for Entrepreneurs," SucceedFeed, Mar. 1, 2019, https://succeedfeed.com/kevin-harrington-quotes.Accessed Aug. 20, 2019.

[238] Jia Yu, "How is a Business Valued on '*Shark Tank*?'" Investopedia, Oct. 20, 2018, https://www.investopedia.com/articles/company-insights/092116/how-business-valued-shark-tank.asp. Accessed Sept. 1, 2019.

[239] Dave Bookbinder, "In the *Shark Tank* It's All About Valuation," *Huffington Post*, Dec. 7, 2015, https://www.huffpost.com/entry/in-the-shark-tank-its-all-about-valuation_b_8721958. Accessed Sept. 1, 2019.

[240] Georgia McIntyre, "What Percentage of Small Businesses Fail? (And Other Need-To-Know Stats)," Fundera, Sept. 11, 2019, https://www.fundera.com/blog/what-percentage-of-small-businesses-fail. Accessed Sept. 21, 2019.

[241] Asheesh Advani, "How to Value Your Startup," *Entrepreneur*, https://www.entrepreneur.com/article/72384. Accessed Sept. 21, 2019.

242 Eddie Earnest, "How to Calculate the Value of Your Early-Age Startup," Envato, Jan. 13, 2014, https://business.tutsplus.com/tutorials/how-to-calculate-the-value-of-your-early-stage-startup—cms-65. Accessed Sept. 21, 2019.

243 Patrick Rodgers, "Pre-Money vs. Post-Money: A Guide to These Key Terms for Entrepreneurs," *Entrepreneur,* Apr. 22, 2018, https://www.entrepreneur.com/article/312333. Accessed Sept. 1, 2019.

244 Alyson Shontell, "Down on Startups: What Happens When No One Thinks You're Worth Billions Anymore," *Business Insider,* Feb. 22, 2013, https://www.businessinsider.com/what-down-rounds-do-to-startups-2013-2. Accessed Sept. 21, 2019.

245 Stephen Key, "How to Create a Winning Video to Pitch Your Idea," *Inc.*, Mar. 20, 2015, https://www.inc.com/stephen-key/the-best-way-to-pitch-a-potential-licensee-create-a-video.html. Accessed Sept. 22, 2019.

246 "Lights, Camera, Action: How to Craft a Compelling Pitch Video," Indiegogo for Entrepreneurs, https://entrepreneur.indiegogo.com/education/guide/campaign-video-creation-guide. Accessed Sept. 22, 2019.

247 "How MVMT's Indiegogo Campaign Turned Into a $100 Million Acquisition," Indiegogo for Entrepreneurs, https://entrepreneur.indiegogo.com/education/case-studies/mvmts-100-million-acquisition-started-indiegogo. Accessed Sept. 1, 2019.

248 "How MVMT's Indiegogo Campaign Turned Into a $100 Million Acquisition," Indiegogo for Entrepreneurs, https://entrepreneur.indiegogo.com/education/case-studies/mvmts-100-million-acquisition-started-indiegogo. Accessed Sept. 1, 2019.

[249] "How MVMT's Indiegogo Campaign Turned Into a $100 Million Acquisition," Indiegogo for Entrepreneurs, https://entrepreneur.indiegogo.com/education/case-studies/mvmts-100-million-acquisition-started-indiegogo. Accessed Sept. 1, 2019.

[250] "How MVMT's Indiegogo Campaign Turned Into a $100 Million Acquisition," Indiegogo for Entrepreneurs, https://entrepreneur.indiegogo.com/education/case-studies/mvmts-100-million-acquisition-started-indiegogo. Accessed Sept. 1, 2019.

[251] Justin Kan, "What Are the Most Common Mistakes Founders Make When They Start a Company?" Quora, June 12, 2019, https://www.quora.com/What-are-the-most-common-mistakes-founders-make-when-they-start-a-company/answer/Justin-Kan. Accessed Sept. 1, 2019.

[252] Alan Spoon, "What 'Pivot' Really Means," *Inc.*, Aug. 10, 2012, https://www.inc.com/alan-spoon/what-pivot-really-means.html. Accessed Sept. 2, 2019.

[253] CB Insights, "From Instagram to Slack: 9 Successful Startup Pivots," Research Briefs, Nov. 1, 2018, https://www.cbinsights.com/research/startup-pivot-success-stories. Accessed Sept. 3, 2019.

[254] CB Insights, "From Instagram to Slack: 9 Successful Startup Pivots," Research Briefs, Nov. 1, 2018, https://www.cbinsights.com/research/startup-pivot-success-stories. Accessed Sept. 3, 2019.

[255] Justin Kan, "What Should Every Startup Know About the World of Fundraising?" *Quora*, June 12, 2019, https://www.quora.com/What-should-every-startup-know-about-

the-world-of-fundraising/answer/Justin-Kan. Accessed Sept. 3, 2019.

256 Matt Egan, "The Two-Year Wells Fargo Nightmare Won't End," CNN Money, Sept. 7, 2018, https://money.cnn.com/2018/09/07/news/companies/wells-fargo-scandal-two-years/index.html. Accessed Oct. 31, 2019.

257 "Sustainable Development Goals," Principles for Responsible Investment, Oct. 12, 2017, https://www.unpri.org/sdgs/the-sdg-investment-case/303.article. Accessed Oct. 18, 2019.

258 "What you need to know about impact investing," Global Impact Investing Network, 2019, https://thegiin.org/impact-investing/need-to-know. Accessed Oct. 30, 2019.

259 Abhilash Mudaliar and Hannah Dithrich, "Sizing the Impact Investing Market," Global Impact Investing Network, Apr. 1, 2019, https://thegiin.org/research/publication/impinv-market-size. Accessed Oct. 31, 2019.

260 Abhilash Mudaliar and Hannah Dithrich "Sizing the Impact Investing Market," Global Impact Investing Network, Apr. 1, 2019, https://thegiin.org/research/publication/impinv-market-size. Accessed Oct. 31, 2019.

261 Kate Gibson, "Toys 'R' Us Bankruptcy Lawyers Get $56 Million While Laid-Off Workers Get $2 Million," CBS News, June 28, 2018, https://www.cbsnews.com/news/bankruptcy-court-gives-toys-r-us-workers-2-million-and-retailers-lawyers-56-million. Accessed Oct. 3, 2019.

262 Chris Isidore, "Amazon Didn't Kill Toys 'R' Us. Here's What Did," CNN Money, Mar. 15, 2018, https://money.cnn.com/2018/03/15/news/companies/toys-r-us-closing-blame/index.html. Accessed Oct. 3, 2019.

[263] Feng Li, Gianandrea Giochetta and Luigi Mosca, "Impact Investing: Can Funds Achieve Both Social Impact and Returns?" London School of Economics, July 26, 2019, https://blogs.lse.ac.uk/businessreview/2019/07/26/impact-investing-can-funds-achieve-both-social-impact-and-returns-at-scale. Accessed Oct. 4, 2019.

[264] Subodh Mishra, "An Early Look at 2019 U.S. Shareholder Proposals," Harvard Law School Forum on Corporate Governance and Financial Regulation, Mar. 5, 2019, https://corpgov.law.harvard.edu/2019/03/05/an-early-look-at-2019-us-shareholder-proposals. Accessed Oct. 13, 2019.

[265] Subodh Mishra, "An Early Look at 2019 U.S. Shareholder Proposals," Harvard Law School Forum on Corporate Governance and Financial Regulation, Mar. 5, 2019, https://corpgov.law.harvard.edu/2019/03/05/an-early-look-at-2019-us-shareholder-proposals. Accessed Oct. 13, 2019.

[266] "Shareholder Activism: Real, Impactful and at Your Fingertips," OpenInvest.com, Feb. 2, 2018, https://www.openinvest.co/blog/what-is-the-point-of-shareholder-activism. Accessed Oct. 11, 2019.

[267] "Shareholder Activism: Real, Impactful and at Your Fingertips," OpenInvest.com, Feb. 2, 2018, https://www.openinvest.co/blog/what-is-the-point-of-shareholder-activism. Accessed Oct. 11, 2019.

[268] "Who We Work with: Starbucks," Fair Trade America, http://www.fairtradeamerica.org/for%20business//Who-We-Work-With/Starbucks. Accessed Oct. 31, 2019.

[269] Mary Ann Azevedo, "Growth With an Impact: The Rise of VCs Looking to Fund a (Profitable) Cause," Crunchbase.com,

Feb. 2, 2018, https://news.crunchbase.com/news/growth-impact-rise-vcs-looking-fund-profitable-cause. Accessed Oct. 16, 2019.

[270] Kiki Yang, Usman Akhtar, Johanne Desard and Axel Seeman, "Private Equity Investors Embrace Impact Investing," Bain & Company, Apr. 17, 2019, https://www.bain.com/insights/private-equity-investors-embrace-impact-investing. Accessed Oct. 6, 2019.

[271] Alan Pierce, "5 Impact Investing Examples that Are Changing the World," Sopact.com, Dec. 12, 2018, https://www.sopact.com/perspectives/impact-investing-trends. Accessed Oct. 6, 2019.

[272] "Protein bars with cricket protein," Exo, https://exoprotein.com. Accessed Oct. 18, 2019.

[273] "Leading a Generation to Change the World," HultPrize.org, http://www.hultprize.org. Accessed Oct. 24, 2019.

[274] Gary Fields, "Aid, Growth and Jobs," Working Paper No. 2012/86, United Nations University, World Institute for Development Economics Research, Oct. 2012, https://www.wider.unu.edu/sites/default/files/wp2012-086.pdf. Accessed Oct. 28, 2019.

[275] "Poor Working Conditions Are Main Global Employment Challenge," International Labour Organization, Feb. 13, 2019, https://www.ilo.org/global/about-the-ilo/newsroom/news/WCMS_670171/lang—en/index.htm. Accessed Oct. 15, 2019.

[276] Matthew Desmond, "Americans Want to Believe Jobs are the Solution to Poverty. They're Not," The New York Times, Sept. 11, 2018,

https://www.nytimes.com/2018/09/11/magazine/americans-jobs-poverty-homeless.html. Accessed Oct. 18, 2019.

[277] Matthew Desmond, "Americans Want to Believe Jobs are the Solution to Poverty. They're Not," *The New York Times Magazine*, Sept. 11, 2018, https://www.nytimes.com/2018/09/11/magazine/americans-jobs-poverty-homeless.html. Accessed Oct. 18, 2019.

[278] Matthew Desmond, "Americans Want to Believe Jobs are the Solution to Poverty. They're Not," *The New York Times Magazine*, Sept. 11, 2018, https://www.nytimes.com/2018/09/11/magazine/americans-jobs-poverty-homeless.html. Accessed Oct. 18, 2019.

[279] "Jobs Don't Always Keep You Out of Poverty. Here Are Cities with High Working Poor Populations," *USA Today*, Oct. 4, 2019, https://www.usatoday.com/picture-gallery/money/2019/10/04/largest-working-poor-poverty-rates-jobs/40235803. Accessed Oct. 25, 2019.

[280] "Jobs Don't Always Keep You Out of Poverty. Here Are Cities with High Working Poor Populations," *USA Today*, Oct. 4, 2019, https://www.usatoday.com/picture-gallery/money/2019/10/04/largest-working-poor-poverty-rates-jobs/40235803. Accessed Oct. 25, 2019.

[281] Sarah Ashley O'Brien "Dog-Walking Startup Wag Raised $300 Million to Unleash Growth. Then Things Got Messy," CNN Money, Sept. 27, 2019, https://www.cnn.com/2019/09/27/tech/wag-dog-walking-softbank/index.html. Accessed Oct. 12, 2019.

[282] Sarah Ashley O'Brien "Dog-Walking Startup Wag Raised $300 Million to Unleash Growth. Then Things Got Messy," CNN Money, Sept. 27, 2019,

https://www.cnn.com/2019/09/27/tech/wag-dog-walking-softbank/index.html. Accessed Oct. 12, 2019.

283 Sarah Ashley O'Brien "Dog-Walking Startup Wag Raised $300 Million to Unleash Growth. Then Things Got Messy," CNN Money, Sept. 27, 2019, https://www.cnn.com/2019/09/27/tech/wag-dog-walking-softbank/index.html. Accessed Oct. 12, 2019.

284 Howard Wial, "What It Will Take for Opportunity Zones to Create Real Opportunity in America's Economically Distressed Areas," Initiative for a Competitive Inner City, Apr. 2019, http://icic.org/wp-content/uploads/2019/04/ICIC_OZ_PolicyBrief.pdf. Accessed Oct. 21, 2019.

285 Jason Keller, Erin Kenney, Mark O'Dell and Elizabeth Schuh, "Opportunity Zones: Understanding the Background and Potential Impact in Northeastern Illinois," The Federal Reserve Bank of Chicago, Jan. 2019, https://www.chicagofed.org/~/media/publications/profitwise-news-and-views/2019/pnv1-2019-opportunity-zones-cmap.pdf. Accessed Oct. 8, 2019.

286 "Recommendation for Opportunity Zones," PolicyLink, https://www.policylink.org/sites/default/files/PolicyLink%20Recommendations%20for%20Opportunity%20Zones%20.pdf. Accessed Oct. 14, 2019.

287 "Building Success from the Ground Up," Enterprise Community Partners, 2018, https://www.enterprisecommunity.org. Accessed Oct. 22, 2019.

288 "See What Makes Fresh Box Farms Unique," FreshBoxFarms.com, 2019, https://freshboxfarms.com/about-us. Accessed Oct. 25, 2019.

[289] Abby Schultz, "How Foundations Are Shaping 'Biggest Experiment' of Opportunity Funds," *Barrons,* Oct. 30, 2019, https://www.barrons.com/articles/how-foundations-are-shaping-biggest-experiment-of-opportunity-funds-1540931428. Accessed Oct. 31, 2019.

[290] Adam Northup, "Community Foundations, Meet Opportunity Zones," Locus Impact Investing, 2018, https://locusimpactinvesting.org/news/blog-articles/opportunity-zones-and-community-foundations.html. Accessed Oct. 28, 2019.

[291] Bruce Katz, "How Philanthropies Leverage Opportunity Zones," The Knight Foundation, Mar. 2019, https://kf-site-production.s3.amazonaws.com/media_elements/files/000/000/327/original/KF_OPPORTUNITY_ZONES_REPORT-LRS.pdf. Accessed Oct. 25, 2019.

[292] "Our Mission," The Working World, 2019, https://www.theworkingworld.org/us/our-mission. Accessed Oct. 28, 2019.

[293] Laura Flanders, "New Era Windows Opens for Business in Chicago," *The Nation*, May 9, 2013, https://www.thenation.com/article/new-era-windows-opens-business-chicago. Accessed Oct. 4, 2019.

[294] Laura Flanders, "New Era Windows Opens for Business in Chicago," *The Nation*, May 9, 2013, https://www.thenation.com/article/new-era-windows-opens-business-chicago. Accessed Oct. 4, 2019.

[295] Laura Flanders, "New Era Windows Opens for Business in Chicago," *The Nation*, May 9, 2013, https://www.thenation.com/article/new-era-windows-opens-business-chicago. Accessed Oct. 4, 2019.

296 "The OZ Reporting Framework" OZFramework.com, 2019, https://ozframework.org/about-index. Accessed Oct. 28, 2019.

297 The US Impact Investing Alliance and the Beeck Center "Prioritizing and Achieving Impact in Opportunity Zones," June 2019, https://static1.squarespace.com/static/5c5484d70b77bd4a9a0e8c34/t/5d1144358bc6b10001a5af3f/1561412661497/Opportunity+Zones+Reporting+Framework+-+June+2019.pdf. Accessed Oct. 25, 2019.

298 Abby Schultz, "Private Sector Looks to Measure Impact of Opportunity Zones," *Barrons*, Feb. 27, 2019, https://www.barrons.com/articles/private-sector-looks-to-measure-impact-of-opportunity-zones-01551278200. Accessed Oct. 9, 2019.

299 "Booker, Scott, Hassan, Young Introduce Bipartisan Bill to Strengthen Reporting Requirements for Opportunity Zone Tax Incentive," Booker.senate.gov, May 8, 2019, https://www.booker.senate.gov/?p=press_release&id=922. Accessed Oct. 9, 2019.

300 Rebecca Weicht and Rana Dajani, "6 Steps to Becoming a Successful Social Entrepreneur," The World Economic Forum, Aug. 16, 2018, https://www.weforum.org/agenda/2018/08/6-steps-to-become-a-successful-social-entrepreneur. Accessed Oct. 7, 2019.

301 Natalie Parletta, "The Man Who Makes Water From Thin Air Wins Half-A-Million Dollar Prize," *Forbes*, Sept. 19, 2019, https://www.forbes.com/sites/natalieparletta/2019/09/19/the-man-who-makes-water-from-thin-air-wins-half-a-million-dollar-prize/#7690fca64cac. Accessed Oct. 21, 2019.

[302] "Winner—Cody Friesen: Creates Renewable Energy Technology," Lemelson-MIT Program, 2018, https://lemelson.mit.edu/winners/cody-friesen. Accessed Oct. 16, 2019.

[303] "Winner—Cody Friesen: Creates Renewable Energy Technology," Lemelson-MIT Program, 2018, https://lemelson.mit.edu/winners/cody-friesen. Accessed Oct. 16, 2019.

[304] "Winner—Cody Friesen: Creates Renewable Energy Technology," Lemelson-MIT Program, 2018, https://lemelson.mit.edu/winners/cody-friesen. Accessed Oct. 16, 2019.

[305] "Winner—Cody Friesen: Creates Renewable Energy Technology," Lemelson-MIT Program, 2018, https://lemelson.mit.edu/winners/cody-friesen. Accessed Oct. 16, 2019.

[306] Hilde Schwab, "World-Changers: Meet the Social Entrepreneurs of the Year 2018," World Economic Forum, Sept. 24, 2018, https://www.weforum.org/agenda/2018/09/world-changers-meet-the-social-entrepreneurs-of-the-year-2018. Accessed Oct. 3, 2019.

[307] Rachel Zurer, "31 Social Entrepreneurs to Watch in 2018," Conscious Company Media, Oct. 3, 2018, https://consciouscompanymedia.com/social-entrepreneurship/31-social-entrepreneurs-watch-2018. Accessed Oct. 11, 2019.

[308] "An Economy that Works for All is Possible," BALLE, 2019, https://bealocalist.org. Accessed Oct. 3, 2019.

[309] "SEA: Champions for Social Enterprise," Social Enterprise Alliance, 2019, http://www.socialenterprise.us. Accessed Oct. 11, 2019.

[310] "Regalii: Helping Immigrants Pay Bills Back Home Safely and Cheaply," WeFunder.com, July 2015, https://wefunder.com/regalii/updates. Accessed Oct. 21, 2019.

[311] "Opportunity Zoning: An Inside Look at How Three Cities Are Aligning a New Tax Incentive With Land-Use Plans to Revitalize Neighborhoods," The Urban Institute, July 25, 2019, https://www.urban.org/features/opportunity-zoning. Accessed Oct. 15, 2019.

[312] "Opportunity Zoning: An Inside Look at How Three Cities Are Aligning a New Tax Incentive With Land-Use Plans to Revitalize Neighborhoods," The Urban Institute, July 25, 2019, https://www.urban.org/features/opportunity-zoning. Accessed Oct. 15, 2019.

[313] "Opportunity Zoning: An Inside Look at How Three Cities Are Aligning a New Tax Incentive With Land-Use Plans to Revitalize Neighborhoods," The Urban Institute, July 25, 2019, https://www.urban.org/features/opportunity-zoning. Accessed Oct. 15, 2019.

[314] Brett Theodos, Brady Meixell, and Carl Hedman, "Did States Maximize Their Opportunity Zone Selections?" The Urban Institute, May 2018, https://www.urban.org/sites/default/files/publication/98445/did_states_maximize_their_opportunity_zone_selections_1.pdf. Accessed Oct. 20, 2019.

[315] Ruth Simon and Kris Maher, "Erie Hit 'Rock Bottom.' The Former Factory Hub Thinks It Has a Way Out," *The Wall Street Journal*, Oct. 7, 2019, https://www.wsj.com/articles/erie-hit-rock-

bottom-the-former-factory-hub-thinks-it-has-a-way-out-11570440601. Accessed Nov. 6, 2019.

[316] "Secure Erie Accelerator," Erie Innovation District, 2019, https://www.erieinnovationdistrict.com/accelerator. Accessed Nov. 6, 2019.

[317] "Quick Facts," Lake Erie College of Osteopathic Medicine, 2019, https://lecom.edu/about-lecom/quick-facts. Accessed Nov. 6, 2019.

[318] Ruth Simon and Kris Maher, "Erie Hit 'Rock Bottom.' The Former Factory Hub Thinks It Has a Way Out," *The Wall Street Journal*, Oct. 7, 2019, https://www.wsj.com/articles/erie-hit-rock-bottom-the-former-factory-hub-thinks-it-has-a-way-out-11570440601. Accessed Nov. 6, 2019.

[319] Jeff Nussbaum, "The Night New York Saved Itself From Bankruptcy," *The New Yorker*, Oct. 16, 2015, https://www.newyorker.com/news/news-desk/the-night-new-york-saved-itself-from-bankruptcy. Accessed Nov. 6, 2019.

[320] Kim Phillips-Fein, "Lessons From the Great Default Crisis of 1975," *The Nation*, Oct. 16, 2013, https://www.thenation.com/article/lessons-great-default-crisis-1975. Accessed Nov. 4, 2019.

[321] "Trends in New York City Housing Price Appreciation," Furman Center for Real Estate and Urban Policy, New York University School of Law, https://furmancenter.org/files/Trends_in_NYC_Housing_Price_Appreciation.pdf. Accessed Nov. 4, 2019.

[322] "Trends in New York City Housing Price Appreciation," Furman Center for Real Estate and Urban Policy, New York University School of Law,

https://furmancenter.org/files/Trends_in_NYC_Housing_Price_A ppreciation.pdf. Accessed Nov. 4, 2019.

323 Amy Plitt, "10 Years After the Financial Crisis, NYC Home Prices Have Bounced Back," Curbed—New York, Sept. 18, 2018, https://ny.curbed.com/2018/9/18/17873488/new-york-home-prices-financial-crisis-recovery. Accessed Nov. 4, 2019.

324 "An Overview of 60 Contracts That Contributed to the Development and Operation of the Federal Marketplace," Department of Health and Human Services, Office of the Inspector General, Aug. 26, 2014, https://oig.hhs.gov/oei/reports/oei-03-14-00231.asp. Accessed Nov. 7, 2019

325 "The $21 trillion Pentagon accounting error that can't pay for Medicare-for-all, explained," Vox.com, Dec. 3, 2018, https://www.vox.com/policy-and-politics/2018/12/3/18122947/pentagon-accounting-error-medicare-for-all. Accessed Nov. 9, 2019.

326 Francine McKenna, "The Investors Duped by the Theranos Fraud Never Asked for One Important Thing," *MarketWatch*, Mar. 20, 2018, https://www.marketwatch.com/story/the-investors-duped-by-the-theranos-fraud-never-asked-for-one-important-thing-2018-03-19. Accessed Nov. 6, 2019

327 Ludmila Leva, "Here are the Theranos Investors Who Lost Millions," Refinery29.com, Mar. 29, 2019, https://www.refinery29.com/en-us/2019/03/225707/theranos-investors-list-elizabeth-holmes. Accessed Nov. 4, 2019.

328 Ludmila Leva, "Here are the Theranos Investors Who Lost Millions," Refinery29.com, Mar. 29, 2019, https://www.refinery29.com/en-us/2019/03/225707/theranos-investors-list-elizabeth-holmes. Accessed Nov. 4, 2019.

[329] "The World Has Gone Mad and the System is Broken," Ray Dalio, LinkedIn.com, Nov. 5, 2019, https://www.linkedin.com/pulse/world-has-gone-mad-system-broken-ray-dalio. Accessed Nov. 7, 2019.

[330] Kate Rooney, "This Year's IPO Class is the Least Profitable of Any Year Since the Tech Bubble," CNBC, Sept. 20, 2019, https://www.cnbc.com/2019/09/18/this-years-ipo-class-is-the-least-profitable-of-any-year-since-the-tech-bubble.html. Accessed Nov. 4, 2019.

[331] Oliver Marks, "Dot Com Bust: Ten Years After," ZDNet.com, Sept. 24, 2010, https://www.zdnet.com/article/dot-com-bust-ten-years-after. Accessed Nov. 4, 2019.

[332] Matt Stoller, "WeWork and Counterfeit Capitalism," Matt Stoller's Big Newsletter, Sept. 25, 2019, https://mattstoller.substack.com/p/wework-and-counterfeit-capitalism. Accessed Nov. 4, 2019.

[333] Matt Stoller, "WeWork and Counterfeit Capitalism," Matt Stoller's Big Newsletter, Sept. 25, 2019, https://mattstoller.substack.com/p/wework-and-counterfeit-capitalism. Accessed Nov. 4, 2019.

[334] Rebecca Aydin, "WeWork Isn't Even Close to Being Profitable — It Loses $219,000 Every Hour of Every Day," *Business Insider*, July 3, 2019, https://www.businessinsider.com/wework-not-close-to-profitable-loses-hundreds-thousands-every-hour-2019-7. Accessed Nov. 6, 2019.

[335] "List of World's 500 Richest People: #145, Howard Schultz," *Forbes*, Oct. 31, 2019, https://www.forbes.com/profile/howard-schultz/#4179214c52c6. Accessed Nov. 4, 2019.

336 "Starbucks Employees Domestic and International 2001-2018," Notesmatic.com, Dec. 15, 2018, https://notesmatic.com/starbucks-number-of-employees. Accessed Nov. 4, 2019.

337 Carina Chocano, "Suzy Baliz's Empire of Odor," *The New Yorker*, Oct. 28, 2019, https://www.newyorker.com/magazine/2019/11/04/suzy-batizs-empire-of-odor. Accessed Nov. 4, 2019.

338 Bernard C. Bailey and Edward B. Rust, Jr., "Commentary: Capitalism is Not Evil, But It Appears Endangered. Here's How to Save It," *The Chicago Tribune*, Mar. 22, 2019, https://www.chicagotribune.com/opinion/commentary/ct-perspec-capitalism-benefits-rebuilding-confidence-0324-story.html. Accessed Nov. 4, 2019.

339 "Warren Buffett On Why He Doesn't Invest in Gold: 'It Doesn't Produce Anything,'" Investors Archive YouTube Channel, June 25, 2015, available at https://www.youtube.com/watch?v=BtN17EGeVVA. Accessed Nov. 6, 2019.

340 "Warren Buffett On Why He Doesn't Invest in Gold: 'It Doesn't Produce Anything,'" Investors Archive YouTube Channel, June 25, 2015, available at https://www.youtube.com/watch?v=BtN17EGeVVA. Accessed Nov. 6, 2019.

341 "Margin of Safety: Risk Adverse Value Investing Strategies for the Thoughtful Investor, Seth Klarman, Harper Collins, 1991, Accessed Nov. 1, 2019

342 "We Company Funding Rounds," Crunchbase.com, https://www.crunchbase.com/organization/wework/funding_rounds/funding_rounds_list. Accessed Nov. 7, 2019.

[343] "Uber Fund Rounds, Crunchbase.com, https://www.crunchbase.com/organization/uber/funding_rounds/funding_rounds_list. Accessed Nov. 7, 2019.

[344] "Uber lost over $5 billion in one quarter, but don't worry, it gets worse," TheVerge.com, Aug. 8, 2019, https://www.theverge.com/2019/8/8/20793793/uber-5-billion-quarter-loss-profit-lyft-traffic-2019. Accessed Nov. 10, 2019.

[345] "Margin of Safety: Risk Adverse Value Investing Strategies for the Thoughtful Investor, Seth Klarman, Harper Collins, 1991, Accessed Nov. 1, 2019

[346] "Warren Buffett: Just Looking at the Price is not Investing," CNBC, Feb. 20, 2018, available at, https://www.yousubtitles.com/Warren-Buffett-Just-Looking-At-The-Price-Is-Not-Investing-CNBC-id-2078087. Accessed Nov. 6, 2019.

[347] "Benjamin Graham — Quotes," Goodreads.com, https://www.goodreads.com/author/quotes/755.Benjamin_Graham. Accessed Nov. 4, 2019.

[348] Drew Robb, "Top Cybersecurity Companies," ESecurityPlanet.com, Sept. 12, 2019, https://www.esecurityplanet.com/products/top-cybersecurity-companies.html. Accessed Nov. 4, 2019.

[349] "Gary Vaynerchuk Quotes," AZQuotes.com, https://www.azquotes.com/quote/1400857. Accessed Nov. 9, 2019.

[350] Alexandra Kerr, "Qualified Opportunity Fund," Investopedia.com, May 28, 2019, https://www.investopedia.com/opportunity-fund-4688682. Accessed Oct. 10, 2019.

351 Alexandra Kerr, "Qualified Opportunity Fund," Investopedia.com, May 28, 2019, https://www.investopedia.com/opportunity-fund-4688682. Accessed Oct. 10, 2019.

352 "The Tax Benefits of Investing In Opportunity Funds," Economic Innovation Institute, Jan. 2018, https://eig.org/wp-content/uploads/2018/01/Tax-Benefits-of-Investing-in-Opportunity-Zones.pdf. Accessed Oct. 4, 2019.

353 Dan Caplinger, "Capital Gains Tax Rates: A Comprehensive Guide," *The Motley Fool*, June 1, 2019, https://www.fool.com/taxes/capital-gains-tax-rates-comprehensive-guide.aspx. Accessed Oct. 19, 2019.

354 "How to Roll Over a Capital Gain Into an Opportunity Fund," Fundrise, 2019, https://fundrise.com/education/blog-posts/how-to-roll-over-a-capital-gain-into-an-opportunity-fund. Accessed Oct. 18, 2019.

355 Matt Kelley, "Opportunity Zones: Establishing and Maintaining Compliance," Novogradac, Aug. 2, 2019, https://www.novoco.com/periodicals/articles/opportunity-zones-establishing-and-maintaining-compliance. Accessed Oct. 12, 2019.

---

iMichael Groathaus, "Some of the U.S.'s Biggest Companies Are Founded By Immigrants," *Fast Company*, July 26, 2018, https://www.fastcompany.com/90202816/some-of-the-u-s-s-biggest-companies-are-founded-by-immigrants. Accessed Sept. 21, 2019.

[ii] Quoted in J.L. Elkhorne, "Edison: The Fabulous Drone," *73*, vol. XLVI no. 3, July 1967, p. 52. Available at http://www.arimi.it/wp-content/73/03_March_1967.pdf. Accessed Sept. 21, 2019.

[iii] "Rocco Forino on the Value of Investing in Entrepreneurs," Rocco Forino Capital, Apr. 15, 2018, https://roccoforinocapital.com/rocco-forino-on-the-value-of-investing-in-entrapreneurs. Accessed Sept. 21, 2019.

[iv] "Rocco Forino on the Value of Investing in Entrepreneurs," Rocco Forino Capital, Apr. 15, 2018, https://roccoforinocapital.com/rocco-forino-on-the-value-of-investing-in-entrapreneurs. Accessed Sept. 21, 2019.

[v] "Rocco Forino on the Value of Investing in Entrepreneurs," Rocco Forino Capital, Apr. 15, 2018, https://roccoforinocapital.com/rocco-forino-on-the-value-of-investing-in-entrapreneurs. Accessed Sept. 21, 2019.

[vi] John Cook, "Jeff Bezos Had to Take 60 Meetings to Raise $1 Million for Amazon, Giving Up 20% to Early Investors," *GeekWire*, Dec. 1, 2013, https://www.geekwire.com/2013/jeff-bezos-60-meetings-raise-1m-amazoncom-giving-20-early-investors/amp. Accessed Aug. 10, 2019.

[vii] Matt Rosoff, "Jeff Bezos Told What May Be the Best Startup Investment Story Ever," *Business Insider*, Oct. 20, 2016, https://amp.businessinsider.com/jeff-bezos-on-early-amazon-investors-2016-10. Accessed Sept. 21, 2019.

[viii] Matt Rosoff, "Jeff Bezos Told What May Be the Best Startup Investment Story Ever," *Business Insider*, Oct. 20, 2016,

https://amp.businessinsider.com/jeff-bezos-on-early-amazon-investors-2016-10. Accessed Sept. 21, 2019.

ix "Marc Benioff couldn't get any VCs to give him money when launching Salesforce—now it's worth $124 billion," CNBC.com, Nov. 8, 2019, https://www.cnbc.com/2019/11/08/marc-benioff-no-vcs-would-give-him-money-to-launch-salesforce.html. Accessed Dec. 3, 2019.

x "Marc Benioff couldn't get any VCs to give him money when launching Salesforce—now it's worth $124 billion," CNBC.com, Nov. 8, 2019, https://www.cnbc.com/2019/11/08/marc-benioff-no-vcs-would-give-him-money-to-launch-salesforce.html. Accessed Dec. 3, 2019.

xi Marc Benioff couldn't get any VCs to give him money when launching Salesforce—now it's worth $124 billion," CNBC.com, Nov. 8, 2019, https://www.cnbc.com/2019/11/08/marc-benioff-no-vcs-would-give-him-money-to-launch-salesforce.html. Accessed Dec. 3, 2019.

xii Polina Marinova, "DraftKings' First Investor: 'You'll See DraftKings as a Public Company," Fortune.com, April 4, 2018, https://fortune.com/2018/04/04/jeff-fagnan-draftkings-public/. Accessed Dec. 4, 2019.

xiii Andrea Browne Taylor, "Slide Show: 8 *Shark Tank* Fails That Turned Into Big Successes," *Kiplinger*, Feb. 22, 2019, https://www.kiplinger.com/slideshow/business/T049-S001-8-shark-tank-fails-that-turned-into-big-successes/index.html. Accessed Sept. 17, 2019.

[xiv]Andrea Browne Taylor, "Slide Show: 8 *Shark Tank* Fails That Turned Into Big Successes," *Kiplinger*, Feb. 22, 2019, https://www.kiplinger.com/slideshow/business/T049-S001-8-shark-tank-fails-that-turned-into-big-successes/index.html. Accessed Sept. 17, 2019.

[xv] Connie Chen, "The 8 Most Successful Businesses That Got Their Start on 'Shark Tank,'" *Business Insider*, June 14, 2019, https://www.businessinsider.com/biggest-shark-tank-success-stories-2018-3. Accessed Sept. 17, 2019.

[xvi]"Sunnyvale, California," DataUSA, https://datausa.io/profile/geo/sunnyvale-ca. Accessed Sept. 21, 2019.

[xvii]City of Waterbury, "Economic Development", https://www.waterburyct.org/economicdevelopment. Accessed July 20, 2019.

[xviii]City of Waterbury, "Economic Development", https://www.waterburyct.org/economicdevelopment. Accessed July 20, 2019.

[xix]Post University, "Post Moving 400 Associates to Downtown Waterbury," Apr. 2018, https://post.edu/blog/2018/04/post-moving-400-associates-to-downtown-waterbury. Accessed July 20, 2019.

[xx] "Waterbury, Connecticut," DataUSA, https://datausa.io/profile/geo/waterbury-ct. Accessed July 20, 2019.

xxi IRS, "Opportunity Zones Frequently Asked Questions", https://www.irs.gov/newsroom/opportunity-zones-frequently-asked-questions. Accessed July 19, 2019.

xxii "The One Percent Have Gotten $21 Trillion Richer Since 1989. The Bottom 50% Have Gotten Poorer," *New York Magazine*, June 16, 2019, http://nymag.com/intelligencer/2019/06/the-fed-just-released-a-damning-indictment-of-capitalism.html. Accessed Oct. 26, 2019.

xxiii "Facts: Wealth Inequality in the United States," Inequality.org, 2018, https://inequality.org/facts/wealth-inequality. Accessed Oct. 26, 2019.

xxiv Hilary Leav, "How Many Family Offices Are There in the United States?" Family Office Exchange, Aug. 9, 2019, https://www.familyoffice.com/insights/how-many-family-offices-are-there-united-states. Accessed Oct. 26, 2019.

xxv Will Keaton, "Ultra-High Net-Worth Individual (UHNWI)," Investopedia.com, Sept. 11, 2019, https://www.investopedia.com/terms/u/ultra-high-net-worth-individuals-uhnwi.asp. Accessed Oct. 11, 2019.

xxvi Alicia McElhaney, "Is Anyone Actually Investing in Opportunity Zone Funds?" Institutional Investor, May 23, 2019, https://www.institutionalinvestor.com/article/b1fjptxryzv07y/Is-Anyone-Actually-Investing-in-Opportunity-Zone-Funds. Accessed Oct. 29, 2019.

[xxvii]Blake Christian, "What You Need to Know About the Federal Opportunity Zone Program," AccountingToday.com, Feb. 28, 2019, https://www.accountingtoday.com/opinion/what-you-need-to-know-about-the-federal-qualified-opportunity-zone-program. Accessed Sept. 24, 2019.

[xxviii] "The Tax Benefits of Investing in Opportunity Zones," Economic Innovation Group, Jan. 2018, https://eig.org/wp-content/uploads/2018/01/Tax-Benefits-of-Investing-in-Opportunity-Zones.pdf. Accessed Oct. 9, 2019.

[xxix] "8 Best Money Market Accounts for October 2018," Bankrate.com, Oct. 8, 2019, https://www.bankrate.com/banking/money-market/rates/#money-market-rates-banks. Accessed Oct. 25, 2019.

[xxx]Marcus Galindo, "Opportunity Zone Program Falls Short of Fundraising Goal Amid Investor Skepticism," Primor.com, July 11, 2019, https://www.primior.com/opportunity-zone-program-falls-short-of-fundraising-goal-amid-investor-skepticism. Accessed Oct. 8, 2019.

[xxxi]Marcus Galindo, "Opportunity Zone Program Falls Short of Fundraising Goal Amid Investor Skepticism," Primor.com, July 11, 2019, https://www.primior.com/opportunity-zone-program-falls-short-of-fundraising-goal-amid-investor-skepticism. Accessed Oct. 8, 2019.

[xxxii]Marcus Galindo, "Opportunity Zone Program Falls Short of Fundraising Goal Amid Investor Skepticism," Primor.com, July

11, 2019, https://www.primior.com/opportunity-zone-program-falls-short-of-fundraising-goal-amid-investor-skepticism. Accessed Oct. 8, 2019.

xxxiiiMarcus Galindo, "Opportunity Zone Program Falls Short of Fundraising Goal Amid Investor Skepticism," Primor.com, July 11, 2019, https://www.primior.com/opportunity-zone-program-falls-short-of-fundraising-goal-amid-investor-skepticism. Accessed Oct. 8, 2019.

xxxiv "Shutdown Delays IRS Regulation's for Qualified Opportunity Zones," Thompson Hine, Jan. 28, 2019, http://thompsonhine.com/publications/shutdown-delays-irs-regulations-for-opportunity-zones. Accessed Oct. 2, 2019.

xxxvMarcus Galindo, "Opportunity Zone Program Falls Short of Fundraising Goal Amid Investor Skepticism," Primor.com, July 11, 2019, https://www.primior.com/opportunity-zone-program-falls-short-of-fundraising-goal-amid-investor-skepticism. Accessed Oct. 8, 2019.

xxxviAlicia McElhaney, "Is Anyone Actually Investing in Opportunity Zone Funds?" Institutional Investor, May 23, 2019, https://www.institutionalinvestor.com/article/b1fjptxryzv07y/Is-Anyone-Actually-Investing-in-Opportunity-Zone-Funds. Accessed Oct. 29, 2019.

xxxviiMarcus Galindo, "Opportunity Zone Program Falls Short of Fundraising Goal Amid Investor Skepticism," Primor.com, July 11, 2019, https://www.primior.com/opportunity-zone-program-falls-short-of-fundraising-goal-amid-investor-skepticism. Accessed Oct. 8, 2019.

[xxxviii]"Facts: Wealth Inequality in the United States," Inequality.org, 2018, https://inequality.org/facts/wealth-inequality. Accessed Oct. 26, 2019.

Made in the USA
Middletown, DE
17 November 2020